Dating, Mating, Relating

Dating, Mating, Relating

*Personal Advertising
and Modern Romance*

PAMELA ANNE QUIROZ

McFarland & Company, Inc., Publishers
Jefferson, North Carolina

LIBRARY OF CONGRESS CATALOGUING-IN-PUBLICATION DATA

Names: Quiroz, Pamela Anne, 1960– author.
Title: Dating, mating, relating : personal advertising and modern
romance / Pamela Anne Quiroz.
Description: Jefferson, North Carolina : McFarland & Company, Inc.,
Publishers, 2022 | Includes bibliographical references and index.
Identifiers: LCCN 2022022335 | ISBN 9780786470419 (paperback : acid free paper) ∞
ISBN 9781476646299 (ebook)
Subjects: LCSH: Personals—United States—History. | Online dating—United
States—History. | Dating (Social customs)—United States—History. | Dating
(Social customs)—United States—Case studies. | BISAC:
FAMILY & RELATIONSHIPS / Dating
Classification: LCC HQ801.825 .Q85 2022 | DDC 306.73—dc23/eng/20220601
LC record available at https://lccn.loc.gov/2022022335

BRITISH LIBRARY CATALOGUING DATA ARE AVAILABLE

ISBN (print) 978-0-7864-7041-9
ISBN (ebook) 978-1-4766-4629-9

Front cover photograph by Yohana Calvo (Shutterstock)

Printed in the United States of America

*McFarland & Company, Inc., Publishers
Box 611, Jefferson, North Carolina 28640
www.mcfarlandpub.com*

Table of Contents

Acknowledgments

Writing a book is a creative collaboration that involves the contributions of many people. I want to begin by expressing my profound gratitude to the 72 women who participated in these studies without whom this book would not have been possible. Though personal advertising has now become normative, some of these participants spoke with me at a time when placing a personal ad was still considered to be a deviant activity. Their candor and willingness to share the details of their stories continue to inspire me. In addition to the formal interviews, I engaged in informal conversations with leaders and participants of offline dating activities and observed multiple activities, including coffee mating, speed dating at two community centers, a church, and a high school, and safari flirting. I also sat through couples yoga. I want to thank the participants and session leaders for allowing me to be there and for offering their (informal) insights into the experience of personal advertising. I also engaged in informal discussions with massage therapists who offered couples massage and with yoga instructors who led "couples yoga" activities. I'm grateful to all of them for their willingness to enlighten me.

I want to thank colleagues and students who, over the years, have assisted me in completing *Dating, Mating, Relating*, and while I undoubtedly fail in my efforts to acknowledge each person, I extend my mea culpa in advance and thank my colleagues at the University of Massachusetts–Amherst who provided me with a grant to initiate this work. I am particularly indebted to my senior colleagues at the Center for Advanced Study in Behavioral Sciences (1996), who encouraged me to pursue my research on this phenomenon by regarding it as "cutting edge." I also want to thank colleagues Barbara Risman and Amalia Pallares at the University of Illinois–Chicago who supported my work and read my chapters. Special thanks to Stephanie Coontz and the Council on Contemporary Families, Frank Furstenburg, my senior mentor at the CASBS, Marla Kohlman, Bette Dickerson, Janet Schipper, and Shawn Bingham.

Acknowledgments

The opportunities I had to present the work at the Illinois Humanities Council and Northwestern University's Kellogg School of Management's Consumer Culture Forum provided different perspectives and valuable feedback that helped to shape the book. I am eternally grateful to the late Ray B. Browne, founder of popular culture studies in the U.S., for his interest in my work at a time when it was most needed. I received incredible assistance from outstanding graduate students Amy Stephenson at the University of Massachusetts–Amherst, Rita Duarte at the University of Arizona, and Jonathon Carroll at the University of Illinois–Chicago. I am also grateful for the wonderful feedback from the many friends with whom I talked about this work over the years and, of course, my dear friend and colleague Dr. Nicolas Kanellos, who has tried to help me become a better writer. It is an honor to have Nick read the manuscript. I want to thank Teresa Abney as well because, without her, this book would not have been published.

I would be terribly remiss if I did not offer special thanks to the patience and support of this outstanding publisher, McFarland, and my editor, David Alff. The financial support of the Healy Public Policy Grant, the Institute for Research on Race and Public Policy, and the Society for the Scientific Study of Sexuality Foundation allowed me to complete the work.

Last, but certainly not least, I want to thank my family; without their support, this book could never have been written.

Tables

Introduction:
Personal Advertising

*Dating, Mating, and Relating
in Modern Society*

Tracing the history of courtship in twentieth-century America, historian Beth Bailey cited changes in society as shifting the domain of courtship from the private sphere to a public one.[1] One of these changes involved the entry of women into the labor market. With the increased participation of women in the labor force, the responsibility for financing dates changed as men and women struggled for control over the courtship system. The new system of courtship applied the rules of the marketplace to personal affairs.

> The new system of courtship privileged competition (and worried about how to control it); it valued comparison; it presented an economic model of scarcity and abundance as a guide to personal affairs. The rules of the market were consciously applied; the vocabulary of exchange defined in acts of courtship [p. 5].

Another shift in courtship has occurred in modern society as economic and social arrangements combined with technological changes to broaden the scope of personal relationships. These changes have stimulated new opportunities for people to meet one another, as different groups now use an array of new scripts for intimate connections. Hooking up, the casual sexual encounters associated with college-age men and women, precedes or displaces emotional ties altogether for a significant number of young people, as sexual behavior is no longer subject to the restrictions of romantic love or dating.[2] The right of the individual to choose his or her own mate, lover, or friend is now a cultural imperative.[3] For older adults, the loss of traditional ways to find partners, the loss of time and access to conventional ways of meeting people,

1

Introduction: Personal Advertising

and the loss of loved ones through separation, divorce, or out-living one's spouse necessitates the development of new alternatives. Personal advertising, the public marketing of the self in a circumscribed space or place to establish intimate relationships, has emerged as a set of activities that offers candidates intimacy while retaining the individual power of selection for participants.

In the twenty-first century, personal advertising has shifted in form and content and now stretches across multiple modalities to include print and digital media, such as personal advertisements in magazines and newspapers, online dating services, social networking sites, and through such other forums as speed dating, "It's Just Lunch" and the use of mobile applications (apps), cell phones, and GPS to engage in location-based dating. Each of these activities appeals to particular segments of the population. The typical online dater is 38 years old, while the typical app user is nearly a decade younger at 29 years old. Participants also use more than a single modality as many people who place personal ads or use online dating services also engage in other personal advertising activities.

According to the Pew Internet Research Project in 2013,[4] one in ten American adults had used an online dating site or mobile dating app. By 2019, these numbers had risen to three in every ten American adults.[5] Added to this, 42 percent of Americans know an online ad placer, 29 percent know someone who has used online dating to find a spouse or long-term relationship, and 23 percent have gone on a date with someone they met through online dating or a dating app.

Aside from the reality that people increasingly engage in alternative lifestyles and live longer, demographic trends indicate that the number of unmarried people has increased significantly, and this population is characterized as more connected, caring, and politically engaged, yet it continues to be ignored in discussions of sexuality, intimacy, and family.[6] In his book *Going Solo: The Extraordinary Rise and Surprising Appeal of Living Alone*, Eric Klinenberg[7] revealed that people were increasingly choosing to live alone; however, this does not mean that they wanted to be alone or that they were alone—there is a difference. It is clear we live in a rapidly changing and complex world, and just as rapidly, people approach these changes by innovating. Indeed, since the late 1990s, online dating and matchmaking services have become what anthropologist Susan Frohlick calls *hypermainstream*,[8] both a multibillion-dollar industry and a normative way to meet and mate.

Although the structural factors and social processes involved in personal advertising are relevant to the formation of personal relationships, until recently, the phenomenon of personal advertising as a form of courtship has received relatively little attention from sociologists.[9] Most of the scholarly attention to personal advertising emerges from social-psychological studies that focus on the traits sought by persons of different sexual orientations or sexes through the use of classified print and online advertisements.[10] Some scholars have examined personal advertising as a way to comprehend race relations in our society.[11] This work has called for rethinking the relationship between race and gender in personal advertising (i.e., Asian males and African American females are more highly excluded from cross-racial relationships than are other groups).

With the explosion of the Internet, communications and media scholars have focused on the discursive strategies used in online dating.[12] Other social scientists have examined conversations between speed daters to determine how some participants manage to connect with one another while others do not.[13] These studies inform us about the persistence of sex roles, how new technology mediates the constructing and performing of identity, and the strategic use of language in mating. However, the emphasis in social psychology and sociology has been on identifying categories of exchange, which include: the qualities women and men are looking for in each other instead of the ways that race, gender, class, sexual orientation, and even disability continue to structure relationships; how these master categories intersect and influence the formation of relationships; and the impact of particular contexts within which identities are performed. Additionally, most studies have focused explicitly on the ad contents, whether placed in print or on the Internet, as opposed to presenting the voices of participants in personal advertising. Such questions about how men and women *do identity* and how they experience personal advertising are rarely addressed.

Dating, Mating, Relating: Personal Advertisement and Modern Romance examines personal advertising as a social and cultural phenomenon that addresses challenges of the modern world in establishing intimate relationships. It presents personal advertising from the perspective of those who actually engage in it. Briefly tracing the evolution of mating through personal advertisements, I draw from the interviews conducted between 1998 and 2015 with 72 women to examine how personal advertising has changed and how it assists them in making interpersonal connections. Because women comprise the respondents in three of the four studies, the book is focused on their perspectives. I also engaged in content analyses of print and online ads and observations of speed dating sessions and other activities, such as "coffee mating" and "safari flirting," which I will describe in detail in the chapters to follow. I spoke with owners of massage and yoga venues to learn more about their forays into personal advertising; several of these businesses included activities such as "couples massage" and "couples yoga," which often became venues for dating. Though they were created with preexisting couples in mind, it was not unusual for people to use them as dating activities. Some businesses did advertise couples yoga or couples massage explicitly as a way to date. These data describe how new modes of dating are generating opportunities to meet people and how these opportunities are navigated.

I pay particular attention to the intersectionality of multiple dimensions of identity (race, sex, and class) and the identity claims in personal advertising as a fluid process that involves the conscious construction and marketing of the self (or selves) to strangers in a variety of contexts. It can also include engaging in intimate activities with strangers, such as when strangers meet for the first time to engage in couples massage or speed dating. People who engage in personal advertising activities describe their motivations, experiences, and insights as they construct an abbreviated identity (or identities), select others as potential mates, establish trust to minimize risk, and literally "do" gender, race, ethnicity, sexual orientation, and even social class.

Jeremy Rifkin[14] suggests that we live in a world where virtually everything is marketed, particularly the self and relationships with others. In the twenty-first century, *romantic tourism* represents the ultimate market-based experience that provides boundless opportunities for individuals to pursue romantic or sexual interests. The following chapters present women who have elected to take advantage of these opportunities.

The Book and Its Origins

The chapters of this book provide the social context within which contemporary personal advertising takes place and the personal stories of participants involved in these activities. My own journey into this research area represents an evolution of interests that began while reading personal advertisements in a weekly newspaper (*The City*) during the late 1980s as a temporary escape from my graduate studies at the University of Chicago. By the time I became an assistant professor at the University of Massachusetts–Amherst, I had begun seeing personal ads in mainstream newspapers, local weeklies, and magazines. I also began to think about this activity in a more scholarly way and to read studies about personal ad placements. At that time, the studies focused exclusively on print ad placements in newspapers or other print outlets. The idea for a study of personal advertising first occurred to me in 1996 when I was struck by the exponential increase in personal ads and print venues for ad placements and the lack of attention to this phenomenon by sociologists. At the time, available studies neglected questions about the structural changes in society and their impact on the increase in personal ad placements. They also failed to address the phenomenology and "success" of ad placements by ad placers.

Besides wanting to provide a sociological explanation for these changes in mating patterns, I wondered what motivated people to use this method of meeting people. How did ad placers construct their identity in circumscribed spaces? Was this form of advertising effective? How did cultural differences impact participants? When I began studying this subject, social stigma was still attached to personal advertising. Therefore, I wondered whether my undergraduate students were correct in their assumptions that personal advertising represented a last resort of desperate, lonely, or unattractive people.

During my summer at the Center for the Advanced Study of the Behavioral Sciences at Stanford University, colleagues encouraged me to pursue the project. I began to study personal advertising formally in 1997. It was also at this time that the Internet was starting to be used to respond to personal ads. Four studies about women "ad placers" resulted over the next 17 years (1998, $N=32$ [16 Women]; 2004, $N=14$; 2008, $N=20$; and 2014–2015, $N=22$). Eventually, I expanded my work on the micro-processes involved in personal ad placements in print and online media to include the array of activities that now comprise the phenomenon of personal advertising. I did this because each new set of activities spawned new innovations. The movement from print to online ads was accompanied by the emergence of video and online dating and relationship services, such as PerfectMatch.com and eHarmony. These were accompanied by services such as "It's Just Lunch" and eventually speed dating. Dedicated online sites and offspring of these relationship services have proliferated, suggesting a demand or at least a willingness of people to try new ways to meet and mate.

I also look at the changing social contexts within which these activities are situated and the impact these contexts have on participants in their efforts to date and mate. The following chapters include a window into the development of interpersonal trust and the increasing role of technology in shaping how people meet and mate in a changing world.

Book Chapters

Chapter 1 offers a brief history of personal advertising as functional and even fashionable during specific periods. Early forms of personal advertising, such as classified ads, were used in dedicated newspapers or print media and took the form of lonely hearts and mail-order or picture brides, where men and women advertised for marriage partners. They could also be found in social clubs where people from diverse social classes and ethnic groups came together for various reasons and occasionally resulted in meeting significant others. This chapter traces the changes in personal ads from the nineteenth century to the twenty-first century, during which technology comes to play in modern-day advertising; it also includes the study of entrepreneurial ways of meeting people through such means as Internet advertising, matchmaking services, video dating, and other types of social networking and dating opportunities.

The focus of Chapter 2 is on the commercialization of relationship formation and how capitalism intersects with science to promote the romance industry. Distinguishing between online, print, and offline spaces, the chapter presents how science and technology are used to promote and profit from the desires and dreams of participants. Particular attention is given to the way different venues frame ad parlance and construction and promote ad success. The organization and context of personal advertising in print, online, and other activities are illustrated using newspapers and websites. These contexts also result in shaping the participation of diverse groups of people.

Interviews with participants provide an understanding of the processes involved in personal advertising and mate selection, as Chapter 3 addresses how identities are presented and performed for multiple audiences. The chapter begins by describing the process of ad placement in print and shifts to explain the impact of the Internet on ad placement as online advertising and speed dating present opportunities to craft a personal profile or multiple profiles for imagined and real-life audiences. The chapter maps the processes involved in "doing" identity in particular contexts—presenting identities to anonymous others, engaging in impression management, and selecting among personal advertising respondents, as participants strategize to minimize risk and optimize success. A comparison of personal ad placers' presentations in real-life and virtual spaces illustrates the impact of mediating forces on framing (or "doing") one's identity for various activities and audiences. Ad placers who have experimented with one or more of these activities present the problems and possibilities involved in making personal connections using these techniques.

Chapter 4 draws specifically from interviews with African American and Latina ad placers to highlight how race and ethnicity continue to impact efforts to establish personal relationships in a supposedly "post-racial" and gendered society. Personal advertising is yet another domain in which the sociopolitical categories of race and ethnicity collapse into the private sphere, with the presumption that private beliefs, values, desires, and behavior are the only factors involved in forming personal relationships. Within this framework, interracial friendships, dating, and marriage are regarded as little more than the choices or tastes of individuals, with the only limits to pursuing mates seen as the result of personal interests. In both offline and online personal advertising activities, racial representations and encounters are publicly negotiated. However, participants describe experiences that contradict the discourse of color blindness and convey how the cultural and ideological spheres of race continue in our most intimate associations.

Chapter 5 moves beyond earlier discussions to address an interesting paradox—understanding how personal advertising reflects the dynamics of trust within a society regarded as increasingly distrusting. During the first decade of the twenty-first century, social scientists debated whether successive generations of Americans had not only lost trust in their institutions but also in each other.[15] Nevertheless, we have seen a dramatic increase in the use of personal advertising as a means of establishing various degrees and types of intimacy. In 2005, the Pew Research Center found that 44 percent of Americans thought online dating was a good way to meet people. By 2019, this number had risen to 59 percent. And while a large percentage of persons who have engaged in online dating describe frustration with the experience, most participants acknowledge they would continue to engage in online dating.[16] How do we explain the increased use of a courtship mechanism that has as its central dilemma how to establish interpersonal trust without the screens that used to be provided by family and friends or even face-to-face interaction? *Dating, Mating, Relating: Personal Advertisement and Modern Romance* draws on the perspectives of a range of participants and describes how personal advertising is used to develop the types of relationships that not only sustain individuals but also form the foundation of a society. The universal need to connect with one another and the techniques presented herein illustrate how people negotiate, innovate, and meet the challenges of the modern world.

Each chapter provides a deep dive into a specific type of personal advertising that draws thousands, if not millions, of participants across the country. The chapters draw on interviews with women ad placers, instructors, and mediators who convey the structure, value, and outcome of the activity. Interviews are supplemented by scholarship, online searches, and observations that provide insights into the activity.

Chapters 6, 7, and 8 each address one mode of personal advertising: speed dating, dating apps, adult dating classes and other activities. Chapter 6, "Speed Dating: The Adult Version of Musical Chairs," focuses on face-to-face meetings in round-robin and abbreviated sessions to present an alternative to online dating. Much like dating websites, speed dating could be found in the cities and suburbs, in bars and churches, and advertised to general audiences as well as niche markets (gay, interracial, seniors). The chapter describes variants of this activity and the scholarly interest in speed dating as one of the few romantic interest activities that model perfectly for researchers to gain insights into the various aspects of mating and dating. The foci of research studies of speed dating are described along with the ways in which context shapes interaction. It also addresses the differences in "doing identity" online and in circumscribed face-to-face meetings. The limited number of participants who engaged in speed dating (ten in my studies) and my observations allow me to describe these events but limit my ability to make any substantive statements on its success. Still, women characterize an element of speed dating that is important to them and that mirrors their discussions about online dating—the importance of choice and selection.

Chapter 7, "Serendipity in Personal Advertising: Couples Yoga, Couples Massage and Adult Dating 'Classes'," presents the in-person dating activities that have become part of personal advertising. I learned about each of these activities through a participant in my interviews. The chapter follows the interviews of ad placers, which describe face-to-face dating activities that emerge from adult dating classes. It also describes other activities that ostensibly were not created for the explicit purpose of dating but became part of the mix of activities in which these women participated, such as safari flirting, coffee mating, couples massage, and couples yoga. The chapter links how women create trust in on- and offline activities to support participation in these activities. I also observed and participated in a couple of the activities, and I spoke with the instructors of the activities to provide added information about how something designed for health, exercise, and even socializing became part of the broader world of dating and mating.

Chapter 8, "Dating Apps: Finding Love Just Around the Corner," focuses on the plethora of location-based dating applications that merge smartphone technology to finding love, sex, and friendship. The chapter begins by examining the history of the telephone and how it changed the landscape of dating not only in the early twentieth century but also in the 1980s when the telephone industry was deregulated. It was this deregulation that led to the intersection of technology and sexual fantasy to be followed by new technology, the smartphone. Location-based dating, otherwise known as satellite dating, grew substantially in the latter part of this century's first decade and was as popular as online dating, at least among the younger population (24–35 year olds). The chapter compares dating apps and how they serve the women who use them. It also combines anecdotal data with survey research which reveals gender differences in app experiences. Finally, Chapter 8 describes new approaches to enhancing app utility and trust for women in the digital economy.

Using survey data gathered from the Pew Research Center and other sources, Chapter 9 addresses what we have learned in the past 20 years about personal advertising. It also addresses personal advertising during the coronavirus (Covid-19) pandemic in 2020. Since my last set of interviews in 2015, the world has been confronted with a new set of challenges to dating and mating in the twenty-first century as a worldwide pandemic has now generated what we are calling the "new normal." The new normal consists of social distancing, wearing masks in public, and decreasing opportunities to meet face to face. Ad placers have adapted to these challenges by returning to some of the older forms of personal advertising that had been eclipsed by dating apps; thus, everything old is new again. Chapter 9 describes the current activities in which people are engaging and how personal advertising has adapted to current health, economic and social crises, and how it continues to play a part in meeting our enduring need to connect with others.

Introduction: Personal Advertising

At the end of the book I offer a "Methods" appendix that takes the reader through each small study performed from 1997 through 2015 and the ways in which the transformations in dating motivated each subsequent study. I begin by describing my original intentions with this work and how they were modified over time. I describe why I chose to focus on women exclusively and how I arrived at my samples. There was no grand plan to engage in four separate studies over time, but my interests in the topic, what each set of interviews revealed, led me to my next study and to a continuing interest in identity and how it is performed, the intersections of identities, how context and structures delimit these performances and why or how that matters. I was always interested in women's phenomenology of participation. In sum, the chapter provides the where, what, how, and why of each study, the different approaches to learning about this phenomenon, and the limitations of the projects and of this book. I hope it answers some questions and that the reader finds it useful.

1

From Mail-Order and Picture Brides to Dating Apps and Couples Massage

The Evolution of Personal Advertising[1]

A young Canadian lady aged 20, brunette, large eyes, blue-grey; hair black, height 5 feet 6 inches accomplished musician, thorough housekeeper, well countenanced. Gentleman answering this must be the soul of honor—that with me is more important than riches—be tall, good-looking and refined, and in every sense of the word a gentleman. I have no use for one who uses strong drink or chews that vile weed tobacco.
—January 8, 1887, *Matrimonial News*

I'm not going to tell you about my good looks, the kinds of undergarments I wear, or how pretty my smile is. My mind is flooded with Dylan, sunsets and stars.... twenties and tired of dating scene DWF seeks emotionally & financially secure, considerate, hard working NS, likes kids, and life.
—December 1997, *The Optimist*

You can state that my age is 21; used to be considered good looking by the girls when I lived in the states, though somewhat uncouth in my appearance now; am hale, hearty, strong and full of fun and frolic; have been, and am sometimes a little wild, but I think I should be steady if I had a congenial partner to love and protect. I am not rich in legacy, though my prospects for the future are as flattering as the generality of young men my age who have kicked their way through the world alone. I am anxious to correspond with a handsome, witty, intelligent young lady, between the ages of 16 and my own age with the view of forming a matrimonial alliance. I don't care if she is worth a cent, pecuniarily, or not if she has the accomplishments and qualities, for possible relationship.
—August 1857, *Freeman's Champion*

11

Shaken & Stirred: A 20s and 30s Singles Mixer
Join us for this after-hours event to connect people in their 20s
and 30s with new friends and potential love interests. You'll
mingle with everybody during short mini-dates. After you've
made the rounds, let us know who has piqued your curiosity,
and we'll let you know if they feel the same way.

—www.genre-x.com, 2011

The Right Stuff is an international introduction network for
single graduates and faculty of a select group of excellent universities & colleges. Proof of status required.

—www.rightstuffdating.com, 2007

A lil about why i'm on this site ... i'm here to socialize & get
to know some new ppl ... see where it goes from there ... i am
a free spirit..I love the spontaneity of life. simple things in life
make me happy.

Intent: wants to date but nothing serious. Personality: Night
Owl.

—*Meet Moi*, http://www.meetmoi.com, 2013

Introduction

Personal advertisement sections can now be found in almost all
major newspapers, not to mention weeklies, popular magazines, church
newsletters, university alumni magazines and, of course, the Internet.
Although personal advertising has proliferated across different venues,
this mode of dating and mating is hardly a new phenomenon. Even in
colonial New England people in the United States used personal advertising in order to secure relationships of various kinds and over the
course of two centuries changed the nature of courtship in America.[2]
The first personal ad in the U.S. was placed in the *Boston Evening Post*
in 1759. In the nineteenth and early twentieth centuries, such big-city
daily newspapers as *The New York Times, The New York Daily Mirror,
The Boston Evening Post, The Washington Post,* and more obscure outlets such as the *Denton Journal* (Denton, Maryland, 1847–1965) and
the *Bismarck Daily Tribune* (1873–1916) provided people with opportunities to market themselves to strangers. In fact, eighteenth- and
nineteenth-century personal ads could be found in newspapers in virtually every region of the country.[3] Such specialized newspapers as the
Wedding Bell and the *Matrimonial News* provided similar opportunities along with some measure of protection from the general public as

like-minded people sought each other through publications used exclusively for these purposes.[4]

At various periods in our history, personal advertising has been used to deal with circumstances that limited opportunities for meeting prospective mates. Early immigrants who wanted European brides to maintain ethnic homogamy, secure inheritance, and companionship as well as progeny often sent written requests for spouses to Europe since few women initially migrated. The practice of placing a personal ad remained largely a gendered one in the eighteenth century, with few women even attempting to place an advertisement and even fewer newspapers in which to place them. Women who tried to place personal advertisements often suffered the consequences. For example, in England in 1727, Helen Morrison placed a personal advertisement in the *Manchester Weekly Journal*, resulting in the mayor having her committed to an insane asylum for a month. Although not mainstream in the U.S., by the nineteenth century, personal ads placed by both sexes could be found as matrimonial agencies and newspapers served both genders who looked to them to secure companionship.[5]

Subsequent migration westward during the nineteenth century, combined with proscriptions against race-mixing (i.e., marriage with Native Americans), prompted many men to advertise for mail-order brides from the East, a phenomenon captured in romance novels and films such as *Sarah, Plain and Tall* (1991) and *Zandy's Bride* (1974). The films provide a gritty picture of nineteenth-century life on the Western frontier combined with the added challenges that occur when two strangers enter marriage without prior intimacy or limited knowledge of one another. They also portray the stark reality of discrepancies in the numbers of men and women in Western territories. For example, in 1899, Idaho had 16,584 men to 1,426 single women. Mariposa, California, had only 108 women out of a population of 4,379 in 1850. These discrepancies, along with similar situations in Utah, Arizona, Wyoming and Washington were undoubtedly why personal ads became so popular.

Stories of mail-order brides and arranged marriages have been a major focus of romance novels which offer a stylized version of the tensions found in mail-order marriages. Though the genre does not limit itself to any period, many stories are set on the nineteenth-century Western frontier. In reality, women were scarce in the newly claimed territories, and mail-order marriages served multiple purposes—companionship, children, and the financial benefits accrued through marriage. In *Buying a Bride: An Engaging History of Mail Order Matches*, Marcia Zug's portrait of marriages formed through personal advertisements as far back as the eighteenth century documents the deception and physical abuse as well as opportunities of empowerment that were common in mail-order matches.[6] For many women, placing and answering a personal ad for the purposes of marriage was an opportunity for financial security. It was also a way for women to exert some measure of control in their lives. Of course, that is not to suggest gender equity between men and women in these periods. Financial gain for men occurred not only from the labor provided by wives and the children they would bear but also from the reduced cost of land for married men as an incentive to help settle the West. In fact, the U.S. government played a central role in encouraging marriage by offering land grants to married men. Beauman cited the *Dubuque Iowa News* in 1838 as stating, "So anxious are our settlers for wives that they never ask a single lady her age. All they require is teeth." One settler in the Kansas Territory complained about discrimination against single men to a local newspaper:

> We learn that at the land Sales at Osawkee, unmarried men were obliged to pay 25 cents per acre more for land than married men. In behalf of this unfortunate class of individuals we strongly protest against this outrageous proceeding. In the states, where girls are plenty, we would shout "Amen!" to all such operations; but here, where "ribs" are so scarce that nearly all our bachelors are made so from necessity, owing to their inability to obtain the article, we do think this taxation levied upon them unjust and tyrannical. Can it be that the incorrigible old woman-hater of the White House had a hand in this matter? It does look reasonable. ~Letter to the *Freeman's Champion*, August 20, 1857.

At mid–nineteenth century, the Civil War—which cost the lives of over 500,000 men—left behind a significant population of widows and single women. Some of them advertised to secure marriage and economic security; others traveled west on their own or with children in tow.[7] Asian immigrants who came to the United States to work on railroads, agricultural fields, mines and sugar plantations (Hawaii) relied on exchanging photographs and letters to secure what became known as "picture brides." Although the Chinese Exclusion Act of 1882 effectively limited immigration and barred Chinese women from coming to the United States, Japan negotiated and agreed to limit the emigration of its citizens if Japanese men could bring their wives and families with them. Japanese men in America also arranged marriages. These marriages were arranged by proxy. Because of the prejudices and cultural norms about interracial marriage, Japanese men in the U.S. often sent for brides from Japan. Such unions comprised approximately half of the brides who came from Japan. The largest numbers of mail-order brides came from Asia and Europe (e.g., Japan, Korea, England, Italy, and Sweden), where traditional customs and arranged marriages between women and men, often contracted to marry sight unseen, were extended to the United States. Financial incentives encouraged families overseas to enter into agreements with men who claimed to be young, wealthy, and handsome. Photographs, however, were deceptive and could be as many as ten years old. The estimated age of grooms was an average of 12 years older than that of their brides. Proxy marriages were legalized in Japan, and brides often arrived in the United States only to discover that their reportedly rich, handsome husbands in America were, in fact, significantly older, not handsome, and rarely property owners.[8] While the measures of securing these alliances were unconventional, the practice of marriage for pragmatic purposes was not.

Social club advertisements provided yet another venue for personal advertising in the late nineteenth and early twentieth centuries. During this time, social clubs served a variety of purposes and ran the gamut of social classes, from elite clubs for the wealthiest Americans to the clubs formed in the bars of poor neighborhoods. Regarded as small-scale institutions that amplified party politics, social clubs promoted civil and political participation.[9] Immigrants, in particular, created and used social clubs to sustain ethnic communities, often in response to discrimination and exclusion from the larger society. Some social clubs, promoted in the *New York Daily Mirror* and the *Maryland Gazette,* also performed the latent functions of personal advertising, as these clubs provided a space for both genders to engage in social discourse that occasionally resulted in people forming permanent alliances. Several descriptions mirrored the personal ads of other newspapers.

Other avenues for mating occasionally involved transporting large numbers of women recruited from one location and taken to another for the explicit purpose of meeting and marrying men. Cathy Luchetti writes about the Mercer Maids, one of several such experiments. Mercer Maids were young women from the east coast recruited for transport to Washington by entrepreneur and matchmaker Asa Mercer. Mercer's motivation for taking women to Washington was to cultivate the proper civic and moral values in the Northwest territory with a promise of marriage, wealth, and land.[10]

... I appeal to high-minded women to go into the West to aid in throwing around those who have gone before the restraints of well-regulated society; to cultivate the higher and purer facilities of man by casting about him those refining influences that true women always carry with them; to build up happy homes and let true sunlight shine round the hearthstone. It is simply a matter of duty on the part of Eastern woman to go to the West, where their presence and influence are so much needed. A.S. MERCER, *New York Times*, 1864.[11]

Despite the good intentions of the Mercer Maid project, participants were also charged for the trip, and the $250 fee served as a filter of social class and "who" could embark on this journey. On his first journey, Mercer recruited only 11 women, several of whom did marry shortly after their arrival. Mercer's second trip was more successful, as he was able to get more than 100 women to accompany him back to Seattle.

Asa Mercer was not alone in these efforts. Businesswoman Eliza Farnham in 1849 also attempted to recruit women for bachelors out West. Farnham was an author and social reformer who became the jail matron at Sing-Sing at the age of 27. She had traveled west in 1835 to encounter a scene she regarded as one of licentiousness and depravity. To Farnham, marital immigration was the key to transforming the West into a civilized place as women would use their influence on their husbands to reform their ways and create a more stable society.[12]

Farnham placed advertisements in New York newspapers and secured the endorsement of her plan from such notable figures as Horace Greeley and William Cullen Bryant. Despite her plans and a response from more than 200 women, illness prevented her from following through on her timeline, and, in the end, she was only able to get a handful of women to travel with her to California.

Fred Harvey, another businessman and possibly the most successful matchmaker—though this was not his primary goal—used female waitresses in his restaurants along the Santa Fe Railway. Harvey House, known as the first restaurant chain in the United States, simultaneously provided opportunities to improve working wages for women and enhanced prospects for marriage. Harvey's girls had to be refined, possess an education, and have good moral character. They also had to sign a one-year contract of employment. Between 1883 and 1950, Harvey employed 100,000 women, a significant number of whom found spouses.[13] It is estimated that over 5,000 Harvey girls married and helped to settle the West.

1. From Mail-Order, Picture Brides, Dating Apps to Massage

The many facets of placing and answering personal ads include opportunities and benefits along with dreams deferred and severe disappointments. The fact that the majority of immigrants were men and that interracial marriage was strictly forbidden resulted in the need to bring wives from their home countries. Though a great deal of attention has been paid to the opportunities for women to marry and immigrate, personal advertising and such projects as the Mercer Maids provided two of the few opportunities for women to have some measure of control over their lives. In an article on colonial women who responded to personal advertisements, Marcia Zug stated that these women were independent, powerful and respected. Rather than referred to as the pejorative "mail-order brides," colonial women who answered personal advertisements were referred to as "Jamestown brides," "King's daughters" and "Casket girls." Zug likened them to modern women who engage in personal advertising and suggested that the narratives surrounding women who responded to personal ads in the eighteenth and nineteenth centuries narrowly describe women's motivations and assets and limited them to being victims as opposed to trailblazers.

Letters, magazine articles and books from the nineteenth century indicated that many women thought of moving west as an adventure or even as an opportunity to gain a measure of autonomy. Many of these women did not marry immediately, and some did not marry at all. Those who had skills that allowed them to live on their own used them (seamstress). Some liked the appeal of more liberal environments like California where property could be held in their names (even after marriage). It also maintained liberal divorce laws which made it far more appealing to women who wanted control over their lives. The perception of women as having only one focus—marriage—is a limited understanding of the appeal of personal advertising to women, even in the eighteenth and nineteenth centuries.

As with any innovation that captured a population of participants, deviant behavior inevitably emerged soon thereafter. Deviant behavior was a common feature of marriage through personal ads, and husbands of picture brides were notorious for the deception worked on women and their families. These husbands were often much older and poor, and marriage to them did little to improve the well-being or social status of the bride, let alone meet her expectations of romance and love. The range of deviant behavior ran the gamut from misrepresentation to illegal behavior as wives could discover they had married a bigamist with multiple wives and children (whose dowries the husband had also squandered). Con artists convinced people in the west to send money they would use to find suitable wives. Instead, of course, they simply took the money and moved on to other nefarious activities. Even matrimonial agencies could be fraudulent and fictitious entities to which people looking for marriage or love would send their money with the hope of having a match made for them. However, it was not only men who used the personal ads to engage in deviant behavior; women also participated in fraud and other activities designed to prey upon ad placers and to engage in socially unacceptable behaviors. Just as in modern times, personal ads at the turn of the century were also used to connect to others who had interests alternative to marriage and other desires for connecting with members of the opposite sex. These included prostitution and socially unacceptable sex practices.

One of the deviant practices that involved personal ads included murder by both men and women. Francesca Beauman (2020) dedicated two chapters of her book on personal ads to the topic of deviance explicit to ad placers and responders. These chapters contained stories of men who placed personal ads for wives and after he persuaded the new wife to give him all of her money (for safekeeping), abandoned her and took her money with him. One of Beauman's chapters focused on Belle Gunness, a mail-order bride and serial murderer who used personal ads to lure, murder, and dismember more than 40 men.

Anonymity, geographic mobility, immigration, and isolation were just some of the factors that made personal ads an activity that attracted unsavory people. And yet, this mode of meeting and marrying continued to attract participants for a substantial period of time. It was assumed that nineteenth- and early twentieth-century personal advertising was practiced primarily for the purposes of marriage, but there is substantial evidence that shows those who fell outside of the mainstream also used ads to find like-minded souls. And the same concerns about social class, material circumstances, and good looks seen in today's personal ads were also factors in nineteenth-century mating. Of course, more practical skills (e.g., housekeeping) and good character (e.g., respectability) were also called for in nineteenth-century ads. Throughout time, these same mating and dating criteria have served those forced to find alternative ways of meeting people.

Everything Old Is New Again

Whether placed in the nineteenth century or today, personal ads serve as windows into people's lives and have the capacity to evoke powerful responses from readers as we become voyeurs of those lives. In many respects, nineteenth-century advertisements mirrored twentieth- and twenty-first-century ads with several characteristics common to both. While nineteenth-century personal advertisements were supposedly focused on marriage, many personal ads and matchmaking services today also claim an interest in "long-term relationships," if not marriage. And just as personal ads in the 1800s were placed in response to social circumstances (e.g., war, migration, and financial incentives), modern personal ads are a response to geographic mobility, demographic and cultural changes, occupational constraints, the limited success of more traditional dating techniques (e.g., meeting people through family or church), and innovations linked to twenty-first-century technology.

Demographic trends indicate that in addition to a divorce rate that quadrupled between 1970 and 1996 and remains significant (one of two marriages are estimated to end in divorce), there has been a rise in the number of people who choose to delay marriage, remain single, and who outlive their spouses. Added to changes in marriage patterns is the increased geographic or spatial mobility of people in the United States, particularly in specific regions of the country.[14] Consequently, shifting forms of community—combined with historical, cultural, and structural changes and the consequential movement in and out of various social groups—encourage people to seek alternative avenues for establishing relationships and finding intimacy.

Personal advertising has also contained an element of secrecy regardless of the period in which it has occurred. Formerly exceptional, advertising for mates has now become commonplace as one out of ten persons claims to have met someone through personal advertising. Still, some continue to regard it as a deviant activity engaged in by individuals possessing unacceptable personal characteristics (e.g., desperate or unattractive people or predators seeking to obtain multiple sex partners) or "social types" that include *the adventurous* seeking excitement and *the shy* and *lonely* seeking people like themselves.[15] Yet personal advertising, refracted through the lenses of race, ethnicity, gender, sexual orientation, and social class, has as much to do with our changing social circumstances and the enduring need to form personal relationships as with personal idiosyncrasies or predispositions. Still, there are important similarities and differences between ads of old and modern ads that can be illustrated by looking at two sets of newspaper advertisements placed in the nineteenth and twentieth centuries.

Matrimonial News *(January 1887) and* Social Connections *(May 1997)*

In the late nineteenth century, a newspaper dedicated to introducing prospective mates was the *Matrimonial News.* Published weekly, this newspaper had editions in Kansas City, Missouri, and San Francisco, California, and functioned like the personals section of newspapers today. The *Matrimonial News* also maintained guidelines for ad placements.[16] These included directions regarding where and when to place ads, cost of placement (which differed for men and women), the format, length, and content of the ad. Special incentives were also offered to prospective advertisers:

> Advertisers should give their personal appearance, height, weight, their financial and social position in life, and a general description of the kind of person desired as correspondents and be careful to write plainly their full name and post-office address so that we may forward their letters in reply.
>
> TO LADIES: We will, as a trial, forward five letters to five personals, insert a free personal and send one copy three months for 50 cents. Or to any lady who will send us five personal advertisements for five lady friends, which we will print free of charge, we will mail Matrimonial News for three months, free post paid.
>
> TO GENTLEMEN: Five letters forwarded to five lady personals, a free ad and a free paper for three months for 50 cents. Try it. Try it. (January 1887).

As part of an attempt to entice readers, the periodical also carried a byline that read "SPICY PERSONALS." But by today's standards, the majority of these ads were anything but spicy.

> 289. I am 18, 5 feet 5 inches, high, weight 140 pounds, auburn hair, dark brown eyes, full; I want a number of gentlemen correspondents from 19–25. Object: let the future take care of itself.
>
> 295. A jolly girl of 18 years, brown hair, eyes that are bluish gray and a

fondness for fun and correspondence prompts to ask for gentlemen correspondents. Photos exchanged.

276. I am a brunette of 18 years rather small, lively disposition, full of fun: would like to correspond with gentleman of culture. Object: good time.

230. A young brunette of 30, refined and genteel and in business for myself would like to correspond with a gentleman of character.... Object, let the future take care of itself.

232. There is a bull in Missouri with a foot that's flat.
   With scads in his pocket and a brick in his hat.
   With an eye that is blue, and a No. 10 shoe,
   He's the bull of the woods and the boy for you.

Personal advertisements in the twentieth-century *Social Connections* were also published weekly and averaged around the same number as those in the *Matrimonial News.* However, personal ads in *Social Connections* were part of a subcontract and were placed in the classifieds section of weekly and daily newspapers in eastern cities. The particular sample for this comparison was placed in the daily *Tribune.* Similar to the *Matrimonial News, Social Connections* also maintained guidelines for ad placement that included a word limit (30 words free of charge), eligibility ("only persons seeking long-term monogamous relationships, persons 18 years old or older"), and restrictions stating what could *not* be advertised ("explicit sexual or anatomical references" or "persons wanted under 18 years of age"). It is striking to see the similarities in personal ads placed 100 years apart.

Consistent with analyses of modern personal advertisements performed between 1970 and 2000, men and women who advertised in the *Matrimonial News* also tended to engage in the trading of traits; that is, men desired specific characteristics in women and women desired different characteristics in men.[17] In the *Matrimonial News,* men most frequently requested that ladies be "intelligent," "refined," or "cultured." Women, or "ladies," as the *Matrimonial News* referred to them, desired that male respondents be "honorable," "of good character," "respectable," or in "good society." In *Social Connections,* such characteristics as "caring," "attractive," "interesting," "fun," "intelligent," and "affectionate" were requested by men. Women cited "sincere," "secure," "honest," "sense of humor," and "professional" as traits important to them. In both periods, men and women wanted age-appropriate mates, which typically meant younger women desired by men and older men desired by women, with age ranges of the desired mate more narrowly defined by men than by women.

Table 1.1. Personal Characteristics
in Advertisements (1887 vs. 1997)

	Matrimonial News (January 1887) 101 ads		*Social Connections (May 1997)* 104 ads	
Variable	Gentleman	Ladies	Men	Women
Advertisements placed	49	52	47	57
Average age of advertiser	25	23	38	36
Most frequently requested characteristics	Intelligent Refined Cultured	Honorable Of good character Respectable In good society	Attractive Caring Interesting Fun Intelligent Professional Affectionate	Secure Sincere Honest Sense of humor
Requested "means" or "financial security"	6	7	1	4
Requested "good looking" or "attractive"	5	3	24	5
Requested "matrimony" or "long-term relationship"	22	23	9	9

Also similar to the *Matrimonial News*, *Social Connections* required that advertisers seek "long-term monogamous relationships," yet only half of the people who placed ads explicitly declared that they were "willing to commit" or expressed a desire for a "serious," "committed," or "long-term" relationship. And while an assumption of marriage has been regarded as the driving force behind personal ads of old, less than half of the gentlemen or ladies who placed ads in *Matrimonial News* declared their objective as marriage. These declarations may have been implicit given the title of the newspaper; however, several personal advertisements placed by gentlemen and ladies clearly included interests alternative to marriage. Perhaps social propriety limited such declarations, but given the explicit purpose of the newspaper and the period when marriage was the normative state for adult men and women, it is doubtful.

Table 1.2. Samples of Relationship Goals of Ad Placers: *Matrimonial News* 1887

Ad #	*Personal Advertisement*
239	A highly respected and cultured young lady solicits correspondence with an honorable gentleman not over 25 years old, good standing, one who is full of fun and can write a joyful good letter. I am 21 years of age, 5 feet 4 inches, weight 125 pounds, dark hair and deep blue eyes and of a lively disposition. As to beauty photo will speak. Object, fun and if the harvest is love so much the better. All letters promptly answered. Photos exchanged.
251	A gentleman fond of amusement asks to correspond and become acquainted with some lady of same disposition; have a good business and can make company very pleasant.—all letters answered.
255	A blonde gentleman of 23 years, height 5 feet 11 inches, weight 160 pounds, wishes to correspond with a lady from 18 to 21, brunette preferred. Object, pleasure and pastime, and perhaps....
243	We are two jolly and lively girls both of the brunette order, having dark brown hair and dark eyes, we are both same age and good friends, 20 years old and of good form; want correspondence with gentlemen fond of driving and theater.
249	I am a young gentleman of 23, height 5 feet 8 inches, weight 145 pounds, am considered good looking; Would like to correspond with some young lady of honor; brunette preferred. Object: company and perhaps...
255	I am fond of fun, age 18, height 5 feet 5 inches, weight 140 pounds, have auburn hair, dark eyes; I want a gentleman correspondent from 20 to 25. Object fun and perhaps matrimony if suited.
211	Am 22, 5 feet 10 inches high, weigh 153 pounds and am pining for a few good lady correspondents; acquaintance formed inter on; lots of fun for winter evenings, everyone write and I will promise an interesting answer.
226	I am a jolly little girl of 17, with black hair and eyes, and tan complexion, weigh 115 pounds, am fond of company and would like to form the acquaintance of a nice gentleman or two, with whom I could spend an occasional evening socially, and if mutually agreeable become friends, with proclivities tending ultimately to the greatest ambition of women.
230	A young brunette of 30, refined and genteel and in business for myself would like to correspond with a gentleman of character—Object, let the future take care of itself.
196	A cultured young lady of 19, medium height, dark hair, brown eyes, considered very good looking, jolly, of good family. Correspondence with gentlemen of means only desired.

Ad #	Personal Advertisement
216	I am a brunette of 21 years of age, height 6 feet, weight 175 pounds, dark hair, black eyes, dress neat and am good looking, temperate and irreproachable in character; desire to correspond with a few young ladies under 21, blonde preferred; give full description of self—object mutual benefit and perhaps...
229	I am an American widow aged 50, 5 feet 1 inch in height, weight 127 lbs., a blonde, good form, intelligent, attractive and in good society, enjoying good health, and self-sustaining and unencumbered and wish to correspond with gentleman of honor and suitable age.

Despite the commonalities between these nineteenth- and twentieth-century newspaper personal advertisements, there were also significant differences. In the modern personal ads women desire "financial security" or what nineteenth-century ads often called "means."[18] However, of the 101 ads placed by gentlemen and ladies, at least during this month of *Matrimonial News*, only six gentlemen (of 49) requested that ladies have "means," and only seven ladies (of 52) asked that gentlemen have "means." Women in the nineteenth century were significantly more dependent upon men for economic security; nevertheless, the primary trait of interest expressed in women's personal ads in *Matrimonial News* was that men be honorable. Women in *Social Connections* also listed financial security as important. Another distinction of twentieth-century personal ads is that they included codes for race, ethnicity, marital status, and ancillary characteristics (e.g., SWMNS=single, White, male, nonsmoker). People in both newspapers advertised for members of the opposite sex within age ranges. However, male advertisers in *Matrimonial News* were an average age of 25 years old, and female advertisers were 23 years old. People placing ads in *Social Connections* were older, with male advertisers an average age of 38 and females 36 years old.

The range of "objectives" or types of intimacy in modern ads was significantly broader than that of their predecessors, with twentieth-century women seeking different kinds of relationships, including casual dating and serious and committed relationships. Equally important, women and men ad placers were likely to seek out other members of the same sex for these relationships, a phenomenon unthinkable in nineteenth-century personal ads.[19] Whereas the only acceptable statuses in nineteenth-century ads were single and widow (or widower), by the twentieth century, women and men could be single, divorced, unmarried parents, gay and lesbian, and even "couples," as modern ad placers were allowed to state not only race and ethnicity but also sexual preferences.[20] However, people did use personal ads to attract like-minded others who were open to different types of relationships not sanctified by the larger society, but these were less commonly found in newspapers. Little attention was given by either gender to physical attractiveness in the *Matrimonial News,* but one of the overriding concerns of most male advertisers in *Social Connections* was the physical attractiveness of women, with "attractive" or "good looking" listed first among their desired traits. As youth and physical attractiveness have gained purchase in the twentieth and twenty-first centuries, our modern social context is reflected in the content of our personal ads, just as the proliferation of personal advertising is a reflection of the social changes that have taken place in our society.

Courtship practices in the United States have been well documented over the decades, with personal diaries and correspondence providing insights into the economic and cultural forces that have shaped these activities. Explaining such practices, Beth Bailey pointed to the various functions of courtship in American society[21]:

> The arena of courtship was sometimes used to maintain or to challenge racial hierarchies; it was a sphere in which the meaning of class was contested. Gender roles, of course, always shaped the historical meanings and practices of courtship. And new technologies—whether central heating, the automobile, movies and record players, or the birth control pill—have made enormous differences in when, where, and how Americans have gone about courtship...[3].

The twenty-first century is no exception. In keeping with Bailey's assertion that no dominant national system of courtship has yet to emerge and that current dating practices lack clarity with respect to men and women's expectations, the phenomenon of personal advertising represents another way in which courtship practices intersect with the social, economic, and technological changes in our society.

Francesca Beauman reminded us how the popularity of personal ads has waxed and waned over the decades. After World War I, reduced parental supervision and the concept of dating gained popularity, which reduced dependence on personal ads. In fact, Beauman argued that until the 1950s, personal ads were in decline. It was not until the 1960s that personal ads began to make a comeback, and by the 1980s, personal ads were de rigueur. By the 1990s, four out of five American newspapers carried personal ads.[22] It bears mentioning that the process of personal advertising generated opportunities important to women in the eighteenth and nineteenth centuries that were similar to how women in the twentieth and twenty-first centuries viewed the value of personal advertising—as affording some measure of control over their own destinies.

Women from both Europe and Asia elected to participate in marital immigration (via personal ads) as a way of having some say in their lives. A law in 1855 bestowed on women who married a citizen of the United States automatic citizenship, stimulating many women to use marital immigration as a means of positively changing their lives. Women in the U.S. who participated in the experiments of Mercer and Farnham also used marital immigration to enhance their economic opportunities. Several did not even marry once they arrived at their destinations. Instead, they worked in traditional and nontraditional jobs to secure their economic situations. Early mail-order brides may have experienced more limitations on their choices but traveling thousands of miles, marrying a man sight unseen, and risking everything on a stranger in a strange land was a choice, and one that was made by women and not just men. Either placing or responding to a personal ad for marriage was a way to avoid the oppressive conditions at home—to escape poverty, foreign occupation of one's country, the cultural restrictions in one's homeland, improve one's marital prospects, and even engage in an adventure that promised a different (and more open) experience in America. There were similarities between the Mercer Maids or Farnham's marital immigrants and the Japanese, Korean and Okinawan women who made the trip to the northwest and who also declined to marry once arrived or who married and divorced or who simply left their husbands to make their economic way alone by engaging in traditional women's work (sewing, cleaning and cooking) and work that was needed in these new territories (teaching, social and political activism). Many of these women were independent, entrepreneurial and willing to try life on their own. Marcia Zug (2016) provided the number of Asian women who dared to divorce their husbands and make their living on their own (105 Japanese divorce cases in Seattle between 1907 and 1920, and 70 percent of these cases were initiated by the wives, who won nearly all of the cases).

European immigrant women also preferred the dangers and risks of marital immigration to the alternatives provided them in their home countries. From the 1830s to the twentieth century, almost 4,000,000 Irish immigrants came to the U.S. These immigrants were roughly divided between men and women, and most of them were young and unaccompanied. From data based on 10,000 civil marriage records, Reginald Byron found a significant number of Irish women went west to marry Irish men who worked on railroads, served in the military, and in the mines. The Immigration Act of 1924 effectively ended Japanese immigration to the U.S. and certainly Japanese picture brides; the Quota Act of 1921 severely restricted immigration from Eastern and Southern Europe. However, these did not alter the reality that women had used personal advertising and marital immigration as a means of having control over their lives. The appeal of modern-day personal ads is much the same, as surveys and qualitative research find the issue of autonomy to be at least as important to modern-day women as it was to the women in the eighteenth and nineteenth centuries who came to the U.S. via a personal ad.

From Personal Ads to Personal Advertising

In modern times, there has been a literal explosion of variations on the theme of "personal advertising," with personal ads placed in newspapers or magazines now accompanied by video dating, Internet personals, matchmaking services such as "It's Just Lunch," speed dating (with all of its variants) and dating apps. Like personal ads in print media, these activities involve the public marketing of the self in a circumscribed medium, space, or place. Whether this occurs through an online advertisement, video clip, or rotating foray in a bar or community center, these activities have the added characteristic of what one writer calls "transitory moments," in which people often meet for a single date, coffee, or a five-minute speed-dating session. Encounters are largely with strangers through a mediator (who is also a stranger) and for a fee, all with the hope of making connections to other people. Indeed, personal advertising is limited only by the medium chosen, not by extant social parameters that have defined and confined traditional dating situations.

Online personal ads and dating services are ubiquitous and include services targeted at a general audience along with particular racial/ethnic and religious groups, sexually oriented persons, older singles, working-class persons, and people with specific hobbies or tastes, such as pet lovers. Some dating sites target groups that may be stigmatized or restricted in some way (single parents, unattractive people, or people with a sexually transmitted disease). Virtually any group imaginable can now find an online dating site designed to accommodate its needs, even wealthy men (and the women who want to date them) or wives who want to cheat on their husbands.

Table 1.3. Online Dating Sites

Racial/Ethnic Groups	Blacksingles.com
	Jewishdating.com
Religious Groups	Catholicsingles.com
Sexually Oriented Groups	allthingslesbian.com
Older Singles	romanceover40.com
Working-Class Persons	bluecollardates.com
Pet Lovers	datemypet.com
Star Trek Fans	startrekdating.com
Gothic Singles	gothicsingles.com
Positive Singles	positivesingles.com (known STD)
Unattractive People	uglyschmucks.com
Wealthy Men	richhookup.com
Seniors	silversingles.com
Lonely Wives	lonelycheatingwives.com

Another personal advertising service for busy professionals is "It's Just Lunch." Started in 1991, it now has franchises in cities throughout the country, including Chicago, Charlotte, and Albuquerque, and operates in much the same way as other dating services. Applicants are screened through interviews prior to being matched with clients, and its staff subsequently attends to the logistics of the date. Like most services, It's Just Lunch also claims enormous success, although "success" is largely undefined or corroborated.

One of the most popular forms of personal advertising is speed dating. Speed dating catapulted into the twenty-first century and is now the model for several offshoots of its own (flash dating, coffee mating, safari flirting, and Just Eye Contact) where parties, bars, dance halls, community centers, coffee shops, and even churches have events that as many as 400 singles at a time pay to attend. Speed dating involves a type of round-robin rotation of people meeting and interacting anywhere from five to ten minutes before moving on to meet the next person. Interactions are guided by a set of rules designed to help avoid presuppositions by participants:

- Persons may not ask where a date lives or what s/he does for a living.
- Dates may not let anyone know whether or not they chose them.
- Men move, and women stay seated.
- The next table is positioned out of the direct line of sight.

- Dates must answer the question, was the person polite and respectful?
- Dates must indicate immediately after each "date" whether they would like to see the person again.
- No dates may be skipped.
- Only seven dates are allowed.
- No telephone numbers may be exchanged.[23]

Like online personal advertising, speed dating spawned several variant activities that use the same premise. For example, the now-defunct Just Eye Contact was a dating service that hosted participants to sit without speaking and gaze into each other's eyes for two minutes before rotating on to the next person's gaze. The premise offered was that people could learn more about each other and achieve greater intimacy without verbal exchange by trying to "see into each other's souls."[24] Coffee mating, cleverly named after a milk substitute trademark, maintains the slogan that it's the perfect way to "circulate and percolate" with members of the opposite sex; its website suggested it "could land coffee daters in the love seat with Mr. or Ms. Right." Safari flirting began with a drink and tips on flirting, followed by "working" the local stores in a defined area (where participants may shop) and a subsequent debriefing in a local bar. Safari flirting parties defined the parameters more narrowly for novice "flirts." Each of these activities relied upon a critical mass of people who wanted to make connections with other people and either perceived the need for assistance in doing so or were interested in alternative approaches to dating/mating. Some of these activities were regionally specific, but it is likely that their counterparts existed under different rubrics throughout the United States.

Throughout our history, we have seen the impact of modern technology on courtship practices, whether in the form of the telephone, automobiles, birth control pills, videos, or the Internet. The latest of these innovations involved the use of cell phones and satellite applications (apps) to form what is called location-based dating, also known as satellite, mobile, or GPS dating. This mode of connecting gave new meaning to the label "transitory moments," as smartphone technology was linked to dating apps that connected user profiles in various ways. Users simply downloaded the app, created a profile name, uploaded a photo (optional), and answered questions about themselves (also optional). Phone alerts notified them when potential mates were nearby, or in the case of one app (Assisted Serendipity) when the male-to-female ratio is optimized in their favor. These were followed by "introductions," and the rest was up to participants. The first mobile dating apps emerged in the early twenty-first century. Although the number of dating apps once paled in comparison to the multibillion-dollar online dating industry, they have grown in number. Some of the more extreme claims referred to mobile dating as "a state of mind," "a way of life," "preserving the magic of serendipitous meetings," and even "good for the environment" because people were meeting people nearby and therefore did not have to use their cars. These mobile apps varied in their marketing strategies and their targeted audiences. However, most apps were explicit in their focus on dating and mating. There were even apps that targeted gays and lesbians, straight men and women, and couples interested in "mobile hookups" (Naughtymeetings.com).

Today, as people marry later in life, elect not to marry at all, seek partners after divorce, live long enough to outlive or seek new partners, move into new regions or new occupations, and participate in jobs not conducive to meeting people, the intermediaries or traditional screens that once assisted in dating and mating are not around or at least not perceived to be adequate. In all its variations, personal advertising is an innovation that performs the work that traditional institutions used to perform but in a way suited to modern society. Everything from telephone, televised, and virtual services to "continuing education" that includes couples massage and couples yoga, where people do not have to know each other prior to engaging in the activity, reflects how entrepreneurs and participants intersect to meet the eternal need to connect with others. In his extensive research of lonely hearts in England, John Cockburn argued that what is clear about postmodern society is that loneliness has increased. It is this to which he attributed the increased use of personal advertising in print media. Whether loneliness has increased in U.S. society, Cockburn is correct in explaining that the source resides not so much in our person or our "selves" as in the context of our lives.[25] Beyond this explanation, however, is the fact that personal advertising is also perceived as liberating, particularly by women, because participants create and perform identities and choose from among a seemingly endless supply of potential mates.

Personal Advertising as Modern Courtship?

The raison d'être for personal advertising is as old as time, with participants who described a process whose origins were grounded in complex changes in family structures, the labor market, geographic limitations, and cultural imperatives. Personal advertising was not done in lieu of other attempts to meet people but as one of a variety of ways in which people attempted to establish relationships. Unlike the fear generated by the 1970s film *Looking for Mr. Goodbar,* in which a sexually liberated woman searched for the perfect man in singles' bars and ultimately met a tragic end by choosing the wrong person, participants in this book perceived personal advertising to increase opportunities and generate greater freedom of choice. The benefits of personal advertising coincided with features of our modern society. In a world of radical individualism, unfettered markets, and consumer capitalism, scientific models of matchmaking operate in tandem with the need of participants to retain control over their romantic choices. Technology (and access to that technology) enables larger numbers of people to engage in these multiple modes of dating, mating and relating. And though early computer dating was biased toward White heterosexual, middle-class users, we now see a multiplicity of sites and activities that serve almost any group and conceivable interest. Francesca Beauman offered reasons for the decline in the use of personal ads as the emergence of dating that occurred in the 1920s.[26] The attraction of personal advertising appears to be increasing in the twenty-first century.

Nevertheless, greater numbers of connections do not guarantee greater numbers of relationships, as many of these efforts resulted in disappointment. Still, these activities have proliferated, and there is no reason to assume they will not continue to expand both in number and type. With the diminished salience of family, neighborhood, and other primary groups as tests of preliminary acquaintance prior to intimacy or commitment, the new practices cited here may well be the primary mode of establishing interpersonal relationships in the future, or other more impersonal techniques may take their place. We live in a rapidly changing and complex world, and just as rapidly people approach these changes by innovating. The following chapters describe how technological changes have affected our most intimate associations, providing the basis for the foundation of family, friendships, and primary associations in general. Already, attitudes have changed dramatically toward these practices, and changes in the formation of interpersonal relations are of scholarly and practical interest. The universal need to connect and the techniques presented here illustrate how people adapt to the challenges of the modern world.

2

"Can't Buy Me Love?"

The Intersection of Romance with Science and Commerce

No examination of personal advertising could be complete without understanding our dependence on science to provide answers to virtually all of life's problems. Although we have developed a jaded cynicism about the progress of science and our cultural wars currently include science as an arena of debate, as in other areas of life, when traditional sources fail to provide opportunities for establishing intimacy, we look to science to provide the answers. Television and Internet advertisements tell us that intimacy can be achieved scientifically. Of course, much of the information is what some would call pseudoscience, but it is still made with the assumption that consumers regard science as having the answers. For example, ExtenZe, an herbal sexual enhancement drug, claims to enhance the size of a man's penis, stating that it's "No Gimmick, Just Real Science" with an ad that points to how "simple capsules have been making a difference in our lives for over half a century, from relieving pain, improving our health, managing our weight and increasing our energy." The advertisement claims that ExtenZe is one of the "mini-miracles of modern times."[1] A number of testosterone boosters such as Force Factor, Alpha King, Max Testosterone, and Ageless Male are accompanied by Boost, a female libido supplement that claims to increase sex drive, intensify orgasms and restore self-confidence, permeate the landscape of supplements offered in drugstores, health stores, and online. KY Intense, a vaginal lubricant, is "scientifically shown to enhance female satisfaction," and Kegel devices are recommended not only for restoring pelvic floor health but also for getting more pleasure from sexual intimacy. And, of course, Viagra and Cialis, two of the most popular male sexual performance drugs, have allowed millions of men to address erectile dysfunction. As in other areas of life, science now provides us with the answers not only to our bodies but also to our hearts, or at least our primal urges.

The more dependent we have become on scientific answers, the more profitable it is for entrepreneurs to sell us the idea that personal advertising has mastered the science of matching people romantically. As a result, modern personal advertising, including mobile dating, has evolved from a spontaneous and relatively cheap way to meet people in the 1970s and 1980s to a growing industry in which the exchange of money for accessing potential mates is linked to a demand for success. And in our data-driven society, these outlets provide an abundance of "scientific evidence" and seemingly foolproof algorithms used to match participants.

Few studies explicitly focus on the ways that science and commerce intersect in the marketplace of romance,[2] and those that do have typically been solicited by matchmaking services as proof of their success.[3] These studies carry the patina of scientific claims to validity. There is no denying that participants are interested in relationships, and businesses are interested in profit, and in a world where almost every aspect of the human experience is commodified and commercialized, the formation of intimate relationships has been subjected to these same processes. In an *access* society such as ours, the mandate for any capital venture is to create discontent along with a product that will reduce it and then to market that product to the public.[4] As a feature of consumer capitalism, *relationship tourism* involves the selective appropriation and consumption of activities, networks, and spontaneous opportunities that promise fulfillment of personal desires, whether they are sexual, platonic, or emotional. In contemporary society, the media serves as the major conduit to promote personal relationships; such activities are advertised, packaged, and increasingly consumed by various groups, domestically and globally.

Though we have tended to separate intimacy and personal relationships from economics, there is substantial evidence that the two are inextricably intertwined.[5] Elizabeth Jagger argued that decontextualizing participants who engage in personal advertising from their historical, economic, and cultural contexts, treats them solely as products instead of agents of social change.[6] To this, I would add that participation in personal advertising must also be situated within specific media contexts to comprehend their role in shaping identity for particular audiences. In early periods personal ads were one of the few ways that women could exercise some degree of control over their lives, and thus, the newspaper was one of the few ways to do this. In modern times, the variety of print media, online websites and dating apps have expanded women's options and the multiplicity of outlets, many of which speak to different audiences, and has provided several different choices. One example of this begins by looking at advertisements in print media, specifically newspapers. The vast majority of personal advertising in the nineteenth and twentieth centuries was done in print mode and occurred within the contexts of newspapers and magazines. The majority of scholarly studies of personal ads in the 1970s through the 1990s focused on ads placed in newspapers.[7] Nevertheless, little attention was paid to the role that newspapers played in shaping the participation of personal advertising.[8] With this in mind, excerpts from the following newspaper study conducted in 1998 illustrate how the medium of the newspaper organized and impacted participation in these reflexive projects.

The Print Context of Personal Advertising: Tribune, *the* Idealist *and the* Mirror

The guidelines for ad placement in three east coast newspapers combined with interviews with their newspaper editors, customer service representatives, and those who placed personal ads in these papers were compared as part of the study of ad placers at that time. Each newspaper maintained Personal Ads sections and served a metropolitan area along with several smaller surrounding suburbs and towns. They were chosen because they marketed these advertisements to the same populations, and they had local reputations as conservative (the *Tribune*), liberal (the *Idealist*), and progressive or avant-garde (the *Mirror*). Editors and customer service representatives conveyed the significance and purpose of the Personal Ads section along with how the newspapers participated in framing ad parlance and ad construction and delimited the population of participants to obtain responses from readers. The organization of the Personals sections within each newspaper was examined with a focus on the lexicon of vocabulary codes, guidelines, and requirements and customer assistance in ad placement. This aspect of the project on personal advertising focused on the impact of context on participation, the organizational matrix of the newspaper, and interactions between ad placers and newspaper representatives.

Guidelines in the *Tribune, Idealist,* and *Mirror* provide an

understanding of why participants chose newspapers and illustrate how newspapers participated in ad construction by deciding who was allowed to participate and what could be said. Like the
nineteenth-century *Matrimonial News*, ad placement for each of these
newspapers was guided by a set of codes, categories of who could be
ad placers, the limitations, and costs. These specifications were accompanied by explicit statements in each newspaper that addressed
issues of liability, such as minimum age for advertising, or in the *Tribune*'s case, the requirement that ad placers be "only persons seeking
long-term monogamous relationships." Each newspaper provided cate-
gorical headings (e.g., Men Seeking Women, Women Seeking Women)
that supplied information about the ad placer and the desired "other"
and included symbols, letters, abbreviations about race/ethnicity, sexual orientation or interest and a host of other relevant specifications.
The codes framed the advertisement's discourse, reduced ambiguity,
and allowed shared construction of meaning. Newspapers also offered
customer assistance to participants to generate an optimal presentation of self, defined by both the newspaper and the ad placer as one
that elicited many responses. Supplementary to the codes was the varying amount of space made available to participants (i.e., the number of
lines of text) within which they had to capture the reader's attention and
evoke a response. To varying degrees, each of the newspapers participated in shaping participants' identity construction and the possibilities for interaction.

Tables 2.1 and 2.2 provide the codes and guidelines of each newspaper. Although the actual number of codes provided by each newspaper did not vary by more than three, the types of codes were different.
For example, the *Tribune* listed only two ad placer categories (Women
and Men) and did not include codes found in the *Idealist* and the *Mirror*,
such as "Gay," "Bisexual," or "Transvestite." Similarly, the *Tribune* and
the *Idealist* included the code "Christian," whereas the *Mirror* did not.
However, the *Mirror* had three codes not used by either of the other two
newspapers: "Transsexual," "Married," and "Couple."

Table 2.1. Newspaper Specifications and Codes for Advertising

Tribune	*Idealist*	*Mirror*
S = single	S = single	S = single
D = divorced	D = divorced	D = divorced
W = White	W = White	W = White
B = Black	B = Black	B = Black

Dating, Mating, Relating

Tribune	Idealist	Mirror
A = Asian	A = Asian	A = Asian
J = Jewish	J = Jewish	J = Jewish
H = Hispanic	H = Hispanic	H = Hispanic
M = male	M = male	M = male
F = female	F = female	F = female
*	B = bisexual	B = bisexual
*	G = gay	G = gay
C = Christian	C = Christian	*
P = professional	P = professional	*
*	TV = transvestite	TV = transvestite
NS = nonsmoker	NS = nonsmoker	*
ND = nondrinker	ND = nondrinker	*
*	*	TS = transsexual
*	*	M = married
*	*	C = couple
n = 13	*n* = 16	*n* = 15

Only codes referring to personal characteristics are included in this table. Codes designed to create a shorthand such as "ISO" (i.e., "in search of") are omitted.

Although the lack of codes or categories did not explicitly preclude a gay person or a transvestite from advertising in the *Tribune*, the lack of particular categories combined with other newspaper specifications and the reputation of each newspaper's political stance inhibited some people from advertising in its Personals section. Several participants supported the idea that context matters.

> What made me decide on the *Mirror* was the first relationship I had. I answered his ad in the *Mirror*, so it kind of worked for him. Secondly, the *Mirror* is mostly (pauses) ... speaking from the gay aspect of it, it reaches the gay community more than the *Idealist* or whatever else they have. The *Mirror* has a larger gay section. That tells me it is more open. The other good point of it was that it was five lines free, cheap and runs for a month.

> The *Idealist* was a good paper because it was basically a feminist oriented paper, and so it was read by a lot of women. It was also modern and progressive, and I kind of hate to use the term, but if I may be forgiven, "politically correct." It was read by the type of people I would choose for friends, so that was a good choice of paper.

Another illustration of the extent to which the parameters of ad placement limited "who" placed "where" was seen when looking at the number of homosexual participants across newspapers for three months. Supporting the earlier comment made by a gay participant, these numbers varied significantly by the newspaper, with gay and lesbian ad placers comprising 36 percent of the *Mirror*'s total population of participants and 20 percent of the *Idealist*'s participants but only 5 percent of the *Tribune*'s participants.

Table 2.2 shows how these newspapers' guidelines varied in how they facilitated ad placements, such as the amount of "free" space for ads, modes of ad placement, available times for placing ads, and advice on ad placement. For example, ad placers could only place personal ads in the *Tribune* via the telephone and a computerized menu; however, participants who advertised in both the *Idealist* and the *Mirror* could mail in, walk in, or use electronic mail (email). Restrictions on "who" could place an ad were also different, with the *Tribune* setting the most significant number of restrictions on ad placement, while the *Mirror* set no formal restrictions at all.

Table 2.2. Newspaper Guidelines for Ad Placements

	Tribune	*Idealist*	*Mirror*
Cost	30 words free	40 words free; .50 per additional word	50 words free (or eight lines); $6.00 per additional line
Mode of Placement	Telephone	Telephone	Telephone, mail-in, walk-in, email
Time of Placement	24 hrs. per day w/o assistance; 8 a.m.–11 p.m. M–F; 10 a.m.–6 p.m. Sun w/customer assistance	9 a.m.–5 p.m. Mon–Fri	Unspecified
Customer Service Representatives (average time spent with ad placers and number of reps)	Five minutes; workers*	Five minutes; classified ads; one classified worker who also assisted w/the Personal Ads	20 minutes; four full-time workers
Ad Limit	30 words	Unlimited	Unlimited
Who can advertise	Persons seeking long-term, monogamous relationships; persons 18 years or older	Single people 18 or older seeking relationships	No specifications**

Dating, Mating, Relating

	Tribune	*Idealist*	*Mirror*
Categories for Type of Relationship	Two; women and men	Six; W-M, W-W, M-W, M-M, Friends, "Something Else"	Six; W-M, W-W, M-W, M-M, Friends, "Anything Goes"
What Cannot Be Advertised	Explicit sexual or anatomical language; persons wanted	Sexual suggestions; anatomical language	No specifications
Statement of Non-Liability	Yes	Yes	No

*The number of customer service representatives for this paper was unobtainable.

**Unlike either the Tribune *or the* Idealist, *the* Mirror *did not set specifications as to who may or may not advertise in the Personals section.*

No doubt, at least some of the ad placements were idiosyncratic and serendipitous, and some ad placers described placing personal ads in more than one of these newspapers. Yet given the distinctions between newspapers with respect to several characteristics, it is likely that the organization of advertising by newspapers, and the perceptions of ad placers regarding these newspapers, influenced how and where persons chose to advertise.

Because the Personals section of a newspaper was not an altruistic endeavor but rather a mechanism for generating revenue, it was in the newspaper's interest to assist ad placers. According to their editors, what essentially began as an experiment or small enterprise for the newspapers eventually became a central feature of two of them. Comparisons of the three newspapers in Table 2.2 provide a glimpse of what the Personals' editor of the *Mirror* conveyed in her interview, that newspapers view the Personals section differently from other advertising sections. Clearly, this had consequences for support, both of the Personals section in general and for ad placers specifically. As the editor of the *Mirror* stated,

> We want the Personals and we really are sensitive to the fact that the Personals, in addition to being a real money-maker, because it is a money-maker, you know, based on our survey two years ago we found that the Personals is one of the most read sections in the paper. So we feel we have a responsibility to make a section that really works in many more ways than dating. What we do is, we turn around and tell our other classified ad placers, "yes, you need to buy an ad in our classified section, because yes, our personals section is one of the most read sections in the paper, and we're apt to display around that section."

2. "Can't Buy Me Love?"

The Personals section in the *Tribune*, on the other hand, was subcontracted, collapsed onto one page, and placed under the general classified ads editor. It, therefore, received little attention from the *Tribune*. Nowhere did organizational support become so apparent as when the editor of the *Idealist* conveyed that the Personals section was in the process of being phased out of the newspaper due to a reported shift in the newspaper's focus.

> We felt like it [the Personals' section] sort of tarnishes and sullies the image of the newspaper. We just, from a marketing angle, try to appeal to a slightly higher demographic of people, you know, older and more educated people. The purpose of the *Idealist* is to provide readership with a sense of community and enthusiasm regarding the community, the world, etc. Personal ads do not fall under this mission. In fact, they are counter to this mission.

While support of the Personals section varied by newspaper, each newspaper did offer some type of assistance in the actual construction of the ad placers' personal ad. At one end of the support continuum, the *Mirror* had a staff of full-time customer service representatives who were available on the telephone, by email or in person, who averaged 20 minutes with each customer.

> It's part of our job to produce quality ads. We try to tease out of people ads that will be interesting, a little quirky, because it makes the person sound like they have a life and because if we get those types of ads in the paper, we get a response for our ad placers.

At the other end of the continuum of support, the *Tribune* relied on its automated assistance that offered minimal information to prospective ad placers (e.g., "be sure to describe the things that are special about you"). One could access a customer service representative by telephone; however, assistance generally consisted of succinct responses regarding the procedure. The average amount of time these representatives spent with customers was five minutes.

It was also through customer service representatives that newspapers helped ad placers to respond to others since this was the primary mechanism by which the newspaper made its money. In the case of the *Mirror*, ad placers were given a script to guide the verbal presentation of self to the potential mate, and participants were encouraged to speak as long as they liked since the caller paid to hear the script. With the cost of extracting messages at $1.99 per minute, it is easy to see why the *Mirror* guided the personal ad construction and encouraged lengthy introductions by participants. Newspaper rhetoric focused on interest in participants' success, yet clearly, the more popular and successful the ads, the more money that was made for the newspaper. Responses to ad placers were the return on investment for newspapers. Regardless of the motivation behind customer assistance, the fact that each newspaper provided different forms of support was not lost on advertisers.

> I think that the people at the *Mirror* are more personal than the people at the *Tribune* paper. And if you have a problem with your ad they refer you to another number. I think the last time I called the *Tribune* there was a new company that was doing it, and it was actually over the phone. You're listening to a computer-enhanced phone voice. If you call the *Mirror* you're speaking to a real person. So I haven't placed one in the *Tribune* recently.

Participants chose ad placement venues for several reasons, including availability and the relative ease of placement, money, or referral. However, interviews with ad placers also supported how the organization of the Personals section by newspapers played a part in encouraging or discouraging participants and groups in ad placement.[9] More importantly, the relative support given by the newspaper was directly connected to assisting ad placers in presenting themselves to others.

Perhaps nowhere have we seen the growth, refinement, and intersections of commerce, science, and romance more transparent than in the organization of personal advertising displayed on the Internet. Personal ads, once placed in newspapers and magazines, have evolved to include interactive multimedia presentations of photography, video, and text along with the use of surveys and "scientific data" by online matchmaking services to promote their websites. In addition, sophisticated profiles of participants are created and matched to optimize goals for building serious relationships. Though many online websites mirror those ads found in print, unlike personal ads placed in print, the virtue of the online ad is that it can present significantly more information than a print ad and can be modified and interactive. Some online sites offer opportunities for a range of encounters that include sex, sex with couples, an affair with a married person, and even bondage and sadomasochistic encounters. The range of services is virtually endless. Online dating sites are competitive and are evaluated by the media industry, which offers annual awards for different features of the sites. In 2011, the iDate awards, described as the industry's equivalent to the film industry's Academy Awards, were presented in several categories in the dating industry to acknowledge the best online dating site; best site design; most innovative company; and best use of technology. The 2020 iDate award categories included "best coach"; best mobile dating app;

best new technology; and best international dating agency; and lest we forget the real purpose of the industry: the awards for best payment system and best marketing program.

Though opinions are divided as to the outcomes of relationships formed online, the increased attention to digital dating suggests not only a need for these activities but also the possibilities of their success. Studies of online personal advertising by communications scholars indicate that anonymity and virtuality afford safe spaces within which participants can share sensitive information that might be more difficult to divulge in face-to-face interactions.[10] The Internet also allows people to connect across diverse geographic and social spaces and thereby facilitates the reshaping, if not total compromising, of current cultural and gendered scripts. And while we retain the lessons learned from earlier dating projects, such as deviant behavior connected to personal ads (i.e., fraud, bigamy, murder), modern women have developed strategies to protect themselves from falling prey to unsavory persons. The virtual context of personal advertising has revolutionized the way we communicate to form relationships and has allowed participants to explore their options and interests by encouraging participation in the globalized commodification of intimacy.

The Virtual Context of Personal Advertising

Scholars have argued that the context of virtual advertising has pressured users to present identities that would attract the desired other, and this has altered the type and amount of self-disclosure. Some have suggested that this was generated by the structure of the website. Regardless of the answers to these arguments the Internet and technology have had a transformative impact on how we meet, mate and date, as the use of dating sites and dating apps has become a normative practice and definitely part of the mainstream. Since the late 1990s, social networking, online dating, and other networked publics have become common practice, even hypermainstream,[11] as dating online is now part of the mix with dating offline. Some of the more prominent online dating services in the first decade of the twenty-first century included eHarmony, Match.com, PerfectMatch.com, Chemistry.com, True.com, and FriendFinder, along with Lavalife and eLove. Each of these sites claimed to provide some unique aspect to their service as it attempted to carve its niche in the marketplace of romance. Most

41

dating sites required monthly or yearly fees; however, Lavalife offered a pay-as-you-go plan. True.com promoted its screening of participants by a criminal records database; eLove attempted to distinguish itself by first screening applicants offline. Some of the largest matchmaking services currently operating are Match.com and eHarmony. Each site presents elaborate compatibility systems, surveys, and experts to legitimize the service and assure client success. Match.com advertises its relationship expert, noted celebrity and Oprah Winfrey protégé Dr. Phil and now Helen Fischer of the Kinsey Institute. Noted Sociologist Pepper Schwartz served as the relationship expert for the now-defunct PerfectMatch.com, which once claimed to have surpassed eHarmony as the most successful matchmaking service in the industry. Initially a website that offered advice on dating and marriage, eHarmony shifted to online dating in 2000, making it one of the oldest online dating systems with the largest media profile. This profile includes websites, television commercials, radio advertising, email, postal mail advertising, and commissioned studies that skillfully promoted its services. As such, eHarmony provided an excellent opportunity to examine the virtual context of personal advertising.

eHarmony

Targeting people who were "ready to settle down for life," eHarmony illustrated the intersection of romance, commerce, and science by charging a fee for the use of its patented and "scientifically proven" compatibility matching system that included 29 dimensions for matching singles (i.e., a 436-item relationship questionnaire).[12] Indeed, science factored prominently in eHarmony's promotional package as it maintained that its success rested on its ability to find one's soul mate, as it referred to over 35 years of empirical and clinical research. eHarmony was the first algorithm-based dating site. Specific research data was even cited to support these assertions and was written into its website introduction. The results of a 2009 study conducted for eHarmony by Harris Interactive found that, on average, 542 people married every day in the U.S. as a result of being matched on eHarmony. This number was more than twice as high as a similar poll from 2007. The number means that from January 1, 2008, to June 30, 2009, 148,311 marriages occurred between people who met on eHarmony (4.77 percent of all the weddings in the U.S. for that period). The study also found that more than 1,130,000 20–54 year olds said they were in a non-married, monogamous relationship with someone they met on eHarmony.[13] Another sizable study was conducted in 2019, the "Singles and Desirability Study,"[14] which was accessible to the public and described for viewers what traits were desirable by men and women. These types of scientific claims, along with media saturation that overwhelmed its competitors, allowed eHarmony to maintain one of the highest profiles among online matchmaking services.

With the onset of the coronavirus (Covid-19) pandemic in 2020, eHarmony added new features as it stated it had "overhauled" the eHarmony experience that included the VideoDate![15] Though video dating preceded online interactive dating sites, it had been revived as a "new" form of dating that allowed participants to remain safe while getting to know prospective mates. So eHarmony initiated the matchmaking process by having participants complete a lengthy profile designed to optimize compatibility between matches, thus maximizing time, energy, and outcome. The website also provided an interactive column that offered advice "24/7" and drop-down menus, including suggestions for maintaining a healthy lifestyle and advice on everything from kissing to date selection and improving self-esteem. Still, the pursuit of romance was not without cost as eHarmony was/is one of the most expensive of online matchmaking services with fees of up to $250 for a one-year membership, but the financial investment for participants who used eHarmony was offset by their personal investment in finding a mate, particularly as eHarmony claimed in its commercials that every 14 minutes someone with eHarmony finds love.

[Linda] It ended up being more expensive than I thought it would be, but I have met some nice men. They're not men that I would necessarily want to be with, you know, anything serious ... but they are professional men and interesting in their own right. And I've at least had someone to attend the many functions that I have to attend for my job, so that has been a nice change, you know, not always having to show up alone at places.

[Karyn] It does cost more to use this, or Just Lunch. Now that's really costly [Just Lunch] and not worth the money in my opinion. I have a couple of friends who used this one, and one of them met her husband this way. They kept telling me that I should try it and told me what it involved, so I finally decided to do it. I did meet some men, though occasionally I found myself wondering whether they [eHarmony] got something wrong. I mean, we did not have anything in common! (laughs). I'm still alone, but I'm glad I tried it. It was a good experience. Who knows, I may even try it again.

[Janet] The way I looked at it is, if I'm serious about finding someone, then I want to do what will help me achieve that. In the short time I've been using eHarmony, I have the sense that people who go through all of the trouble to fill out the profile, which really is a bit of work, are really serious about meeting someone. I mean it takes some time to put it together and some thought. I still expect to meet a guy who has two ex-wives and possibly one he's stilled married to! But I think it's less likely to be the case with something like this [eHarmony] than with bikerchicks.com, you know? [laughs].

Through one interview, I learned about one of the more exclusive matchmaking services only to learn much later that it had an advertisement in my alumni magazine.

The Right Stuff

Nowhere was the impact of context on personal advertising more obvious than in dedicated sites, such as The Right Stuff dating service (TRS).[16] The Right Stuff dating service was an international network through which participants met and formed personal relationships; that is, so long as they were graduates and faculty of selective colleges and universities. As a networked public, The Right Stuff served a highly circumscribed group of participants who had to demonstrate their membership in an elite group of private colleges and universities and a few select public universities, such as the University of California–Berkeley. A list of "excellent" schools was provided by the site and included Haverford, Cambridge, Vassar, Williams, Northwestern University, the Art Institute of Chicago, and Yale, to name a few. Yearly membership was $150 with a $35 registration fee, and applicants were provided a set of guidelines to build a profile and given recommendations about the length of their responses.

In addition to the profile, there were eight possible forms of proof required for participation. These included a copy of their diploma, fundraising letter addressed to the applicant, a page from the alumni or faculty directory that included the applicant's name, alumni or faculty card, alumni magazine with an intact computerized address label, school transcript, correspondence from the university of the applicant that indicated applicant was a graduate or faculty member, or email message sent to the alumni email account of a TRS school. Akin to other eugenic-minded dating sites (e.g., DegreeDate, EliteSingles, Good Genes), The Right Stuff was one of many dedicated services that attempted to capture a particular niche of the singles population.

[Penny] I have a degree from Harvard, and I've attended private schools all of my life. Frankly, I was tired of wading through the volume of people to find someone with whom I could actually connect. I know all about the popular dating sites, but I don't believe that everyone understands the difference between one educational experience, for lack of a better phrase, and another. I mean just because someone fills out "x" number of years of education or checks a box that says they have a "college education," you cannot assume that person will have the same ideas or goals or even the same experiences. I know this sounds pretty harsh and possibly provincial, but I wanted to meet people who were like me, who had the same values, similar educational experiences and goals ... people to whom I wouldn't have to always explain my choice of words or any of my choices, you know? The Right Stuff sort of implied I would meet those types of people without wasting a lot of time and energy. I know how this all sounds but I'm just being honest.

Though both eHarmony and The Right Stuff did offer several dating opportunities for participants, the number of potential matches outstripped their success, mainly when "success" was defined by participants as a long-term, serious or compatible relationship.

[Jocelyn] I met a number of guys and learned a great deal, not just about them but also about myself ... what I wanted, what I could and was willing to do to get it. So I have no regrets about trying it, but I can't say that I found Mr. Right or my "soul mate" [gestures as if to place quotes on the term soul mate]. I didn't. In fact, I sometimes wondered if they got my profile mixed up with someone else's because some of the men I met were not even close to being what I stated I was looking for!

[Sheryl] I still don't know how to characterize the whole thing, as worthwhile or an enormous waste of time! I met some real boors who were so full of themselves that all I could think of was, if this is what I am about, then I really need to take a step back and reevaluate! I definitely had a number of dates, at least one date a week for about four months (if I chose to go out with a guy). So in that sense, I would call it a worthwhile effort. However, I would also have to say that for every match, I ended up dating relatively few, and most of those were one-nighters, or at most two or three, but nothing materialized. There wasn't anyone who I considered having a real relationship with, so in that sense, it obviously wasn't what I had hoped it would be.

Between 2000 and 2010 the number of online dating sites exploded with sites varying in their degrees of regulation. Most of these sites relied on advertising to make money; however, they evolved from free sites to a graduated fee structure tied to the type of access the user desired.

Personal Advertising in Offline Spaces: Speed Dating

A myriad of personal advertising activities accompanied online matchmaking services and social networks. One of the most popular of these activities to emerge in the first decade of the twenty-first century was speed dating. Unlike matchmaking services, the cost of speed dating could range from a nominal sum to moderate fees for participation ($5 to $75), with fees paid at each speed-dating event. Speed dating occurred in a variety of settings, but the format was fairly similar across contexts. Whether in bars, restaurants, coffee shops, or church centers, the speed-dating format typically involved semi-scripted and round-robin sessions with participants meeting for a designated period to determine their interests in a future date. Participation was scripted (i.e., certain questions may not be asked of the other), and varying numbers of mini-dates were slotted by the event.

No participants could be skipped, and dates were arranged by a mediator. Typically, men moved from table to table, and women remained seated. This dating format has been lampooned in such movies as the comedy *40-Year-Old Virgin,* when friends of the main character, Andy (played by Steve Carell), tried to assist him in his effort to lose his virginity. Andy's friends and workmates David, Jay, and Cal signed him up for a speed-dating session in which they also participated. They met a variety of strange women, including David's former girlfriend on whom he remained fixated. Unlike the characters in the movie, participants in my studies did not describe bizarre encounters when speed dating. And though they struggled with their initial participation in the activity, they were positive about the format.

[Lisa] At first it was difficult to get into the flow, but once I went through one or two sessions, I began to get more comfortable with the format and have some fun with it. One thing I kept in the back of my mind was that at least if it wasn't working out with that person, you know, if I felt awkward or absolutely had no physical attraction to him, I wouldn't have to remain in the situation for very long. After going on too many awful dates to mention, I have to say that doing it this way was a relief.

2. "Can't Buy Me Love?"

[Anne] I did it because my girlfriend begged me to do it with her, so I did. Honestly, I thought it was a joke at first, but I ended up really enjoying myself. We went to this community center. It was sponsored by a church, and they called it speed *relating*, you know, as opposed to speed *dating*. It ended up lessening the pressure of thinking of it as a date, and I think it helped me relax and enjoy meeting people. And there were a lot of people! I remember the director or minister or whatever saying there were nearly 400 people there that night! At first, I was really nervous. I mean, before it began, there were men who stood around the room like they were stalking their prey. A few of them even had the nerve to walk around the tables and look at you like they were deciding if you were going to be good enough ... it was kind of creepy. I didn't know what to expect, but I didn't expect to see so many people. But then I started thinking if there were that many people who wanted to meet people and were willing to do it this way, then maybe it wasn't so crazy after all. I mean, this *is* the suburbs, right?! I didn't actually meet anyone that I wanted to date, but everyone I did meet was polite, and it was okay, you know.

Events like "Speed Tennis" used sports as a way for participants to stay fit with the subtext of meeting people. Safari flirting offered participants lessons on how to "flirt" with the added bonus of shopping as you practiced flirting to meet potential dates/mates. And while "couples massage" and "couples yoga" implied preexisting mates who engaged in these activities, several of these services were also ways in which strangers met (with a purpose).

Even though many online matchmaking services and offline activities marketed their services as finding romance, women participated in these activities for different reasons, and the costs of participating varied substantially. Some activities and websites explicitly stated the primary focus of participants was mating, while others may have served the romantically inclined as well as those who were looking for platonic encounters. Even on websites geared toward establishing meaningful or long-term relationships, such as eHarmony, people could be found who were not genuinely seeking serious relationships and even those who were already in serious relationships, including married participants. The formation and supervision of romantic relationships have been physically, geographically, culturally, and digitally dispersed.[17] Consequently, new, more dynamic scripts and possibly emergent institutions were replacing former conventional roles and institutions.

47

Location-Based Dating

One of the most recent innovations in personal advertising involved using cell phones and satellite apps to form what is now called "location-based dating," also known as satellite, mobile, and GPS dating. Location-based dating applications are smartphone software that uses the Internet to facilitate romantic or sexual relationships between strangers. Dating apps are simply shorthand for "application" software that can run on any electronic device (e.g., smartphone). The first mobile dating apps emerged early in the past decade (around 2003), with the rest following midway through the decade. Although the number of dating apps originally paled in comparison to the multibillion-dollar online dating industry, by 2011 they had exploded to rival online dating sites. However, dating apps were used predominantly by persons under 30 years old. The most popular of these dating apps is Tinder. Tinder was launched in 2012, but by 2019 it was regarded as the most populated of dating apps, with estimates of 6,600,000 to 7,860,000 users worldwide.

Of the six mobile dating websites that I examined in 2011, location-based dating was promoted as a "global network for meeting people," "the mobile matchmaker," and an assisted way to "get your game on." Some of the more extreme claims refer to mobile dating as "a state of mind," "a way of life," "preserving the magic of serendipitous meetings," and facetiously, even "good for the environment" (because people are meeting people nearby and therefore don't have to use their car). These mobile apps varied with respect to how they were marketed and their targeted audiences. For example, Grindr was advertised as an "all-male social network," which was so successful that its founder developed Blendr, a site for straight women, and Tinder, an enormously popular app. Skout advertised as a social network site where one could meet "new friends or activity partners." However, most mobile apps were explicit about their focus on dating, and there was even an app that targeted gay and straight persons, as well as couples interested in "mobile hookups."[18]

The way that romance intersected with commerce was also visible in satellite dating. Though most were advertised as "free," several apps provided different types of memberships (for a fee), with the premium membership offering not only the ability to receive introductions and send "winks" but also the ability to see who looked at your profile. Like several of their online counterparts, some mobile services used "scientific" techniques for matching, such as "chemistry" surveys, proposed as assisting users in optimizing their date match.

Some apps also built in some type of security measure to allay user concerns. For example, Skout and MeetMoi provided only general or approximate location information as opposed to targeting the specific location information of a member or members. Assisted Serendipity simply notified the user when the "scales of love tip" in his/her favor; that is, when the male-to-female ratio of people in one's favorite bars, clubs, coffee shops or restaurants shifted to optimize meeting a member of the opposite (or same) sex. At one point, Skout marketed its app to two communities, an adult community and a teen community of users that it restricted according to age-appropriate groups "based on school grades" ("members could only communicate with peers close to their age").[19] As an assurance that members were secure, the site also claimed that "we ban over 40,000 devices each month for violations," though just how secure participants felt knowing that the site had to ban this number of devices regularly was anyone's guess. Each of the sites had some statements about their origins. However, Skout and Grindr presented the most details along with multiple buttons that offered access to the app's blog, press coverage, security measures, user interviews and stories, and events that link the virtual world with the real-world events sponsored by the app, and even an online store, as some sites vacillated between presenting their services as facilitators of social networking versus dating. Again, the population of participants who engaged in location-based dating was a younger population who preferred to use smartphone technology rather than "filling out forms" online. They also enjoyed the rapidity with which they could download, swipe and access a number of potential matches.

Reporters questioned whether the "old school" way of online dating had been replaced by GPS dating. Between 2012 and 2015, media outlets such as *CNN*, the *New Yorker*, *The New York Times*, and National Public Radio featured segments on this new approach to meeting and mating. Supposedly, technological communication provided an intersection of interest to communicate personally yet self-protectively through online advertising and matchmaking services, but this was perceived as less accurate in mobile dating ... at least by women. According to NPR's Lauren Silverman, GPS dating reflected gender disparities, with men users of mobile dating apps who outnumbered women by a ratio of four to one.[20] Added to this, deviant behavior similar to the behaviors linked to placement of personal ads in earlier periods (i.e., fraud, murder) was also linked to online dating sites and dating apps. In fact, during this same period (2012–2015) crimes related to these activities increased by nearly 400 percent, indicating that while the technology has evolved, the risks related to dating and mating have remained remarkably consistent.

One example of criminal behavior occurred when a man who was already serving time in prison acknowledged how he swindled women out of money by responding to profiles on dating apps. By selecting women whose profiles signaled loneliness or "desperation," this young man in his 20s managed to bilk multiple women of thousands of dollars.

"I would go for older women and look for the desperation," he said.

> "Keywords would be like 'I just want happiness' or something like that. I'll act cool and if she talks back, then I know she's interested from my pictures [he regarded himself as good looking and used real photographs of himself].
> From then, that's when I start putting my game on, selling you dreams like
> 'I want a kid with you.'
> I just say everything she wants to hear until she's fallen in love."

Despite these (and other) behaviors, the number of mobile dating apps continued to expand, and established online services such as eHarmony were expanding with them, adding a mobile app to its retinue of services. Scholars attended to the dating app market and offered advice about how ad placers could optimize their chances in the dating app market. Using a Google algorithm to examine messaging and demographic patterns among dating app users in four cities (New York, Boston, Seattle and Chicago), University of Michigan researchers Elizabeth Bruch and Mark Newman found that writing lengthy messages did not produce positive results and that the time of day when messages were sent also mattered. In keeping with prior research, women's views of men's desirability peaked at the age of 50, while men's views of women's desirability peaked at the age of 18, showing that perhaps we haven't evolved as much as some have argued. This research provided practical advice to ad placers that included: (1) send many messages; (2) play "out of your league" because fit often pays off; (3) keep messages to 40 words or less (think "Tweet"), and (4) be patient.

Personal advertising has expanded the boundaries of self-presentation, as well as the possible spaces within which romance or intimacy may be established. Not only do online relationships develop into offline relationships; both online and offline relationships shift in substance and intensity. In *The Purchase of Intimacy*, Sociologist Viviana Zelizer challenged the idea that markets undercut the maintenance of interpersonal relations and reminded us that all social relations, even intimate ones, entail economic transactions and rely upon culturally meaningful institutional supports.[21] Zelizer's array of examples illustrated how economic activity was linked to negotiating, supporting, and maintaining a variety of intimate relations, such as providing personal care for loved ones that may include elderly or child care, adoption, subsidized college education, or even wedding presents. As an old social practice that has evolved into a modern phenomenon, personal advertising can be included in this list as commercial transactions and multimodal communication combine to expand the boundaries and opportunities for intimacy in ways consonant with our new social structure.

3

"Doing Identity" in Personal Advertising

The modern personal advertisement or online profile frames an invitation for intimate private interaction through the public marketing of an *abbreviated self* (*selves*) that is consciously created and presented to others. Online advertising and matchmaking services and face-to-face encounters, such as speed dating, present opportunities to craft a personal profile or multiple profiles for imagined and real-life audiences. The identities or selves are social constructions as well as personal ones that result from living in our society, with the cultural imperatives that men and women are taught to value. What complicates this process is that we have multiple cultures and subcultures, multiple intersecting identities, and multiple audiences. This chapter maps the processes of "doing identity" in various personal advertising situations, as ad placers presented identities to anonymous others, engaged in impression management, and selected a date. Regardless of their context, personal ads represented a frozen moment of doing identity.

Scholars have argued that the context of websites has altered the doing of identity and that identity in virtual time is different from doing identity in print, with both impacting the type and amount of information disclosed to the audience. It is the abbreviated aspect of personal advertising on virtual platforms that necessitates a more strategic identity performance as ad placers have fewer cues to help them comprehend information presented by others. The promise of a future face-to-face meeting also motivates participants to present authentically (for those who use websites as transitional to a face-to-face meeting and for those using dating apps).

To get a fun take on what is meant by "doing identity," I recommend the film, *Must Love Dogs*. This romantic comedy centered on a 40-year-old divorcee (Sarah, played by Diane Lane) whose family was determined to find her a man by creating a profile of Sarah and placing her personal advertisement on PerfectMatch.com. As it turned out, Sarah's father, a widower, began placing advertisements at the same time, which gave the audience a view of their gendered experiences in dating. The film offered a humorous look at the process of personal advertising as it took us through a series of Sarah's unsuccessful dates with men who either wanted someone younger and sexually compliant or merely different from Sarah. On these dates, Sarah consoled a depressive date who cried uncontrollably, arm wrestled another date at the bar to see who paid for dinner, was told by a lawyer date that he really was expecting (and wanting) someone much younger (male date: "I mean, eighteen is legal, right?"). Sarah was at the upper end of the age range he had provided online.

We were able to see the contrast between Sarah's and her father's experiences. Sarah's father was having the time of his life meeting and juggling women. During a family gathering, Sarah's father asked her to take one of his dates home. (He had invited three women to the gathering and had selected the woman he wished to remain with him.) As Sarah drove Dolly to her home (played by Stockard Channing), a discussion began about men, dating, and the Internet, which gave a glimpse of "doing identity" and the logic offered by Dolly, who was 60 (responding to Sarah's admission that her husband left her for a younger woman).

> Dolly: They always go younger, don't they? When they're 80, they want 60, when they're 60, they want 40. Hell, when they're 80, they want 40, and they get it too! goddam supply and demand ... we ought to kill the guy who thought of that one.

(A ping is heard, and Dolly interrupted her conversation by moving to her computer.)

> **DOLLY:** Uh-oh, got a live one. [She began typing on her computer.]
> I LOVE THE INTERNET. PART FANTASY. PART COMMUNITY. AND YOU GET TO PAY YOUR BILLS NAKED!
> [DOLLY LOOKED AT SARAH.] YOU'RE ON THIS, AREN'T YOU?
> **SARAH:** [nodded yes]. Hmm hmmm. PerfectMatch.com
> **DOLLY:** What, just one site?! Honey! You gotta put more bets on the table! I'm on at least ten. You get to try out different personalities ... like here, I say, "I'm into opera, antiques, poetry in the original Greek."
> [DOLLY SWITCHED TO ANOTHER WEBSITE WHERE HER PROFILE WAS DIFFERENT AS WAS HER DRESS STYLE.]
> ON THIS ONE, "I LIKE TO SKYDIVE, RIDE MOTORCYCLES, AND ENJOY A RODEO."

SARAH [SMILED]: But you don't *do* any of those things.
DOLLY: It's an ad. It's like those cars that say they get 30 miles to the gallon.... I mean, who knows? You just want someone to take you out for a test drive.
SARAH: I'm just not comfortable advertising myself this way.
DOLLY: Honey, when you get to be my age, and you're approaching your expiration date, it pays to advertise. [Dolly patted her computer.] ... This baby never sleeps. It's working for me 24 hours a day; God bless its little Pentium chip heart!

In this three-minute scene, we were treated to the way that at least some women looked at doing identity in personal advertising, a version similar to the responses of many of my participants over the years. When I began this research, personal advertising still had a stigma attached to it, and many people viewed these activities as exclusive to shy, desperate, or unattractive people. Personal advertising is no longer considered a deviant activity, and it has undergone a virtual explosion. My interest in identity formation brought me to the study of this work as I interviewed women to gain an understanding of their experience. Ad placers described how they "do" identity by constructing an abbreviated self (or selves) to establish a variety of relationships.

Doing Identity

Identity is a narrative of the self that conveys a multidimensional and dynamic construct.[1] "Doing identity" refers to how identities emerge in interactions with others and how understandings became tied to existing discourses of master categories by which we sort and understand people, such as gender, race, social class, and sexual orientation.[2] Unlike Dolly in the movie *Must Love Dogs*, doing identity was not about a lack of authenticity but rather presenting an identity that was viewed as appropriate to the situation. These dimensions mattered just as much in cyberspace as they did in real life.

According to Anthony Giddens, identity in modern society is a reflexive project in which the self must be routinely created and sustained.[3] We actively shape, reflect on, and monitor our identities, crafting our narratives as we go through life. The emphasis here is on "doing," understanding identity as dynamic, fluid and occurring across multiple and intersecting discourses. As the audience changes, so too does the performance, underscoring the importance for the researcher of the need to look at the contexts in which doing identity occurs.[4] Thus, at best when we read a print ad or online profile or observe a speed dating session, we capture identity in a single moment in time or a picture of identity because identity itself is a lifelong task, ever changing and evolving.

Doing identity in personal advertising is often an ambiguous and problematic endeavor. The challenge to advertising oneself in print, online, or in speed dating and dating apps resides in the need to provide several sorts of information in delimited space and time; hence the self is abbreviated. Regardless of whether the performance occurs in the more limited domain of print media, cyberspace, where it is often presumed that no boundaries exist, on video, or in the more nuanced activities of safari flirting, the identity presented must be viable in the marketplace of romance—as an individual separate from the other advertisements, one must clearly convey goals, intentions, desires, as well as the characteristics of the desired mate who will read the advertisement and respond to it.

The characteristics of personal ad placers and the parameters of print, face to face, and virtual contexts are only part of the ad contents. To be viable, an adequate identity lists the characteristics of an attractive self, the pleasures the self would like to share, and a description of the self's "other" for the shared experience—what Sheldon Stryker referred to as an *organized structure* reflecting the "I am"–"I want" responses of the ad placer to him- or herself.[5] Successful ads convince the "other" that the self in the ad could be the person sought by the reader of the ad. Without such an exchange of self and other, the ad does not reach the marketplace.

Emile Pin and Jamie Turndorf described the dilemma for persons who must present the self when meeting strangers as involving the choice of a multiplicity of roles, audiences, and normative systems.[6] This is the ad placer's dilemma: she must choose and market an identity to anonymous "others" without the traditional screens that family, friends, workmates, or neighbors used to provide. The mediator is also a stranger as in the case of speed dating. The identity performed depends on the audience the ad placer is trying to reach and the ad context. The irony of identity work in personal advertising is that the performance is necessarily abbreviated, yet the desired outcome of this activity can be of great significance to the ad placer. What accounts for the proliferation of personal advertising in the twenty-first century? One of the most powerful features of ad placement is the control it offers the ad placer. Ad placers are the authors of their own lives in these abbreviated texts;

they not only present themselves to their audience, but they also get to voice what they want in a desired mate and select from among those who respond to their ads. As part of these self-produced narratives, ad placers revealed a variety of circumstances for placing ads.

Why Market the Self to Meet People?

In the late twentieth century, demographic trends revealed that in addition to a steadily growing population of divorced persons, there was also a rise in the number of single persons under the age of 44.[7] This group of singles included those younger generations who had postponed marriage and those divorced persons who were often older. Currently, millennials (age 23 through 38) are the largest segment of the U.S. population. This demographic is more educated, more racially and ethnically diverse, and slower to marry than previous generations.[8] Added to the changes in marriage patterns was the increased geographic and spatial mobility of persons in the United States, particularly in specific regions of the country. Though these patterns have changed in recent years, it is probable that the rise in personal advertising was at least partially attributable to these patterns of geographic and occupational mobility, shifting forms of community, and the consequential movement in and out of various social groups. As far back as 1997, ad placers described a variety of life experiences and social situations that played a role in their motivation to engage in personal advertising. Marie, a rather shy woman who worked full time as an activity coordinator in a nursing home, described the constraints of her job regarding her efforts to meet men.

> I work in a nursing home. I work a lot of hours, and basically, the sorts of people I work with are elderly. They're all elderly, and it's just a very closed work environment. You don't meet a lot of people. And as for my social life, I have a social life, but basically, if you want to meet men, it's over at the bars. I did that for years, and it's just the same types of people all of the time. So, the only option was to place an ad.
>
> [Verna, divorced working mother] Not only do I work at home, but I was also married for ten years and have a seven-year-old daughter. I don't make that much money, and I don't have anyone who I can leave her with. I mean, I cannot afford to hire babysitters all that often, so my opportunities to meet men are really quite limited.
>
> [Sarah, an assistant professor] Well, I'm actually from here [an east coast city], but I've been away at graduate school and so coming back I realize,

possibly more now that I'm an adult and in a different situation, that this is a small place, so opportunities are going to be limited. It's great for families, or at least it was great for me growing up here, but I think it's going to be more difficult to meet men of my age. I used the personals in grad school and found it to be okay.... I'm sure I will try it here.

Chris, a (trans) private investigator with a soft voice and cautious manner, talked at length about the limits of her job for meeting people.

My line of work is not at all conducive to meeting people. I am a private investigator. Given the nature of the work, your encounters with people consist of secretive or guarded conversations and often hostile encounters. It is not a nice or friendly business to be self-employed in. I did try lots of sports, volunteer work, and other stuff, but I've also used the ads on and off for about six years at the same time.

Chris was like most of the ad placers I interviewed over the years, who pursued multiple avenues for meeting people, including going on traditional dates, joining volunteer groups and health clubs, patronizing bars, engaging in sports, and pursuing such hobbies as line dancing and choral singing.

Lacey, a divorced mother of two sons and a former beauty queen, was depressed about turning 40 and determined to find a second husband. In addition to personal advertising, Lacey had developed a strategic plan that involved multiple ways to meet men.

[Lacy] A woman has to put out as many signals in as many ways as possible, you know. You need to cover all the bases. Besides ads, I also go to Home Depot and walk the aisles. You can meet a lot of men that way [smiles]. You figure out where they'll be most likely to shop, you know, which aisles, and you just strike up a conversation ... ask for help ... that's a sure-fire way to get a man's attention. I also have a membership at Gold's Gym. I meet men, plus I get to stay in shape [laughs]. And there, you just ask for help with the weights. Men love it when a woman needs their help. The bookstore is another good place, you know, Barnes & Noble, or really any bookstore. You just hang out in certain sections, home improvement, computers, history.... I also refuse to go to things where I know there won't be any men. It's just not really worth my time.... I met this lawyer who I really liked, and I think he likes me, so I sent my boys back to their father's because I think it might've been discouraging for him to always see me as a mother and not just as a woman.

Despite the diversity of dating activities in modern times, ad placers suggested that their existing social capital had failed to provide sufficient resources for meeting men (i.e., family, friendship, and work networks). They regarded personal advertising as a value-added process and believed they did not have much to lose by trying it.

How does one frame an invitation for private interaction through a print or online ad, speed dating session, or dating app? Contrary to popular assumptions, personal advertising may look like an isolated or lone endeavor, but the process was a social one, particularly for women, who often relied on friends to assist them with creating their advertisements and who participated in particular meet-up activities with friends, such as in speed dating. Just as our identities are the result of living with and among others, *doing identity* through personal advertising is also a social construction, and simultaneous to personal ad construction was the choice of where to place the advertisement, a choice that ad placers made with some discretion and purpose. It was also a choice that shaped the performance.

Constructing an Abbreviated Self

Doing identity in personal advertising is a reflexive process. Personal ad placers described to me how they dealt with the challenges of presenting themselves to others. An important part of this process was the contexts chosen by the ad placer. Having selected a place for an advertisement, the ad placer confronted how to present the self within that context.

Regardless of the particular modality (print, virtual or face-to-face dating), each context had guidelines that set the parameters of dating. As Chapter 2 illustrates, personal advertisements in newspapers often had age limits for participation, word limits (for cost), what types of activities were acceptable (i.e., only one newspaper accepted advertisements to meet "couples") and age parameters. Online advertisement sites and matchmaking websites also set rules of participation (e.g., eHarmony.com, ChristianSingles.com, EliteSingles.com). One is able to observe the commodification that occurs in doing identity as participants packaged and presented themselves within these established parameters. With ad placement in print or online, participants had to economize because they were both selling themselves and looking for a mate. With dating apps, doing identity involved photographs and a more superficial presentation of self because the speed of swiping made selection a quick process, forcing the ad placer to provide a concatenated self-description. Likewise, ad placers relied on predominantly superficial characteristics to make the first contact.

The first step described by most women was to read other advertisements prior to creating their own. Personal ad placers explained how they reviewed other personals as a means of comprehending how to proceed within the chosen context (online, magazine). If the activity was in person (speed dating or dating apps), ad placers typically knew someone who had engaged in the activity and sought her/his advice before engaging. Few ad placers entered an activity without any prior knowledge, even if that knowledge was indirectly acquired. All of the women (1997–2015) engaged in online and, in 1997, print advertisements, and the majority of them characterized constructing their identities as a social event, occurring within support networks of coworkers or friends. Each woman described having discussed the activity with at least one and typically two or more persons before doing it. Ad profile creation involved the woman's reflexive exercise in presenting herself, but it also involved soliciting the perceptions of others (friends and coworkers, and rarely family members).

[Sandy] I told this to most of my friends, straight and gay. Some were like, "Oh, that's good," and some said, "Oh, you're not going to meet anybody interesting." ... Most of my friends feel that I'm very brave because they feel it takes a lot of courage to do it [engage in personal advertising]. Some even gave me advice on what to say.

Several women described the creation of personal advertisements as literally a collective construction, effected with confidantes after dinner was served, at a bar, at work, or in one's home.

[Karen] I asked four of my dearest friends to sit down with me over dinner and to help me write the ad. It was a fun experience, you know, to have others tell you what it is about you that is appealing. But it was a bit scary, too [laughs]. You never know what will come out in those moments!

As recently as 2015, personal ad placers were also aware of negative attitudes that still existed about personal advertising, and they perceived a social stigma still attached to it. Not everyone in their social circles approved of the activity or took it seriously, and negative responses were even more pronounced when the activity was unorthodox, as in couples massage. When asked whether she shared her activities with family, Nia responded emphatically,

[Nia] Wow! No way. I could never discuss any of this with my mother. She'd say, "What's wrong with you?! You crazy?!" [laughs]. I mean, she knows I'm pretty open to life and will try many things, but I don't think she really wants to know about it [laughs]. I have to admit that when he (her date) suggested it, at first, I thought it might even be a setup. You know, something shady or kinky. But once he told me about the place ... and I checked it out, you know, to see that it was legit ... once I spoke with the woman who does this, I thought, "What the hell, why not?" So, I did it. And really, all it was was both of us getting a massage at the same time, in the same space. Nothing much to it. It sounds more exotic than it is. It was a little weird, but okay.

Couples yoga, speed-dating sessions, and dating app hookups often involved friends who accompanied the ad placer. Few women described engaging in these activities alone. An example of how participation in these activities is embedded in existing social networks is found in the comedy, *The 40-Year-Old Virgin* with Steve Carell. Carell plays a 40-year-old man (Andy) who has never had sexual intercourse with a woman, even though he defines himself as heterosexual and he lives alone. Andy's workmates decided they would help him with his "problem." Their strategies included taking Andy to a speed-dating session at a nearby restaurant, in which they also decided to participate. The event was titled, "Welcome to Date-a-Palooza! 20 Dates in 1 Hour." The implication in this scene was that one has to be open to having fun and experimenting with ways to meet people.

> **ANDY:** I know what this is.... I saw this on Prime Time Live.
> **DAVID:** All right Ninja Man, we've given you all the advice we have to give. Now, you have to put it in action.

The tables were set with men remaining stationary and what looked and sounded like a police siren that signaled rotation for women to move to a new table. In real life, interactions were limited to a few minutes (three to ten minutes), but in the film, we only saw brief highlights of interactions with various women. In the first interaction, Andy used the advice of his friend Cal (played by Seth Rogan) to answer each question posed by the women by restating it as his question to them. For example,

> [Woman] "How are you?" [Andy] "How are *you*?"
> [Woman] "I'm fine." [Andy] "You're *fine* then?"
> Ultimately, this results in the woman asking him if he is retarded.

After the first rotation, Andy met Gina (pronounced JI-nah), a bisexual woman who spent most of her time with women but who wanted to shift back to dating men.

> [Gina] "Look, I'm gonna be real honest with you. Um ... it's been a

long time since I've been with a man. I've spent a lot of time with the ladies. Looking to get back up on that pogo stick ... you know what I'm saying?"

[Andy] "Excuse me?"
[Gina] "You're a good-looking man."
[Andy] "Thank you."
[Gina] "Very pretty. Real soft, delicate features. You're real feminine, you know, which is good for me because that would be a simple sort of transition, you know what I'm saying? ...maybe throw a little rouge on ya ... tuck your sack back ... you game?"
[Andy] "No."

Just as people used to double date, many participants engaged in personal advertising with a friend or friends, either out of curiosity, for support, as a good time, or for security.

"I'm the One Your Mama Warned You About"

One feature of the abbreviated self, particularly in print and online profiles, involved provocative headers or titles above the advertisement/ profile in order to pique the reader's interest (e.g., "Brain Candy" or "Guided by the Stars"). The ad header was a cue that initiated the dating process and helped to attract some readers (and potential dates) and sort out other readers. This rhetorically succinct device could be part of marketing, revelation or even political resistance. Ad placers used these headlines creatively to reveal appealing or unflattering characteristics of themselves—to stand out among other advertisements and to sort those who would be interested from those who would read the header and continue their search. It was here that they were able to produce those provocative headers that attracted people who didn't mind and may even have appreciated the "Rubenesque" woman or man, such as "Bewitching Big Babe," or the "Full-figured," presumably euphemisms for being large or overweight. Other ad headers, such as "HIV positive" or "Herpes Hero," were used to disclose important information about the ad placer in an effort to sift through potential dates and eliminate those who wanted to avoid persons based on such information.

"Love to Laugh"
"The Right Stuff"
"Looking for Love in All the Right Places"
"Only the Serious-minded Need Reply"
"I'm Your Destiny"
"If Covid Doesn't Take You Out, Can I?"

Dating, Mating, Relating

[Wendy] I don't know why, but my biggest problem is coming up with a title. The site offers you advice on making yourself stand out, you know. And they tell you the title is important, that this is the first time the reader will "see" you? So, it has to be clever. I think that sort of got into my head, and I was afraid that if I screwed it up, that's it.... I ended up using songs in my titles, you know, like one I created around Christmas. I used the song title as my ad title, "All I Want for Christmas Is You." I thought it was okay. I'm not very good at the titles, though, and I don't know how much difference it makes.

In the movie *Must Love Dogs* Diane Lane showed the Internet's flexibility as she experimented with presenting different identities on multiple websites as the lyrics to the song "Don't It Feel Good to Let Yourself Go" played in the background. Her first identity was as a bicyclist on SeekingNewLove.com. Her header read, "Handles Great! But Watch Out for the Curves!" Her second identity, created on DatingHopes.com, showed her with a violin, stating, "Come Play My Instrument! First Lesson Free!" Her third identity, on Reel-in-Love.com, showed her in fishing gear with the header, "What's Your Angle? Fishing for the Big One!"

Although the film presented experimentation and disingenuous identities, no woman with whom I spoke claimed to engage in creating fake or inauthentic identities. At the same time, most of the women placed more than one advertisement and created different identities. They also characterized the construction of self as an ongoing process and a learning experience. Research suggests that the promise of a future face-to-face meeting motivated participants to engage in the authentic *doing of identity* rather than misrepresent themselves and face the person who would be likely to disengage. This was even more likely with the use of dating apps as the explicit endgame of dating apps is to have a face-to-face meeting with someone.

[Linda] Over the years I've done personal ads, I've worked on the writing. The first one I did, I just described myself using lots of adjectives, and I described the man I wanted to meet using lots of adjectives. I worked on different ways of expressing ... using my writing style to speak as well as the actual words I was using. My goal was to achieve the perfect ad.

[Barbara] Earlier, I was very specific. I tried various approaches, being very specific about who I was and being more open. And once I tried an ad that I had calculated would have broad-range appeal, just the ad that I could write that all the men would want to answer [smiles]. That was a disaster [laughs]. I learned that it's a good idea to be specific about who I want and what I want. I think it's something you have to learn by doing, and I've made some regrettable mistakes, and I've had some adventures ... but it's been interesting.

3. "Doing Identity" in Personal Advertising

Nearly everyone described having placed multiple advertisements and presented different identities simultaneously, as a utilitarian exercise.

> [Laura] I just sat down; I looked at ads and just wrote what I thought said things about me. I've had various things. Right now, I have one that says "Independent Redhead" because that's how I really feel about myself. I had one that said, "Looking for a Challenge," because I've been told that I'm a real challenge by others. The one that I have that's going to start this week is "Heart and Soul." That site sort of requires a flashier ad, you know? I guess I've got about three or four ads placed at any point in time.

According to Sheldon Stryker, the self is organized in two ways: (1) as a set of discrete identities existing in a hierarchy of salience, with the presentation of any given identity having a probability factor attached to it; and (2) as a set of responses of an organism to itself (a reflexive process).[9] The women I interviewed described themselves as having a rotating mix of identities that existed in shifting systems of social arrangements. The projection of an identity was purely situational, relevant to the desired interaction of meeting someone. However, unlike the character Dolly in *Must Love Dogs*, who saw herself as moving toward her "expiration date," no ad placer with whom I spoke claimed to engage in "fake" identities or disingenuous presentations.

That is not to say, however, that context did not impact identity management. The women who also used dating apps suggested that they relied more on the superficial than the written word simply because the app was structured in a way conducive to this.

> [Vicki] There's only so much space you have to say anything about yourself so it's really the photograph that matters. I wish I could say I pick men based on their qualities, but the truth is, I go by how they look. You really have to rely on your photographs, and I put the best ones I have up there. It is superficial, but that's what it is.

Because personal advertising exemplifies courtship situations that are structurally isolated, these women merely presented multiple identities to enhance their chances for "success." One woman referred to her activities as being a "shape shifter." For *Star Trek* fans, this phrase conjures the image of Martia, a character from the planet Dominion whose ability to morph into various creatures and humans (from a child to Captain Kirk's double) enabled "it" to elude its enemies . Lois's approach of placing different advertisements on multiple sites was portrayed as a desire for acceptance rather than as an attempt to intentionally mislead or be disingenuous.

[Lois] It's not a matter of lying; it's just a matter of self-perception and what people define. I think that people just try to shape themselves in a way that the other person's going to accept them. Maybe it is lies…. I don't know if it's really lies; people try to chameleonize themselves—you know, become shape shifters. I think people want to be accepted, and we put our best foot forward to achieve that.

The Dating Game

One of the benefits of personal advertising was that ads were placed in anonymity, guaranteeing advertisers confidentiality with respect to their identities. However, a dilemma for women who participated in personal advertising was that the "other" was also anonymous, a stranger. Thus, the benefit of anonymity was also the cost of leaving the ad placer to select and arrange dates with others in the absence of the traditional cues by which we evaluate and make our best "first guess" about persons. The selection of persons to date, particularly in online sites, speed dating, or dating apps, occurred in a relative vacuum of information, forcing personal ad placers to rely upon their own perspicacity concerning the written text or spoken word. Many personal advertisers stated they had previously underestimated the significance of traditional and nonverbal cues and gestures until they began placing ads. Another feature of ad placement was that the audience of potential mates might not consist of the idealized other whom the ad placer sought.

On the other hand, attachments whose origins began through personal advertising could be grounded in more substantive interactions than those whose initial meetings were face-to-face meetings, which were often based on superficial characteristics. Because of the anonymity of personal advertising, self-disclosure and subsequently achieved intimacy could actually be greater.[10] Whatever the drawbacks of personal advertising (the work, risks, and possible disappointments), ad placement continued to grow, as have various innovations of these activities.

There were three benefits to online dating. First was the ability to access a multiplicity of partners, and while the majority of them may not have resulted in a positive match, the endless possibilities they presented supported the fantasies of finding that "perfect soulmate." These endless possibilities (i.e., the large number of connections) also offset the disappointments many women experienced in online dating. A second feature of online dating was the ability to use online communication to get to know someone before meeting him. Matching was done by many websites where women asserted their interest in a serious or romantic outcome. These sites used algorithms whose positive outcomes were debated and challenged, and yet the intersection of romance with science provided many women a sense of serious purpose and even security in this process.

Nearly every woman I interviewed conceded that personal advertising was fraught with challenges and anxieties, but the unanimous and compelling response was the sense of empowerment these activities provided to these women. The level of anxiety differed among women, with younger women less concerned (women in their 20s and early 30s) than older women. Some ad placers spent a fair amount of time developing strategies to mitigate their concerns. Concerns included those about physical safety (attracting "some nut") and the risk of exposing themselves publicly, as well as fear of rejection (i.e., not receiving any responses). Women spoke at length about equivocations, fears, conversations with friends about their fears, and the strategies used when meeting and dating men.

> I always leave my information with at least two friends, you know, where I'm meeting him, what time, when I expect to be back, and so forth. That way, if anything happens, they can call for help or something.
>
> The first time I meet a man, I choose the place and the time, usually in the afternoon and usually at a coffee shop. There's a Starbucks that I go to where I'm known. I feel safer that way. I'm not paranoid, but I try to be smart about things.

Strategies to minimize risk before meeting someone face to face included spending time with the person on the telephone (in 1997) and online (2004, 2008, 2015) and trying to get to know him prior to meeting in person. Several women described conversations (with potential dates), looking for clues that might offer whether they should *not* meet the person. These included assessments of how aggressive and self-absorbed she perceived the man to be and how at ease the ad placer felt in her communications with him. Nearly all the women had arrangements to assure their safety. In the absence of available cues received in face-to-face interactions, ad placers relied on other strategies to assess a potential mate. Several women talked about looking for subtle indicators that revealed or at least helped them to form their impressions of potential dates. Some of these signs were how rapidly the "other" responded to their email, how much he wrote and how he wrote it (his "style").

Charlotte developed an interview schedule to help her sort through responders and evaluate their compatibility as well as to look for signs of (physical) risk. She acknowledged that this caused her to "lose most of them," but she used her interview schedule anyway. Regardless of the diverse strategies used to reduce risk, almost all the women could recall at least one negative experience.

According to several women, the trick was to be able to assess the credibility of the ad respondent/potential mate while at the same time applying the filters and strategies they used in their presentation of self. Not everyone engaged in this reflexive exercise, but many attempted to use the same rules they applied to assessing others when presenting themselves as a metric of how they believed others would assess them. This was a balancing act to engage in doing identity with eliciting the most positive impression of their identity performance. Some women described this as a complex process and one in which they were always engaged when dating online.

The other side of presenting themselves was the approach they took toward men. A common refrain among women ad placers was the enjoyment of having some measure of control over the dating/mating process through personal advertising. Many women were engaged in romantic tourism, shopping for the "right" or "perfect" or "perfect for me" man or relationship. Instead of feeling that they were impotent and commodified in the process of dating, women who engaged in ad placement, dating apps, or any mode of personal advertising felt empowered. They could exercise some control, declare their goals and preferences, choose their date/mate, and reject others, regardless of the outcome. Regardless of the science of algorithms and their utility for matching people, the mere ability to choose to participate, fashion her profile or identity, select her mate was what many of these women were seeking. The act of choosing was almost as satisfying as the outcome.

And despite the media promotion of eHarmony and its 300-item survey created by Neil Clark Warren and Galen Buckwalter to create compatible matches or Pepper Schwarz's 100-item Duet Total Compatibility System developed for PerfectMatch.com or even Helen Fisher's matching system developed for Chemistry, it would appear that the assumption of pseudoscientific matching was not infallible or perhaps even preferable. At least half of the ad placers described a situation when they received a negative response from a date met in person (e.g., a look or comment of disappointment). Some ad placers recalled experiences that ranged from humorous and inconvenient to surprising and even frightening. Janet explained how a misprint of her personal ad caused her a great deal of trouble.

> [Janet] I had this line in my ad, you know, the title ... that was supposed to say, "Easy Going," but the newspaper left out the word "going," and of course, you know what happened. I couldn't believe the number of creeps I had calling me! I would get calls asking what kind of sexual things I would do. And that is not the worst of it!

Jerri described how a disagreement evolved into being harassed on email.

> This guy I had been talking with, Doug ... we had progressed from email to speaking on the telephone.... I liked him and thought we hit it off. We had a disagreement about children or something. It was some hypothetical situation ... nothing about us. Honestly, I don't even remember what it was, it seemed so silly to me to have a disagreement on it. Or at least I thought it was a difference of opinion, you know. But he became belligerent. I don't think I realized how angry he was at the time. So anyway, we ended the conversation and I knew he had gone a bit cold but it seemed okay. Like an hour later I received this email. From him. It required I open it, and when I did, it was the most disgusting picture of a guy sodomizing a woman. I was in shock. No words, nothing. Just the picture. I decided something must've been wrong. You don't do something like that just because you have a disagreement. I dropped him right away.... I stopped responding to him. But he sent me another one of those.... I just deleted it, and he finally stopped. It was very strange and somewhat jarring. I thought we were getting along real well ... but after I got over the shock, I was glad it happened. I could've gone out with the guy, and that would've been much worse.

Melissa recalled a date that involved deception and a first encounter that revealed her date was a transvestite.

> [Melissa] The guy sounded really nice on the phone. I just figured okay, I'd go to his apartment and meet him, and hopefully, everything would be okay. I know ... really stupid, right? Well, he answered his door in lipstick, a wig, a sheer [stops] ... a guy dressed up in girls' lingerie! It was kind of like seeing Phil Hartman on *Saturday Night Live* with lipstick on his face! I just stood there in shock for a minute, you know? And he acted like this was normal, no big deal ... then I got hold of myself and left. I've never even told anyone about that night.

A more serious situation occurred for one ad placer when she found herself being stalked by a man she had dated one time.

> [Wendy] This was the worst mistake of my life. I talked to him on the phone a few times before I even agreed to meet him. He sounded really nice, really stable. He described himself as "I have blonde hair, da, da, da...." So, I let

67

him come to the house and meet me. Big mistake.... The only blonde hair he had was right here [points to the periphery of the head]. The really scary thing about it was that a couple of days later, I get a call at work, and somebody else answers the phone. I'm like, "Is this you?" And he says, "Oh, yeah, it's me from the other night! Don't you remember, honey?" He had tracked me down at the place where I worked! At first, he just kept calling. Then, he started showing up there and everywhere I went! It took forever to get rid of him!

Another serious encounter occurred when a "bi-curious" ad placer found herself under the control of what she referred to as a dominatrix. This had happened long before the interview; nevertheless, Grace's voice trembled, and she became teary as she recalled the incident.

[Grace] I met her several times ... and you know. Then, one day, we're at her home, right? It was like this big transformation! She tells me that she is an Ex-Mistress of Dominance and a neo–Nazi supporter! She turned out to be a man-hating dyke with heavy-handed pronouncements of what she would and wouldn't listen to! I won't even mention what she did to me that night. It was awful. I have to tell you that there are some extremely flaky and messed-up people out there!

Given the effort, the social-psychological and physical risks, and the multiple disappointments involved in personal advertising, how did women assess this activity? Slightly less than half of women ad placers described positive experiences and a modicum of success in establishing various types of relationships. Slightly more than half of them were relatively unsuccessful in establishing relationships and portrayed the experience as a hassle.

Any time you open yourself to strangers, you're going to meet a variety of persons. When romantic love comes into it, all kinds of neuroses will find their way into it. People are fraught with inappropriate and unrealistic expectations, fears, and neuroses. They're looking for "Prince Charming." When I was young, I was more adventurous. I took these meetings with equanimity. Now, I think that the best use for personal ads is in connecting for friendship or a specified interest. There's less problem connecting with people in a platonic way.

Women ad placers also regarded personal advertising as an alternative to the bar scene, providing at least the illusion of power to select partners as opposed to the more overtly sexual encounters experienced in bars.

They're [men] usually heavy drinkers, and from what I've met, to be honest and blunt, they're looking for one-night stands. They're looking for ... they are basically almost "anonymous, let's go home, have sex, goodbye" type of people. That's not all of them, but I would describe the scene … that's 90% of them that go to bars. That's not for me.

Even with its drawbacks, personal advertising was viewed as having several positive aspects to it. Women addressed the liberating effect of being able to speak with men candidly and without the concern that typically accompanied meeting someone at work or through a friend or family member. These women suggested that since the person is unknown and unseen, they were able to ask questions, provide direct answers, and state their wants and needs, oblivious to the social pressures that constrain them in more traditional encounters. Thus online technology lessened self-consciousness and created a sense of control and freedom for women.

Interestingly, even those ad placers who described their efforts as disappointing intended to continue personal advertising. The reasons offered for their persistence revolved around the difficulties in meeting people to establish personal relationships; despite its problems, personal advertising only increased their chances for establishing intimacy.

[Jane] It's been good, and it's been bad. When it's been good, it just seems like everything falls in place. Timing is essential. If anybody ever does participate in trying to meet people this way, it's an experience that I don't think they would ever forget. It's such an incredible learning experience on the ins and outs of just talking to people and trying to draw people out.

[Karen] Yeah, I'll probably try again, just to see who else I could meet, if anybody. I think the biggest thing for me is because I'm so cheap. I don't have money to waste, and it's a pretty cheap way to meet people. At least the dating sites I use. You know, what are you losing? You have total control. You place the ad. You decide the place … where … for the introduction. You retrieve the messages, and you can decide for yourself. It's not like you're on the spot or anything. What the hell, you might as well try.

[Sue] It's nothing like the dating I did as a teenager, you know? Where you waited and waited for the guy you liked to see if he liked you. And then you waited to see if he would ask you out; you know what I mean? I was always trying to figure things out, but I never felt I had control over things like what I do now.… Honestly, I still don't think I could ask a man out … not on my own. But when I do the ads, I can do that. I mean, I can have more control.

Doing identity in personal advertising revealed the multiple aspects of this process: reflexive, social, and situated within multiple structural constraints, including occupations, geographic location, and marital and parental status. In their descriptions of these processes, ad placers

69

assessed themselves as reference points, even as they sought the help and participation of friends and others. Doing identity was also a relational construction operating in culturally sanctioned practices. As part of this practice, women ad placers (and prospective dates) looked for what was presented about the self and what was not presented, using various strategies to determine whether or not to meet a person or to continue interacting with him. They relied on cultural interpretations since interaction was not possible until at least some meaning had been assessed. This further complicated exchange, as meaning varies within cultures and between subcultures (e.g., racial/ethnic groups).

It was also clear that the context of advertising shaped the doing of identity with online advertising offering ad placers the opportunity to reveal aspects of identity in a more progressive way. Dating apps structured the doing of identity in ways that forced the ad placer to wrestle with how much to reveal about herself before she met someone. And that information was available to anyone who "swiped." Thus, the former provided more opportunities to engage progressively while the latter limited one's ability to manage risk and identity even as it connected users almost immediately. Dating and mating were literally transformed through technology as new forms of matchmaking emerged.

Most of the ad placers in my interviews conveyed serious intent on connecting with other people to establish a romantic and enduring relationship. Because of this goal, ad placers carefully navigated doing identity as something that required authenticity and strategies. Researchers have weighed in on both sides of the question, arguing that technology stimulates authenticity (because the ad placer is anonymous, and therefore disclosures are less impactful) and deception (depending on the ad placer's goals, lying may be acceptable for the same reasons; she was anonymous and there was no consequence to being disingenuous).

The advertiser's conveyed meaning may or may not have been the potential "other's" received meaning. Despite such drawbacks, personal advertising and placing oneself in "thin trust" situations have continued to increase. Why?

Personal advertising appears to expand the pool of prospective mates, and technology makes the pool of possible mates a global one, perhaps blurring ethnic, racial, sexual, regional, and even national boundaries as people connect with one another in distant locations. Personal advertising allows participants to fantasize about anonymous others, creating and recreating the ideal mate or partner. These fantasies may evaporate once reality sets in (i.e., meeting the person), but there is an endless capacity and need to continue the search for a perfect or suitable match, even if it means meeting scores of unacceptable strangers.

In the advent of matchmaking services, the emotional connection is enhanced by narrowing the field through any means necessary. With so few cues available to them online, and even fewer with dating apps, women looked for anything that provided some evidence to move them in a positive direction (meet the person face to face) or toward terminating the interaction.

Interviews with female ad placers indicated a feeling of empowerment as they declared interests, presented identities, selected among respondents, and expressed themselves to anonymous others. The benefits of speaking candidly, asking questions, providing direct answers, and stating their wants and needs apart from the social pressures that constrained them in more traditionally generated encounters offset the drawbacks of these activities. And even though the risk may be perceived when social contact occurred, safety precautions and strategic arrangements often restored a sense of control or agency. A modern form of courtship, such as personal advertising, did engender anxiety; however, it also generated the perception of more options and greater freedom to pursue those options. And if one can be philosophical, like Jane, it was a way to connect to others and learn about people while also learning about oneself.

In many respects the technology of the Internet and online dating has altered how we meet and mate in very positive ways. It has improved opportunities for men and women to meet each other and therefore enhanced their well-being. In fact, this is likely one of its best features—the ability to provide large numbers of potential dating partners. However, there were also problems with online dating when too many people to choose from overwhelmed participants and disappointed them. Other limitations to the impact of online dating had to do with how participants wrestled with assessing potential dates/mates and how to present themselves but also with how they thought about others. Romantic tourism tended toward a shopping mentality where people run the risk of commodifying people and in this way limits the potential of what these dating and mating techniques had to offer. Such interactions could result in premature and rapid assessments of others and subsequently aborting interactions without allowing relationships to develop. Conversely, technology enabled people to connect rapidly and perhaps without sufficient attention to the risks involved. The question is really to what extent the technology and format of dating has changed how we think about and interact with people.

Personal advertising was a social activity, creating new relationships while situated in existing social arrangements with their cultural imperatives. It involved friends, coworkers, and imagined audiences. Chapter 4 illustrates how digital dating and other personal advertising activities still follow cultural scripts, as men and women continue to be situated (online and offline) within broader gendered, racial, socioeconomic, and political contexts.

4

The Color of Love

Black and Latina Ad Placers[1]

African-American Goddess Waiting to Exhale
Full-figured, artistic, creative, adventurous, lonely but not desperate,
seeks SBM, 35+ who can appreciate all of the above.

Unclaimed Treasure Looking for Love
SHF 29 attractive, mother of two, refreshing, sweet and classic. Enjoys
movies, dining out, beach, church and quiet times. Seeking modern SW/
HM, 30–40.

James Bond. Intelligent, cool and funny!
Dancing, grown up discussions or just hanging out, mixed w/romance.
NO Droopy pants, N/S, N/D, N/Drugs.

One of the realities of modern U.S. society is our changing demographics, as our younger population is also becoming browner and less racially prejudiced. These changes have not only impacted our politics, but they have also changed the landscape of courtship and personal advertising as interracial dating is at an all-time high.[2] In the first decade of the twenty-first century, the argument was that systemic racism no longer existed, and racial discrimination was now a matter of individual tastes or beliefs. This argument resulted in privatizing the discourse on race, defining racial problems as private ones with individuals' beliefs, values, and preferences assumed to be the only factors involved in forming personal relationships. Similarly, until the "Me Too" movement, many held the assumption that sex discrimination and sexual harassment was a thing of the past. This also made public discussions of sexism difficult to engage. These difficulties were exacerbated in arenas not typically viewed as social ones, such as the formation of personal relationships.

This chapter presents African American and Latina women who participated in various forms of personal advertising between 2004 to 2015. It presents the synergism of race and racism, sex and sexism, sexuality and heteronormativity and how these systems continue to pervade interpersonal relations. Patterns found in personal advertisements and interviews suggest that establishing relationships continues to be located within inequitable social arrangements. Ad placers' narratives revealed common experiences, and yet their responses to these experiences were diverse. Women of color conveyed how personal advertising remained rooted in modern society, where people choose their individual affiliations yet continue to be defined by their group affiliations. These ad placers allow us to explore how identity work is engaged when women lay claim to multiple and intersecting identities in different contexts and the responses to their claims.

Intersectionality in Personal Advertising

Personal advertising has largely been seen as reflecting individuals' identification, lifestyle, and tastes. Race, gender, social class, and sexuality are divorced from economics, politics, and power and the intersections of these master categories within social arrangements. Instead, ad placers are seen as their own agents of self-fulfillment, operating in the marketplace of romance free from constraints. Research has typically addressed personal advertising as the trading of individual traits and preferences as opposed to the intersection of identity markers embedded in a society characterized by cultural scripts and inequality.[3] Supplementing this latter view is that real-world assumptions and stereotypes about groups are brought into virtual spaces and interactions. Preferences are not merely inclusionary; they are also exclusionary, as members of certain racial groups are excluded from consideration by ad placers, with existing social arrangements setting the parameters for doing identity.[4]

In personal advertising, race and gender presentations are privately negotiated in public spaces. Race is regarded here as important not only because it signals differences in people's experiences but also because it is experienced in ones' most intimate associations. And while race refers to a set of socially constructed identities, these constructions have real meaning for those who have racialized experiences. Perhaps nowhere is the reality of multiple, intersecting, and shifting identities better exemplified than in personal advertising, with its practices of inclusion and exclusion, desire and rejection, and efforts to exercise and reproduce privilege and power at its essential level. By presenting their experiences with personal advertising, African American and Latina women convey the complexity of identity processes that occurs when multiple identities intersect in different cultural contexts, particularly when people engage in interracial dating.

There has been an increase in interracial dating and a reduction in prejudice against interracial marriages, with approximately 15 percent of married couples now interracial.[5] Interested ad placers can now find online dating sites dedicated to interracial dating, such as Swirl. com, InterracialDating.com, Interracial.com, and Interracialdating-Central.com, to name just a few. Even mainstream websites have added a category targeting people interested in interracial dating: SilverSingles, Cupid EliteSingles (AfricanCupid), and eHarmony. Nevertheless, despite a growing, mixed-race population and an increased willingness by ad placers to cross-racial borders, racial homophily remains the dominant practice for marriage and long-term relationships, and interracial dating is found to be unevenly distributed among racial/ethnic groups.[6] Even as new technology enables the crossing of racial lines, researchers have found the Internet and dating apps also facilitate maintaining the racial divide.[7] Though some research explores the notion of a racial "dividend" in response to multiracial ads placed online, the women with whom I spoke and who pursued interracial dating conveyed decidedly racialized experiences when meeting ad responders in person, regardless of how they (the women) presented themselves in their personal advertisements.

Until recently, few studies of personal advertising devoted attention to race and ethnicity, and those that did assumed racial dividends based on the racial group's position in our society.[8] Some researchers have suggested that much like "attractiveness" or "financial security," race is a trait that can be traded for other traits or achievements in the dating market (e.g., a Black male with high educational or occupational achievement dating a White female of lower socioeconomic status).[9] However, relegating our most intimate associations to little more than resource exchanges fails to capture the intersectionality of identities and the larger context within which these exchanges are made. Expanding on social exchange theories, Belinda Robnett and Cynthia Feliciano analyzed personal ads as a mechanism to understand race relations in our society and found a race-gender dynamic (i.e., Asian males and Black females were more highly excluded from cross-racial relationships than were other groups).[10] This work called for rethinking the intersections of race and gender in personal advertising.

75

Dating, Mating, Relating

Feminist scholars developed the intersectionality framework to explain the social and economic positionality of women of color compared to other groups. Intersectionality focuses on how concurrent identities of race, ethnicity, gender, social class, sexuality, and the structures of inequality in which ad placers are embedded affect how women view and experience their world.[11] Scholars who use the intersectionality paradigm argue that focus on a single identity marker (race, gender, class) fails to adequately capture the complex social arrangements in which behaviors are embedded. Rather, individuals negotiate multiple identities and challenges within multiple social contexts, thus requiring a more nuanced understanding of what happens in modern society or, in this case, modern courtship.

I use this framework to understand personal advertisements placed by African American and Latina women in a local Chicago newspaper, *The City. The City* was chosen because personal ads had been placed in it for more than 25 years, and the format of the newspaper encouraged responses from people with a variety of relationship objectives (i.e., restrictions on ad placers were minimal and the available codes were suggestive of a variety of possible associations). Ad placers also produced many creative personal advertisements offering voyeurs an opportunity to learn more about ad placers than other venues. Though print advertisements have been displaced by online ads and dating apps, research has determined that personal advertising in both print and virtual media share enough commonalities to generate similar analyses and outcomes.[12] The discursive patterns in a sample of 52 personal ads placed by African American and Latina ad placers in 2004 illustrated how language and the lexicon of codes used in personal advertising explicitly marked race and allowed both ad placer and ad respondent to mentally map one of the most enduring and visible criteria for sorting people.[13]

Table 4.1. Personal Ads Placed in *Weekly Reader*

Black Female Heterosexual	28
Black Female Lesbian/Bisexual	3
Hispanic Female Heterosexual	20
Hispanic Female Lesbian/Bisexual	1
Total Number of Personal Ads	**52**

Personal advertisements were treated here as cultural scripts that reflected the accepted values, practices, and desires accessible to others.

These scripts were understood implicitly because identities were regulated by norms that guided behavior and assumptions about groups and other symbolic expressions of power and privilege. All cultural scripts are performed by individuals, embedded in our existing social arrangements and perpetuated through our institutions (family, media). One enduring cultural script was the script that set the limits for men and women's behavior in a sexual relationship. For example, Kathy Bogle's research informed us that in *hooking up* activities on college campuses, the cultural script for casual sexual encounters between young men and women maintained different expectations for each group.[14] Even in a world of transitory sexual encounters without obligation, these expectations addressed how often, what types, and with whom young women could have sexual encounters before being labeled as a "slut," whereas there were no such limits for young men, whose social status remained unaffected by the number or type of sexual encounters with women. The cultural script displays the rules of participation that occur in a seemingly open situation. The personal advertisements of women of color revealed how ad placers created, revised, and reinforced their identities in cultural contexts that often challenged the cultural script.

The utility of the intersectionality framework was that it helped us recognize how these cultural scripts represented the confluence of social circumstances. Personal ads provide *collapsed contexts* in which women managed multiple identities. Collapsed context refers to what happens when many social groups exist in one space (e.g., SBF). Obviously, we are limited in what we can say about any woman by analyzing personal advertisements, but this limited knowledge is also what the ad responder must assess in deciding whether or not to approach the ad placer. For example, we can interpret a person's social class by examining the ad placer's interests and education. Sociologists assume that personal tastes and interests or hobbies are a critical aspect of social class and education—"enjoys opera, fine dining and restoring planes/cars" is considered to be the tastes and hobbies of middle- and upper-class participants since these activities cost money. The least discussed master category in studies of personal advertisements is social class. Ad placers' interests also provided a good example of how meanings vary within cultures and between subcultures, thus complicating exchanges—"Executive," "Professional," "Intelligent and Educated." These words represented the ad placer's perception of social class and her location within this construct rather than any objective index of economic or social class. More importantly, the ad placer's conveyed meaning may or may not have been the ad reader's received meaning (e.g., a teacher may regard him-/herself as a "Professional" but may not be regarded as such by someone reading the ad). Cultural scripts provided guidance for behavior and communication, but they could not solve the dilemma of multiple cultural scripts. In U.S. modern society, we have multiple cultural scripts that complicate our lives and our choices.

Neal Lester and Maureen Gobbin's analysis of interracial ads characterized ad placers as engaging in the act of defiance and transformation, arguing that the mere act of ad placement to date interracially constituted a public act of defiance of norms.[15] Ad placers in *The City* who were interested in interracial dating highlighted some aspect of identity interpreted as having cross-cultural or cross-racial appeal, in short, something that made the ad placer acceptable to someone of another race. At the same time that race of the potential mate was stated as irrelevant by ad placers, ad placers strategically identified some aspect of the self that was designed to mitigate the impact of race or to lay claim to the *dividend* of race (e.g., "dark-skinned" juxtaposed with "but very pretty" or "African American with biracial features"; or "Good looking BF with hazel eyes"). Implicit in these discursive strategies was recognition of the social circumstances in which ad placers tried to form relationships with members of other races, subtly demonstrating the impact of domains of oppression on identities.[16] To identify oneself as "biracial" is different from describing "biracial features," just as to describe oneself as dark-skinned takes on a different meaning when the "but very pretty" and "professional" are added. The "biracial features" and "very pretty" and "professional" were designed to mitigate race as it was or might have been perceived by ad respondents.

Table 4.2. Phrases in African American and Latina Personal Advertisements

Race

"race unimportant"
"BF w biracial features seeking M of any race for relationship"
"Brown/Black Latina"
"Carribean Black Female"
"Good looking BF with hazel eyes"
"I'm a generic female sought by all races and types!"

Class

"college educated professional with many interests seeks appropriate counterpart"

"seeks man who can enjoy the finer things in life like I do"
"executive seeks professional, classy and sophisticated, no local yokels
PLEASE"
"likes music, muscles, movies, the mall, and board games"
"enjoys opera, concerts, fine dining, and restoring cars/planes"
"like to read good books, spend time on my boat, and good wine and good
company"
"Me-professor, loves: knowledge, space, travel, am cultured, educated,
athletic"

Relationship Orientations
"grown up discussions or just hanging out, NO droopy pants"
"I am self supporting and want you to be too. I don't want to be your
momma! No weirdos or drugs!"
"I'm the box of chocolates that your mom talked about!"

Juxtaposed with mixed-race were social class descriptors, "very attractive, intelligent, educated mulatta"; and "BF with biracial features.... Executive. Great figure." Personal advertisements made explicit how race, gender, and social class presented simultaneously as participants' discursive strategies relied upon the use of cultural interpretations since an interaction was not possible until at least some meaning had been assessed. They also show how racial categories were malleable. Race and gender were both constructed by the discourse in these personal advertisements as ad placers engaged this activity in a politicized racial and gendered sphere.

"HF seeking WM or AM"
"I'm dark skinned, but very pretty, nice figure, spontaneous, and professional F."
BF seeking "Any race"
"BF w biracial features seeking M of any race for relationship. Executive, 5'10", great figure."
"BF—race unimportant"
"Very attractive, intelligent, educated 'mulatta.' Must be 6' 2" & over, 40+, professional w. good sense of humor. Race unimportant."

It is also possible to interpret stereotypes or behaviors of particular groups as declarations of interests and the desired characteristics sought in a mate revealed assumptions about their group. For example, Black females seeking Black males made explicit demands that, on first glance, implied stereotyping of Black males. (Certainly if White women made such statements about Black men, we would call this a stereotype.) The common descriptors in each of these five advertisements were "no drugs or addictions" and "secure."

"I am a professional and secure lady seeking a professional and secure guy. Into hanging OUT—not hang UPs, so no drugs, or major issues please!"

"Intellectual, attractive and financially secure. Seeks financially and emotionally secure, classy, M. No drugs."

"I am self-supporting and want you to be too…. I don't want to be your momma! No weirdos or drugs!"

"I'm a big girl—emotionally secure, financially sound, and fun. No drugs/heavy drinking. Financially secure."

"Seek secure guy 25–30 for friendship and possibly more. No addictions. No mind games."

Wherever they are found, personal ad contents reflect the consequence of living in our society with its cultural imperatives, messages, cues, and values that men and women, African American and Latina, working class and middle class are taught to know are important to each other.

I also interviewed 27 women (17 African American and ten Latina) who participated in various forms of personal advertising between 2004 and 2015. Narratives suggested that ad placers were individuals whose markers of race, class, gender, and sexual identity produced commonalities but whose responses to those common experiences were quite diverse.[17]

Table 4.3. Profiles of Participants in Personal Advertising

	Age	Race/Ethnicity	Sexual Orientation
Anita	43	African American	Heterosexual
Joanne	27	African American	Heterosexual
Sanji	26	Asian	Heterosexual
Charlotte	54	African American	Heterosexual
Brenda	27	African American	Heterosexual
Maria	24	Latina	Heterosexual
Jean	38	African American	Heterosexual
Nia	26	African American	Heterosexual
Josie	38	Latina	Heterosexual
Arnetha	31	African American	Heterosexual
Marta	34	Latina	Heterosexual
Jane	52	African American	Heterosexual

	Age	Race/Ethnicity	Sexual Orientation
Verna	36	African American	Heterosexual
Silvia	45	Latina	Heterosexual
Janet	39	African American	Heterosexual
Alicia	38	Latina	Heterosexual
Janice	38	African American	Heterosexual
Meredith	46	African American	Heterosexual
Nilda	37	Latina	Heterosexual
Rosa	49	Latina	Heterosexual
Carol	56	African American	Heterosexual
Barbara	52	African American	Heterosexual
Michele	32	African American	Heterosexual
Carmen	29	Latina	Heterosexual
Sharon	25	African American	Heterosexual
Sheila	31	African American	Heterosexual

Interview participants were solicited in the same weekly Chicago newspaper (*The City*). I also posted flyers to solicit participants (i.e., a coffee shop, two spas that promoted couples massage as a personal advertising activity) and at the Discovery Center (one of Chicago's independent adult education centers). In the first study (2004), more than 25 people of color responded to recruitment, with 14 who engaged in both print and online advertising (nine African American and five Latinas). In the third and fourth studies (2008 and 2015), 13 women responded who had placed online advertisements and engaged in other personal advertising activities (eight African American women and five Latinas). Ad placers were offered two options for an interview: face to face or telephone. All of the participants chose in-person interviews, and the questions they were asked focused on the same set of questions asked of all ad placers: motivations for advertising, types of relationships sought, the processes involved in identity construction and performance (both online and offline), how they selected persons to date, strategies used in meeting others, experiences with advertising (e.g., meeting others), and the meanings ascribed to these activities and their outcomes. However, these participants were also asked whether they perceived race as an important factor in their activities and, if so, how.

Dating, Mating, Relating

"I Know What I Want and What I Don't Want"

Interviews with personal ad placers amplified our understanding of identities and contradicted images of Black and Brown women cynically presented as despondent failures of modern society and its changes—the sexual revolution, radical feminism, careerism, changes in media, and technology.[18] These women described how perceived opportunities for self-fashioning abounded in the modern dating world. And just as White participants described "doing" multiple identities simultaneously, women of color also described placing multiple ads and highlighting different identities in different venues.

> [Janet] When I began using personal ads, I really worked on writing what I thought would be the perfect ad. I was so caught up in how I presented myself. Then I decided to use a couple of ads to see if one would work better than the other. I think it's okay. I mean, I regard it all as a learning experience. So, I usually have a couple of places where I'm placing ads, you know, one paper in the [neighborhood] and one on the Internet. The Internet is fun because you can play with it more. Change it. The problem there is picking a site. There are so many.... I debated about whether to try [a] site created for blacks, but in the end I decided to go with Match because it's been around a while and I know people who have used it. Besides its listed as a good dating site for African Americans.... Later, I learned to focus more on who I wanted, you know, what I was really looking for, but I also learned that I need to be a bit more open. If you maintain this fantasy male image, you're going to be sitting around very disappointed. Earlier, I was very specific. You need to be clear about who and what you want, but you have to also be open to meeting people. If you want to meet people, you have to be prepared to meet a lot of men that don't fit your ad or your ideal.

Placing multiple ads and highlighting different identities was regarded as nothing more than maximizing one's opportunities to meet people. Multiple identities (by the same ad placer) did not involve fundamental identity alterations or deceptions. In other words, race and gender were not changed, denied, or elided in any of the personal advertisements placed by women. Rather, different identities were where tastes, the audience, and identities merged.

> [Anita] I don't see any difference between having multiple ads and meeting men playing tennis or at some other place. It's all the same. I do use different sites, and I try to make the ads different. I don't want to place the same ad on different sites, you know. So, I'll talk about some things in one ad and some things in another, but the basic things stay the same. I mean, I'm not one of those kinky people who play with, you know, what it's like to be a man and pretend I'm someone else. And I'm certainly not going to say I'm a

White girl! Right?! That wouldn't make any sense and isn't what I'm looking for anyway.

One distinction between Latinas and African American ad placers was the limited options perceived by the latter. Most studies on interracial dating reveal African American women as comparatively least desired among racial groups. This reflects a reality of African American women who were more likely to talk about the difficulties of meeting men.

[Joanne] I'm a professional woman, and I want a man who has his—together. A man who has his own identity and who can take care of himself.

[Janice] There just aren't that many ways to meet a man. I don't want to date men outside of my race, you know, White men. I wouldn't be comfortable doing that. I have a friend who tried that, and it didn't work out. And I just don't find them that attractive ... so that means I date less. I don't have many chances to meet men ... so, I decided I might as well try placing a personal ad. Honestly, it's been pretty much the same situation.

Participants also conveyed how their identities were modified and navigated based on interactions or anticipated moments with potential mates.

[Nia] I do go out with White men and men of different races. I'm open to people and new experiences. I'm probably more cautious, a little more hesitant, a bit more reserved. That's natural for a first date anyway, but I confess I probably have shields up, you know, I'm more in defense position when I first meet them. It takes longer for me to really relax and be myself ... and usually, it's all fine but sometimes you realize he's got this mind-set, I'm not sure how to say this.... Some men have a preset idea of what I will or should be like, and that is a huge turnoff. I usually can pick up on that within the first ten minutes of the conversation.

Strategies associated with gender, such as risk management (i.e., assuring physical safety when meeting men face to face), were described by most women who expressed concerns about shifting from online encounters to meeting men in person.

[Meredith, emphatic] I never EVER meet anyone at night on a first or even a second date. I insist on picking the place. Always in daytime. Always a safe place. Somewhere where people know me, you know, like my local Starbucks. I'm really careful about those things because you just never know. I know some women who use ads, and they do the same thing. You have to be careful, safe, you know.

Rosa, a lawyer, spoke about the disappointment of waiting for someone who either didn't come to the meeting or (as she put it) who might not have liked what he saw.

[Rosa] I have had some moments that I'd like to forget [laughs]. I had a date arranged with a man who I had spoken with on the telephone a few times, and he seemed nice. So we decided to meet at Jake's (a deli). I arrived, you know, maybe five minutes late but not more than that. I waited and waited, but he never showed up. I was a bit disappointed, but mostly I just felt foolish. I never heard from him again. So, I thought maybe he did show and just didn't like what he saw and left [laughs]. There were only a couple of people there besides me, so ... who knows.

With few exceptions, race figured prominently in women's personal advertising experiences, though in different ways—the limited options of African American women who wanted to date African American men, wariness about interracial dating, and culture clashes that occurred even among those who desired to date interracially. Each of the women described what she interpreted to be racialized experiences in her encounters. Regardless of their stated interests and identities, when meeting men, particularly White men, participants described being viewed through the lens of racial/ethnic stereotypes.

[Janice] I know what I want and what I don't want, and so I was careful to state that in my ad. But I still received responses from men that are absolutely insane! To be honest with you, I'm always suspicious when I see an ad by a White man who's specifically looking for a Black woman. I figure the guy's into some type of Master-Slave thing, you know? Especially those ads that say things like, "knows how to treat a man"! I don't think you find that too often, but I have seen it, or things like that. Anyway, this man responded to my ad saying he'd like a little hot chocolate! Can you believe it?! [indignant]. It doesn't matter how I see myself. Well, I've always known that. You can't be Black and not know that.

[Nilda] I try to be careful because even though I'm open to meeting men who are from other races.... I've dated White men and a couple of Black men.... I realize you have to be extremely careful. You know, Black folks have a built-in radar for racism. So, I feel like I am on my heels about what I say when I date a Black man because something I may not even be thinking about in terms of race, he responds to, and then I'm defensive. It can be difficult. It's almost automatic, you know? But I do have to admit I worry more when I agree to meet a man, a White man, that he's going to expect me to cook and clean for him, you know what I mean. And I have gone on dates with men who really were looking for their stereotype of a Latina.

Despite the cautionary tone, most women reported being satisfied with their lives and elected to "ignore the downside" of personal advertising.

[Jane] You know, I like to think I'm an adventurous person. I mean, I have a job that I like. I make enough money. I get to travel all over the world, sometimes more than I want to because of my job. I admit I did get lonely sometimes, but I'm certainly not desperate. So, placing a personal ad was not that big of a deal. In fact, it's been enjoyable. Until I met my boyfriend, I still dated in the so-called "normal" ways, and so this was just another way to maybe meet some interesting men.

For Maria, placing an ad represented "starting over."

[Maria] Even though I'm the mother of three children, I haven't had any luck with men. Certainly not with their father! I know that I'm older, but people tell me I'm attractive. I think I am. I still want a relationship with a man, a good relationship with a man of my age who recognizes and values a woman who's maybe learned a few things about life! [laughs]. If there's a Latino man out there who can deal with me and not be caught up with the issues of his father, even better! [laughs]. If he's a good man, I don't mind if HE has kids! If I can do it this way [through advertising], even better. I like getting men to respond and choosing which ones I'll look at or talk to. It's much better than waiting for a man to come over to you at a bar and having this long conversation only to learn he's a loser!

Several women characterized themselves as privileged, with privilege linked to class (e.g., education, financial security, job satisfaction) or personal experience (e.g., opportunities to travel, having many friends). A couple of participants juxtaposed privilege (as a comparative view of self) with family members, friends, or members of their racial/ethnic group. One woman even linked privilege to her ability to participate in personal advertising.

[Rosa] I'm a Latina who makes a pretty good living. I have a condo. I have a respectable job. I have friends and family who love me. I can afford to join eHarmony and look for a man. Not that it's that expensive, but I have a lot of friends who couldn't afford it. So, I feel like I'm one of the lucky ones.

Personal advertising provides a unique illustration of the intersectionality of identities as they were lived and used to achieve intimacy. Patterns found in both personal advertisement texts and interview narratives illustrated how establishing relationships among women who were members of heterogeneous collectivities reflected an awareness of existing social arrangements, stereotypes, and values. However, they also suggested agency and resilience among women who presented identities innovatively and engaged in pursuing relationships that transcended boundaries. Opportunities for self-fashioning and refashioning were described as plentiful in a world where both people and goods circulate widely. They allowed us to examine personal ad placers individually and highlight how identities oscillate because of context, social location, and desires. In short, as Leah Warner observes, identity is a "moving target," and this is particularly evident in online advertising.[19]

A focus on the identity markers of race and gender gave way to emergent and intersecting categories of race, sex, and social class through examining the texts in written advertisements. Equally important, even with the caveat of risk maintenance and annoying stereotypes encountered, these women were not "despondent people who are missing out on one of life's greatest adventures" (i.e., marriage).[20] They stated quite clearly that personal advertising was the adventure (not marriage), a celebration of independence, and it was regarded as added value in the dating arena ... and as an outlet for those who perceived their opportunities to be limited. Despite stereotypical assumptions, disappointing encounters, and limited success, these women viewed personal advertising as a modern form of courtship and as an opportunity, not the last chance. While some perceived their ability to engage in these activities as a privilege, most described awareness of societal parameters within which they were required to form relationships.

Certainly, personal advertising is rooted in modern society where African Americans and Latinas choose their individual affiliations and yet often continue to be defined by their group affiliations. As such, personal advertising reflected the politics of sexual desire and romance, race and gender relations, and social class position and tastes as these occurred simultaneously, not independently. As with earlier forms of dating and mating, personal advertising provided opportunities to learn about "others" in a form suited to its particular historical moment.

Women of color used their *cultural toolkits* to strategize dating and mating as they sought sexual fidelity and/or love. As Ann Swidler explained, these toolkits were comprised of a multitude of emotions, ideas, values, and strategies of action that were based on how personal ad placers saw themselves but also how they perceived themselves to be seen by others.[21] Women of color comprised a significant part of this dating population, and as Virginia Rutter suggested, diversity and mating are complex.[22] Black and Latina personal ad placers described what race identity means to them as the identities they presented were conditional, contingent, and dynamic. Personal advertising itself confounds the mating process focused on generating intimacy by simultaneously conflating identities that are both private and public, ascribed, and achieved. This is why this approach to dating in the twenty-first century requires a more complex analysis.

In the early part of this century, scholars and pundits debated the "post" nature of our current world, as we are now supposedly beyond being identified or discriminated against according to our ascribed membership in groups.[23] Modern society is said to be comprised of multiple, fragmented, and dynamic identities that defy categorization and simple binaries and move us into transnational and transcendent spaces. The social transformations of our modern world make it possible to step across the color line through the multiple choices and identities presented and desired. And while some personal ad placers sought to do this, believing in this fluid, anonymous and modern world, too often they were confronted by just how fluid and "modern" is our society.

Written texts of personal advertisements and the narratives of participants indicated that master categories and their intersections remained salient to both participants and others, not merely because of personal idiosyncrasies or because of the codes made available by different ad venues but because they were embedded in our social arrangements and our institutions, where the intersection of romance with commerce and the variety of relationships for which it held promise emerged and were sustained. Given recent events, such as "Black Lives Matter" and the protests that have occurred along with signals of awareness (Black students at West Point, police brutality, debates about the importance of the confederate flag and monuments, renaming of professional sports teams), it seems clear that the U.S. has had an awakening to the reality that race still matters very much indeed. With the "Me Too" movement, accompanied by protests, marches, an emergent "women's vote," and the increase of women holding political office, we are also reminded about the ongoing cultural scripts that define gender. With the recent recognition of African American women's role in helping to elect President Joe Biden, we see how the intersectionality of identities matters in our politics. It is, therefore, reasonable to conclude that if it matters in the many ways just presented, it surely continues to matter in our personal relationships.

5

Building Trust
in a Distrusting Society

In recent decades, social scientists have argued that successive generations of Americans have not only lost trust in their institutions but also in each other. And while trust in institutions waxes and wanes, it is thought to redound. In other words, trust is resilient, particularly when it comes to our trust in institutions (government, family, schools). Scandals in the Boy Scouts and even the U.S. presidency may rock our trust in institutions, but we tend to recover faith in them. Even the significant breach of trust by thousands of priests in the Roman Catholic Church who throughout the world molested children has not altered the support of many Catholics, at least not enough to cause them to dissociate from the institution. Unfortunately, studies show that this has not occurred with trust in persons, as trust in individuals has steadily declined over the past 50 years.[1]

In his book *Bowling Alone: The Collapse and Revival of American Community*, Robert Putnam argued that our diminishing trust in others was a consequence of generational shifts and loosened social ties in the past century.[2] Putnam characterized modern society as having mostly adverse outcomes, such as weakened traditional bonds that used to connect people to each other and their communities. Americans no longer joined civic groups or volunteered sufficiently in activities that promoted trust and cooperation. According to Putnam, who used surveys to measure the degree of social isolation and volunteerism, the generation of the Great Depression and World War II was a more trusting generation due to the economic and political needs of the time, while Baby Boomers and subsequent generations have weakened bonds and connections in civic participation, resulting in the greater social isolation now experienced in our society. Much of this was attributed to the growth of media and technology.

Others scholars, such as Everett Ladd,[3] disagreed with this thesis and saw modern society's potential to increase opportunities for individual choice and hence the social connections that yield intimacy.[4] Robert Samuelson also took issue with Putnam, calling his theory "bunk" and offered instead a pragmatic view of participation in social groups; he suggested that Putnam's nostalgic view of participation neglected the motivation for participation as rooted in segregation, prejudice, and escape from the drudgery of working-class jobs.[5] This perspective suggested that instead of a decline in participation and hence, social trust, what we were experiencing was "more relaxed, less traditional patterns of social connection shaped by the new ways Americans live and work."

We have been divided in our interpretations of modern society, with some fearing that the times augured the decline of community, social ties, and trust, while others found omens that championed the social ties between people. Regardless of where we fall on the continuum between these polar views, most of us can agree that our society has experienced shifts in community. And though the concern regarding social ties and trust tended to focus on the larger implications for maintaining our democratic system, the concept of trust and the opportunities it made possible could also be applied to the world of personal advertising.

Personal advertising characterizes what Robert Putnam[6] referred to as a "thin trust" situation; that is, one where trust is extended beyond the radius of people known personally to the "anonymous other," with the presumed goal of establishing "thick trust" relationships (i.e., personal relations that are multi-stranded, intimate, and embedded in reciprocity). In addition, the social contexts within which personal advertising has occurred have been regarded as increasingly distrusting ones. However, during the same period that our trust has supposedly diminished in persons and institutions, we have also witnessed the proliferation of personal advertising activities. Women and men, young and old, have been meeting online, at day spas (couples massage), in speed-dating sessions, and through dating apps. At a time when issues of diminishing trust, attenuated social ties, a cultural divide, and the collapse of community have been touted, how do we explain the dramatic increase in personal advertising, an activity that involves "thin" trust situations? How does a courtship mechanism that has as its central dilemma establishing interpersonal trust without the screens of traditional institutions work? How do ad placers build interpersonal trust so that anonymous others become acquaintances, friends, lovers, and even significant others? How do we situate personal advertising within Putnam's larger picture of the decline of trust relationships in our society?

One argument supports Putnam's position that personal advertising represents an example of attenuated social ties and resources that traditional institutions used to provide. A different argument is that personal advertising exemplifies the expansion of opportunities to make interpersonal connections. Regardless of which position is more persuasive, personal advertising presents situations of "thin trust" that for many reasons have more to do with our changing social structure and technology than with personal idiosyncrasies.

Trust and Social Isolation

To address the questions posed in the prior section, we must examine how our society and the concept of trust have changed over time. According to many scholars, trust is what makes social life possible, and, without it, modern society could not function. There are two dominant ways to focus on trust: as an emotional or psychological state and as an action or behavior. They may occur simultaneously, but it is not necessary to have deep faith in the outcome for one to engage in trusting behavior. Although perhaps difficult to imagine, some argue that trust behavior can occur without believing in the outcome. Certainly, we engage in both aspects of trust, but it is the latter—as an action or behavior—to which I give my attention.

Trust as a behavior requires us to relinquish control over something we value (e.g., money) in order to acquire something that we want. As researchers of trust have pointed out, it is our daily trust behaviors that allow a complex modern society to function. When we use the ATM machine, we trust the bank to deposit our money into our account. It is the depositing of money in this manner that represents trust behavior. When we see a red traffic light, we trust that traffic will stop. When we use Uber, we trust the driver to show up, charge less than a taxi, and take us to our destination safely. Getting into the car is the trust behavior.

In *Power and the Structure of Society*, James S. Coleman traced changes in our society that resulted in new social structures and new forms of trust relations.[7] In his study of the evolution of modern society, Coleman noted the shift from natural persons in hierarchical societies lacking social mobility to societies comprised of corporate actors that enabled collective action. These corporate societies generated greater freedom for individuals; however, as corporate actors gained rights comparable to natural persons, individuals lost control over the corporate actors. As corporate actors gained power, individuals lost power. Change in the structure of society also resulted in a new form of trust: *institutionalized trust.* Institutional trust referred to relations that were dependent on formalized guidelines, legal contracts, and operating procedures to formalize trust relations. These guidelines provided a measure of security for the individual so that if the trust were broken, s/he would have some recourse. Institutionalized trust helped to alleviate uncertainty, but it was never sufficient, primarily because the world became more complicated than we were able to anticipate or codify. For example, our system of jurisprudence was developed with individuals in mind. It was not designed for the reality of corporate actors, and it did not evolve to enable it to adequately address the deviance of corporate actors. Even today we apply the legal system created for natural persons to complex corporate structures and often fail to adequately address the new social reality. This has serious consequences for natural persons. Some have suggested that corporate actors have taken control of our system of jurisprudence (and our political institutions) so that corporate deviance is almost impossible to regulate.

If an individual steals, our criminal justice system has clearly defined procedures for punishment and restitution. However, when a corporate actor steals, as shown in Susan Shapiro's *Wayward Capitalists*, prosecution and punishment are more complicated and often limited.[8] Shapiro focused on how representatives of public corporations—accountants, stockbrokers, and lawyers—defrauded investors, and the complicated process of investigating and prosecuting offenders.

More difficult still is how to punish corporate actors accused of harming or even killing people. One of the more familiar cases of this occurred when the Pacific Gas and Electric Company (PG&E) was accused of contaminating water that caused cancer in the Hinkley, California, community. PG&E's role in Hinkley's groundwater contamination resulted in literally hundreds of people employed by PG&E getting ill and dying from cancer. Instead of facing prison, the company entered into binding arbitration, reflecting a system that failed to properly address harmful acts by corporations because it was difficult to determine individual culpability and because corporate actors often had powerful legal teams at their disposal to minimize the consequences. James S. Coleman concluded that in modern society natural persons were in an asymmetric power relationship with corporate actors with respect to the violation of social and legal norms.

Another massive change occurred in modern society as technology and social media profoundly changed the way Americans related to each other and derived meaning from social interactions. The concept of *social isolation* emerged in modern society. A common theme in the United States is how technology has been a disruptive force in our lives as it generates social isolation and loneliness.[910] However, Paolo Parigi and Warner Henson offered a theoretical argument that social isolation took a new form in America as social media altered isolation from a structural position to a process in which relationships were more easily created by technology.[11] The so-called increased fragmentation of modern society also led to increased interactions among those who felt more comfortable interacting with smaller groups of like-minded people.[12] In this view, technology was not a mechanism of isolation but a source for innovation. In its own way, disconnection or isolation could therefore become a resource, a repository of ideas and innovative behaviors.

Researchers also argued that we were experiencing another change in our society which was changing our trust relations. Just as our system of jurisprudence had been unable to accommodate the outcomes of industrialization, segments of our society were not prepared for the impact of the technological revolution and how it changed our world. Rachel Botsman argued that the institutional form of trust of the twentieth century was no longer an acceptable form of trust relationship in the digital age.[13] Institutional trust was now being replaced by twenty-first-century forms of trust relations that included *distributional trust*, which was accountability-based.

Learning to Trust Strangers

Historically, we moved from an economy based on exchange between persons to an industrialized economy run by corporate actors. We are now part of a new and emerging economy that has been ushered in by technology: the *sharing economy*. The sharing economy is defined as a way of sharing a resource with other people through a digital platform (information or assets). Its defining characteristics are that access to resources is temporary, sharing happens safely, and interaction occurs with strangers. The sharing economy revolves around interactions between people and consists of (1) sharing platforms, (2) peer-to-peer employment markets, and (3) peer-to-peer platforms for sharing and circulating resources.[14] Diverse types of consumer relationships were stimulated by the Internet as younger generations are now more interested in "access" than in "ownership." In this world, *distributive trust* has become essential as users must calculate risk and assume that online service providers will meet their stated behavioral intentions.[15] Trust is now *flowing* through society, decentralized, transparent, and accountability-based. Among the examples are the ratings of Airbnb home exchanges and rentals, Lyft, and Uber; these allow us to understand how a system that includes worldwide users and connections is based on distributive trust.

In the case of home exchanges and Airbnb, guests rate their hosts and housing accommodations, and these ratings are likely to affect subsequent business. Botsman argued that such online situations made us more accountable and in a way that was visible to everyone.[16] This explanation allows us to understand the success of Amazon, eBay, and other online businesses that are based on trust; as every day, 5,000,000 people take a "leap of trust" and ride in an Uber car. And regardless of claims that it is unsafe, those who elect to use Uber use the name, photo, and rating of the driver as a means of reducing uncertainty. One of the primary systems of trust-building and accountability in the sharing economy is how users of platforms evaluate them and share information. Trust is at the core of the sharing economy and is as vital to the sharing economy as it has been to our prior economies. Without it, there is no sharing. Consequently, technology is creating new institutions and enabling new mechanisms in which to place trust. We're learning to trust strangers.

We have moved from living in a world where social connections once required a considerable investment of time to a world where connections are widely available and relatively easy to establish. Behaviors in the real world, which on the surface appear to be nearly impossible (i.e., creating interpersonal trust), become almost routine within certain segments of the economy and online.[17] A surprising amount of trust can be built relatively quickly and early on (through technology), but trust fades as interactions continue.[18] As more information is acquired, over time, trust diminishes. The paradox is that technology makes it easier to establish trust, but over time it also makes it more challenging to build stronger ties as people gather more information. In the evolution of research on trust, we now see a view of trust that explains why people are increasingly willing to engage in an activity that, at first glance, would not appear to be a trust-evoking experience. Technology makes it possible for people to trust strangers, while at the same time, it may be weakening the bonds that unite individuals. It is within this new type of distributive trust that we can understand how the popularity of personal advertising activities has exploded in modern society.

Framing Trust and Personal Advertising

In the digital environment, where making connections is ubiquitous, learning to trust strangers is a type of generalized trust that many ad placers hope to transform into "relational" or "thick" trust depending on the type of interaction. The Internet has provided the means for people to communicate with each other, but the greater connectivity is only the beginning of the process. In the same way that consumer activities rely on a generalized and distributive trust in making connections and holding businesses and persons accountable through reviews, ratings, etcetera, the greater number of connections generated by personal advertising do not translate into more relationships, such as "long-term relationships" or enduring relationships and marriage. It is here that concepts of trust and social isolation become salient to the individual in a way that is different from making a purchase on eBay. It is not the number of connections but rather the quality of those connections and what people manage to mine from those connections (substance and depth) that matter. Thus, social isolation can now exist with persons who have many connections, but when few of those connections have deep meaning or substance, few become sustained connections that meet the individual's needs, as most of the ad placers in these studies indicate several dates but few lasting relationships.

Like other interactions online, personal advertising also requires trust built from digital connections and highly delimited encounters when done face to face (speed dating, couples yoga). Institutions provide the knowledge necessary to engage in trusting relationships, and it is the institutional arrangements that obviate the need for trust as institutions provide the information that reduces uncertainty.[19] Because personal advertising occurs without the support of institutions, one can imagine significant risk and loss for persons engaged in activities designed to establish intimacy. Although ad placers are tasked with the challenge to build trust, it is important to remember that while personal advertising is not embedded in institutions, the people who participate in it are frequently embedded in trusting relationships (e.g., friendship and family networks). Women in these studies reveal how their personal advertising activities are constructed and engaged with friends who support their participation. Perhaps these worlds do not intersect, but the ad placer's existing trust relations are critical to her participation.

The model of trust-building in personal advertising unfolds as a five-part process: (1) the use and reliance on existing trust relationships; (2) connections and interactions with responders to ads; (3) strategies to minimize risk; (4) engaging in risk-taking; and (5) a commitment to the utility/practice of personal advertising. These elements are commonly described by ad placers, but women differ in their use of time to make determinations involving risk. Personal advertising requires trust created between ad placers and ad responders to be successful, with "successful" defined as sustained connection and interactions. This means moving from the choice of a site or venue to connection, interaction and development of generalized trust (or distrust and disconnection), a strategic plan for dating, the date (again with the potential for disconnecting). With face-to-face interactions, such as coffee mating, much of this process is the same; however, the in-person interaction occurs first, and the participant must engage this review process similarly, with a delimited time frame but with more information (cues, first impressions based on the physical appearance and the conversation). Ironically, in keeping with the argument that distributive trust is more easily built, despite the effort to minimize risk, several ad placers characterized personal advertising as accelerating the trust-building process.

Two elements drive trust situations: uncertainty and vulnerability or risk. Ad placers used a number of tools to decide when to place trust. One woman used an interview schedule. Another relied on an artificial timeline (of two weeks) and multiple email interactions to determine whether to proceed to a meeting. Another woman analyzed the timing of interactions—how rapidly the "other" responded, what time of the day he responded and the quality of the response (i.e., was it truncated and meaningless or substantive). Still, another relied on her "intuitive response" to the ad responder. Women also relied on the assessment or knowledge of a friend, the reputation of a center or venue, and online reviews.

Another reminder from our trust experts is that while connections (generalized trust) can be built rather easily, that trust fades over time as interactions continue. This is very common among personal ad placers. As more information about the ad responder is acquired, ad placers often end interactions (or the ad responder terminates interactions).

These are also the limits of a sharing economy grounded in digital trust-building.

In personal advertising, "first impressions" were important as the ad placer and ad responder either talk on FaceTime, Zoom, What's App, email, or when they meet. These initial impressions were used to continue, repeat, or cancel further interactions. The next stage or test was the actual meeting, where several false impressions or "fake" performances could be more easily detected. For example, if a person described herself as attractive or slim or young, these characteristics were revealed in face-to-face contact. Here, the absence of information could signal a fake presentation and result in distrust or complete termination of the interaction. These factors suggested that persons who were seriously engaged in these activities would be unlikely to present inauthentic performances to guarantee credibility and ongoing interactions.

Ad placers described situations of "thin trust" as those where the ad responder elicited a minimal sense of sincerity, respect, or confidence. It was with those "others" who convinced ad placers that their interests were in some way shared that "thin" trust evolved into a "thicker" trust relationship. Regardless of the measures used by personal ad placers, when a date turned out to be disappointing, the ad placer reviewed and re-evaluated his or her trust process.

As a reminder, in our contemporary and digital environment, the most valuable aspect of trust relationships is their decentralized character, transparency, and ways in which interactions and persons can be held accountable. While dates do not receive reviews that are placed online in the same way that Airbnb, Home Exchanges are reviewed, and there is no single solution to trust-building in this new environment, dating companies and websites do depend on their reputations and can be evaluated by users. Trust relations in connection with intimate relations can exact a high toll since the value placed on intimacy (loving and sexual relations, friendship) is directly proportional to the value of the relationship—as the risk increases, more trust is required. If a woman intends to place herself in a physically intimate situation, greater trust is required relative to FaceTiming or Zooming, email communications, or even meeting in a public place for coffee. And as the stakes get higher, the issues of trust and distrust also expand.

Personal ad placers described the factors that promoted interpersonal trust and addressed why/how trust evolved in some cases and not in others. They provided examples of interactions that stimulated distrust. They also described attempts to restore trust after trust was disrupted. It was this built-in uncertainty that characterized personal advertising. However, if the ad placer found a source of connection (either online or in the real world), the reward gained through distributive trust was supported (by preexisting trust relationships) and resulted in positive connections that may or may not have evolved into sustained relationships. This was why disingenuous performances of ad placers (or ad responders) were thought to work against their interests; a misspoken word, a misinformed idea or evaluation could signal a "fake" performance on the part of one or the other and generated distrust and, in the case of personal advertising, ended the interaction. Thus, the differences between perceived "real" performances and "fake" performances became the basis for the development of trust or distrust.

On the other hand, because the initial performance of identity was so abbreviated, it was possible that added information acquired during interactions was not fake at all; it may simply have been *more* information than one could convey in a profile or personal advertisement. And this information may have altered the ad placer's initial impressions. In short, distributive trust was an iterative, dynamic process subject to multiple challenges.

> [Charlotte] In the beginning, I was pretty naïve about it and much less discriminating. I've learned to talk longer, never to say that I'll answer every response, and to essentially screen them. I'll ask questions like "What is their living situation?" "Do you own a house?" as an indicator of class I guess; "What are your dreams?" "What would you like to be doing in the next five years?" "Where would you like to live?" "What happened to your previous relationship?" … You'd be amazed at what that brings out!
>
> [Jane] Overall, I've had some incredibly positive experiences. With the exception of two men, the people I've met have not been social outcasts or losers. They've been great. Great dinners. Great jobs. Part of the fun of placing ads is the incredible detail, personal detail you'll get almost right away. It's one of the differences in this case. You know, you don't have the initial embarrassments that you have in the traditional meetings. You don't have to worry about the initial issues because since you're all doing this, you've stated that you're in a particular situation.

The Challenge of Finding Love Through Distributive Trust

How do we situate personal advertising within Robert Putnam's portrayal of our society as diminishing in trust and reducing the ties persons have to one another? Does the fact that personal advertising is now mainstream support the argument that it increases opportunities for establishing social connections? Are personal ad placers an atypical population of persons predisposed to trust?

One might say that the phenomenon of personal advertising supports Putnam's thesis that "thin trust" situations increasingly characterize modern society, as opposed to the "thick trust" situations of old. However, many ad placers with whom I spoke were engaging in this activity to form relationships of "thick trust," whether that meant sustained friendships, sexual relationships, or "long-term" relationships (which had different meanings to ad placers). Personal ad placers also relied upon primary groups and social ties to assist in their efforts. They simultaneously engaged in and utilized traditional sources to achieve the same goals. They persisted even in the face of fear, social stigma, and physical risk and despite setbacks and unhappy outcomes from advertising. Why? Perhaps the answer lies in a broader understanding of what it means to be a single person in the twenty-first century.

Being single in twenty-first-century America no longer carries the stigma it once did, and in fact, as Chapters 8 and 9 show, many single people are happy being single and do not engage in romance tourism. Doubtless, economic and cultural factors also weigh into our new realities. The freedom that comes with being single is the freedom to choose when, where, and how to alter that status. And just as industrialization ushered in a new social structure that produced corporate actors, it also changed "natural" persons—persons in the twentieth century were different from those of the nineteenth century. It was early in the twentieth century that women's roles and opportunities changed substantially as they entered the labor force and demanded birth control. Eventually, these demands included abortion rights, legal protection from violent husbands, and equal opportunities in schools, equal pay for equal work, and even the chance to become president. Although most of these demands have yet to be fully realized, the forward movement of equality for women in the twenty-first century is undisputed.

Similarly, the twenty-first century and its new innovations not only shape how people connect with one another; it also produces new persons. One example of this is how children who grow up in this century only know a world of technology and dynamic relationships and learn differently than did their parents. Clearly the benefits and popularity of dating apps are consonant with the features of our sharing economy. Mobile dating is perfectly suited to a young, technologically savvy, and mobile society in which relationship tourism has become a way of life for millions of people. Perhaps it is not that we are less trusting but simply that trust itself is changing form as are persons, and the challenges we experience or observe are the challenges of overlapping systems as one system gives way to a new system, a system that is different but still grounded in accountability. It may simply be that the mode of trust is different, and the system of accountability is different. The ways that we meet, mate, befriend, and love are not better or worse than before; they are merely different.

6

Speed Dating

The Adult Version of Musical Chairs

By minimizing the conventional issues involved in dating, such as financial investment, personal advertising literally transformed the landscape of dating and mating. The relative ease with which one could date and mate, particularly when combined with a mediator, provided some level of protection and expanded personal advertising and its participants. One of the face-to-face dating innovations of the twenty-first century was speed dating. Speed dating first emerged in the late 1990s, but it proliferated in the early to mid–2000s, rivaling online websites in its variations and numbers. Speed-dating events were advertised in neighborhood weeklies, mainstream newspapers, online, and as adult dating classes. They were often presented as an alternative to the traumas of online dating. Events could regularly be found in the city and the suburbs and occurred in bars, restaurants, coffee shops, community centers, high schools, tennis courts, university student unions, and churches. Although my interviews and observations were in the Chicago area, online searches showed that speed dating was a national and international phenomenon. Next to dating apps and online dating sites, speed-dating events were probably the most common activity in which people met strangers through the use of a mediator for the purposes of romance. Described as analogous to meeting at parties, speed dating was regarded as an excellent research activity to understand attraction and personal relationships and as a real-life opportunity to meet and mate.

Like advertising on the web, speed dating provided access to a large number of potential mates in a single event. There were five characteristics of speed dating. First, there were two populations of participants (men and women). Second, participants from these two populations had not previously encountered each other. Third, speed dating involved a known, formal, single setting. Fourth, parameters of speed dating assured that people would meet several members of the other population in controlled and limited encounters. Fifth, organizers and facilitators created the possibility for interested participants to engage with each other in less structured situations.[1]

This modern dating activity could consist of smaller groups (ten to 40 participants), but it also featured large groups of people looking for potential mates (up to 400 participants in a modified speed-dating format). Women typically remained seated at a table, and the men rotated from table to table as a bell or buzzer signaled the end of each rotation. Participants were provided forms to assist them in evaluating meetings and keeping track of potential mates. At the end of the session, the event coordinator matched mutually interested daters and subsequently shared email addresses with them to enable a future date. Many events specified an age range and sexual orientation, but others were open or unspecified. Registration was typically required, with limits placed on participation, but occasionally people could register at the event. Many speed-dating events were dedicated events—for Christians, African Americans, gays, interracial persons, neighborhoods, seniors, divorced persons, wine lovers, persons with children, and many other groups. Events could include drinks and snacks or even dinner and alcohol. Undoubtedly, the quality of events varied, but their popularity suggested that people were willing to try speed dating.

There were features of speed dating that eased participants' concerns about meeting strangers. One was that participants could attend with friends, making it a social occasion with a party-like atmosphere. Another feature was that all participants were "responders." Though their choices may not have been reciprocated, there was no public rejection or negative experience because of the structure of speed dating. If the person desired also desired the participant, information was exchanged through a mediator. Some of the other advantages of speed dating included time limits and rules for dating, or as one participant said, if she didn't like the person, she knew she did not have to stay in the situation or see him again. The parameters of speed dating minimized the difficulties even when the mini-date was a bad one. Both feedback and gratification were delayed, which allowed participants to avoid embarrassment. In brief, speed dating afforded relatively unobtrusive ways to meet a variety of persons without much stress. Reportedly, speed dating resulted in more successful dates than did online dating websites.[2] Whether this activity had a higher probability of resulting in long-term relationships than participation in other personal advertising activities was uncertain because we do not have research comparable to that kept on Internet dating.

Like dating websites, speed-dating events often had labels designed to pique the reader's interests. For example, Meet-Market, Ready-Set-Date!, Swipe Less-Date More, Kismet Konnections, and many more. Also, like websites, many speed-dating events were designed to serve niche markets, for example, Chocolate and Milk (Black Women and White Men), *Jewish Melting Pot*, and Queer Zodiac Speed Dating, Made for Jew! Speed Dating, and Cougars and Cubs (older women and younger men). This was the modern dating activity most often featured in films and television such as *Frasier, Sex in the City, Reba, 60 Minutes, iCarly, Law and Order*, and many more others.

Scholarly Interest in Speed Dating

Speed dating was possibly one of the most researched of the modern dating activities as psychologists and social psychologists were able to examine multiple aspects of romantic interest using experimental design and because speed dating provided a natural setting within which scholars could control for a number of factors that might influence the outcome of the meetings. Issues like romantic attraction, gender and race preferences, and the impact of communication on success in connecting with a partner and differences in dating have been examined by scholars.[3] As in other dating activities, the most important indicators of a man's preferences for a woman were her attractiveness and age, whereas the most important features of men to women were their race and intelligence.[4]

Additional research on speed dating included how background music impacted romantic interest and how attachment anxiety affected early stages of relationship initiation,[5] the interchange of mate selection,[6] the correlations between laughter and attraction during speed dating,[7] discussion of relationship histories in speed-dating interaction,[8] the impact of age on motives for speed dating,[9] and the accuracy of mate selection in predicting the development of a relationship between daters.[10] Scholars have even explored the "dark" side of speed dating or how traits such as narcissism impacted mate selection.[11]

Relationship experts Paul Eastwick and Eli J. Finkel conveyed the features of speed dating that make it so attractive to scholars and daters.[12] As a tool for research, (1) speed dating presents a situation where real people meet in dyads and in controlled settings; (2) it offers participants some indication that participants are available; (3) the structure of the speed-dating session enables people who do not possess great confidence to meet highly desirable persons; (4) the speed-dating format assures that unpleasant dates will end in a relatively brief time.[13] Research on speed dating supports the fact that people can arrive at a judgment about potential partners rather quickly. Houser and colleagues argued that speed dating was a far more effective means of finding a mate than blind dates or serendipitous meetings.[14] Speed dating blurs the line between research and real life.

Speed dating even worked its way into the academy and corporations as a protocol to facilitate engagement, develop networks, and improve well-being. It has been suggested that speed-dating protocols in higher education helped institutions to foster interdisciplinarity, establish research collaborations, improve classroom dynamics for students, connections to commerce, and support for funding efforts and innovation. Requirements that students participated in structured discussions with their peers encouraged engagement by students who would otherwise have lacked the confidence to express their views to a large class. The phrase used is that students become active learners, which improved engagement and retention.[15]

Having read somewhere that speed dating was the adult version of musical chairs, I wanted to see for myself how it worked and whether the type of speed-dating activity revealed any differences in participation. I observed several speed-dating activities over the years. These included coffee mating, Just Eye Contact, and speed dating at two community centers, a church, and a high school. I also observed a speed-dating class, Speed Dating Bootcamp, and participated in a speed tennis event. One observation of speed dating occurred after interviewing a woman (Anne) who described the activity as having 400 participants. My observations of speed-dating sessions in the Chicago area found that they ranged in size but skewed toward much smaller groups (i.e., 20 to 40 participants). I was curious to see if the number of attendees was as large as her estimate. The following represents speed-dating events I observed.

Love Is All in the Eyes

One variant of speed dating was Just Eye Contact. The speed-dating format was the same except that instead of talking for a limited period, participants were directed to gaze into the eyes of their contact for two minutes before rotating to the next person. This activity was also linked to science. Eye contact impacts our perception of people as we supposedly rate strangers with whom we make eye contact as more similar to us. According to the creators of this event, eye contact was also supposed to convey interest in the other person. It was supposed to reflect an interest in what they were saying (when people interacted), and it was promoted as deepening a relationship and promoting honesty between people. Its primary justification was that eye contact was essential to building relationships between people. The longer the gaze, the stronger the interest. The type of gaze was also supposed to convey attraction and when a pair was not suitable for each other. When coupled with body language (e.g., a smile), the intimate gaze could have an even more significant impact. Christian Jarrett extended the impressionistic aspects of eye contact to include intimacy.

> The chemistry of eye contact doesn't end there. Should you choose to move closer, you and your gaze partner will find that eye contact also joins you to each other in another way, in a process known as "pupil mimicry" or "pupil contagion"—this describes how your pupils and the other person's dilate and constrict in synchrony. This has been interpreted as a form of subconscious social mimicry, a kind of ocular dance, and that would be the more romantic take.[16]

Indeed, psychologists have argued that if people were willing to pay attention to it, they could learn a great deal about a person simply through eye contact. Eye contact could convey multiple emotions as well as interest: anger and attraction. Gender differences were also noted. For example, it was suggested that when a man maintained eye contact with a woman for a lengthy period of time, it conveyed his interest in that woman. In fact, prolonged eye contact could indicate mutual interest. Gazing into each other's eyes could result in a *micro-moment* of positive connection.[17] When body language was added to eye contact, the connection could be enhanced. According to some, maintaining eye contact encouraged people to be honest with you.

In Just Eye Contact, the argument was that when there was a failure to sustain eye contact or the person you were meeting avoided making eye contact, it meant there was either no connection or that something was wrong between persons. Also, there were different types of eye contact: the *lingering* glance, the *second* glance, the *unconscious* glance. *Lingering* eye contact occurred when the partner sustained eye contact longer than expected. This indicated interest. The *unconscious* glance referred to a situation when eye contact occurred, but one of the two strangers abruptly looked away. This may or may not have had any meaning. The *second* glance occurred when you made eye contact, the eye contact was broken, but the other person returned to gaze into your eyes (after breaking eye contact). Instructions included tips for interpreting eye contact that was accompanied by other body languages, for example, when a *lingering* gaze was accompanied by smiling or a *second* glance was accompanied by a shift in body language to display openness. Despite the patina of scientific validity, eye contact created possibilities for multiple meanings. Since a three-minute window on the gaze was structured for participants in Just Eye Contact, the motivation for prolonged gaze between participants could be confounded by the structuring of time of the activity. Nevertheless, the guidelines, introduction, and tips for interpreting eye contact were the basis of Just Eye Contact.

[Laurie] I've done speed dating, so it's not like I was new to this. I look for things that are different. Even though it had a different twist, it's still speed dating. I do think eye contact is important, but I don't really think it worked out the way they wanted it to [the organizers]. First, it was just too long to be staring into someone's eyes.... I mean, two minutes is an eternity when you're just supposed to look at someone and not speak ... especially someone you don't know, even if you think he's cute. After a while, there's only so much time you can spend looking at someone. Especially when you're doing it up close. I think most of us felt awkward, and it just didn't work.

Speed Dating Bootcamp

Speed dating events were also offered as adult dating classes under several different titles. Most of these were single classes (one-time events) that consisted of an introduction to speed dating along with guidelines for participation. The class I observed was called Speed Dating Bootcamp. Though the substance of the class was essentially the same as other speed-dating events, the instructor spent time introducing class members to the concept of speed dating, its history, purpose, and format. The class was held at an adult learning center with chairs set for participants to face one another, which did create the feel of a class since there were no tables, music or ambience, simply pairs of chairs facing one another. Women were to remain stationary, and men were to rotate every five minutes. The instructor began by asking members whether they had engaged in speed dating before this class. The class was limited in size to 20 participants who were supposed to be between the ages of 25 and 40. Since only a few people raised their hands, I concluded that most of the participants were familiar with this dating format. Participants were provided a sheet with suggested questions to help guide the conversations, and they were advised not to ask questions about people's jobs or where they lived. The instructor told them they would hear a bell that would indicate the end of the session and request that they politely end their conversation and adhere to the time frame. She also asked if anyone had questions.

The class functioned the same as other speed-dating activities with a slightly lengthier introduction, a sheet of information (tips) given to each participant, and a debriefing at the end of all of the rotations. The debriefing began by asking participants how they perceived the experience. This was followed by informing participants they would receive information regarding their matches via email.

Coffee Mating

Another variation of speed dating was coffee mating. Coffee mating was also one of the dating classes. Unlike Speed Dating Boot Camp, this activity took place in a coffee shop. Advertisements for coffee mating used a near northside coffee house that urged people to attend coffee mating where they could "circulate and percolate." At the time of my project, coffee mating was part of multiple attempts to carve a niche in the speed-dating world by changing the location and time where speed-dating events were held. Instead of evening events, coffee mating sessions occurred in the morning and afternoon in a neighborhood coffee shop a few miles north of where the boot camp class was held.

Located in a neighborhood characterized as bohemian, Joe's Coffee Shop (pseudonym) was large enough to have the main room, backroom, and a small enclosed outdoor area where customers could also be seated. The look of Joe's Coffee Shop was deceptively small as a view from the street, but it was actually large enough to accommodate coffee mating without closing its doors to the rest of the public. The front part of Joe's was filled with used couches, worn love seats and oversized chairs, a coffee table and end tables, and a bulletin board that was filled with local notices, messages, events, solicitations (for massage, yoga, and some other activities). Plants were placed around the room and in the front window of Joe's. Local artists' work hung on the walls. When I visited Joe's, most of the customers seemed to be in their 20s or possibly early 30s. As one moved from the front of the shop toward the center, to the right was the counter where one ordered the coffee, tea, bagels, pastries, and assorted breakfast foods. In the center were some small tables at which people could be found reading, socializing or on their computers. Two bathrooms were on the left side of a narrow hallway, which led to the backroom that held more tables and chairs. If one continued straight back, the room led into an open outdoor area that had five tables with red canvas umbrellas under which customers could sit. I learned that Joe's not only held coffee mating events but also open mic poetry slams and, occasionally, live music.

I learned about coffee mating from one of my participants and decided to observe a session to get a sense of the differences between various forms of speed dating and the types of venues in which speed-dating events were held. The one feature of this activity that struck me was the relative ease of participants compared to the boot camp class. Joe's provided a very relaxed atmosphere and seemingly, clientele. I attributed the laid-back demeanor of participants to the difference between Joe's and the artificial nature of the classroom setting, where the only items available at the learning center (boot camp) were chairs facing each other. In the boot camp class, there were no tables, background music, or ambience. It's also possible that the time of day and location might have influenced participants' ease. The director of the coffee mating sessions casually commented that she believed coffee mating drew a different set of participants compared to nighttime events at bars or restaurants. Since I did not engage in any formative assessment of the differences between speed-dating contexts or participants, I cannot offer more than descriptions of these events. One of my ad placers did suggest that the context of events may have played a role in who participated and how they experienced the activity. Georgia explained her attraction to coffee mating as the preferable format and location for her first time to try speed dating.

> [Georgia] I really enjoy my latte in the mornings. My coffee shop is one of my favorite places. I wanted to try it [speed dating] by doing it in a place that made me more comfortable. It's not just about meeting people. It's about meeting the *right* person. I don't have a chance to meet many men in my job, so I have to find or create opportunities to meet someone. This seemed like a good way to do it. To me, having coffee is a more enjoyable way to meet someone.

Speed Tennis

It was not uncommon to see the format of speed dating appro-priated in several contexts. For example, at my university, we have an incredibly successful "speed networking" event sponsored by our Women's Studies program. I have used a "speed relating" for-mat in my research methods classroom to enable graduate students from different disciplines to briefly meet and learn about their peers before selecting the research group in which they would collaborate on a project. There seems to be no limit to the ways in which the speed-dating protocol has been applied. And within the dating world, speed dating has been used in Zumba classes, culinary classes, and sporting events. Cycle speed dating had cyclists pair off and cycle together to get to know one another while engaging in a commonly loved activity. Another sports event was speed tennis. Though adver-tised as speed tennis, the format did not technically subscribe to the speed-dating format, though it does have some parallels with cycle speed cycling.

A limited number of participants played on four courts reserved at a large, public indoor sports complex in an affluent suburb of Chicago. Participants were paired into mixed doubles teams who played together for 20 minutes or whichever team managed to first win their fourth game. Participants then rotated to another partner. Because a partici-pant had not shown up, I was invited to fill in and became not only an observer of speed tennis but also a participant. Unlike cycling, where two paired cyclists ride parallel to each other and, therefore, speak more easily, speed tennis did not offer the same opportunities. The structure of a traditional mixed doubles team is that one participant plays at the net while the other starts at the baseline. Traditionally, both doubles partners capture the net (meaning that both partners play at the net). However, in modern mixed doubles, one partner often remains at the baseline while the other partner plays at the net. And though they are supposed to communicate frequently, communication is (supposed to be) focused on strategizing the team's next move. Consequently, there was not the same opportunity to engage in small talk or get beyond sim-ple introductions. Despite the structural limitations of the game, any-one who plays tennis knows that the amateur game provides as much social opportunity as it does exercise. When men and women play together, there are opportunities to interact prior to, during, and after the match.

[Jean] I love tennis, and I love the people who play tennis. It's a great way to socialize and get some exercise. It's always been a part of my life, and I can meet people by joining a club or playing in outdoor leagues. When I heard about this from a friend of mine, I thought it was perfect. I can play tennis AND meet men! And the men are supposed to be single even though it doesn't always turn out that way.

Unlike other speed-dating events, there were no exchanges of information or formal evaluations by participants. Instead, the event was held every two weeks, and those who remained interested returned to play. Though participants were said to rotate, the director knew that the activity resulted in some participants dating while others simply took advantage of "being able to play the best sport there is and enjoy the company of some great men and women."

Dating at the Coliseum

Because of my interview with Anne, I learned about an event that was undoubtedly the largest (speed dating) event of which I was aware. Though this event was another appropriation of the concept of speed dating, it did follow some of the format. This weekly "Meet and Greet," in which Anne participated, involved a projected 400 participants. The large attendance, and the fact that Anne described it as a speed-dating event, stimulated my interest in whether the night she had attended might have had an unusual turnout, and I wondered how the format could be adapted to such a large group, so I attended three times. Although I had secured permission from the event director, I realized once I attended that it would have been easy to attend without having contacted anyone. I could not count the number of attendees, but given the size of the center, the number of tables (each of which seated ten persons), and the obviously large size of the crowd, I believe Anne's estimate was accurate. Also, the director of the event agreed that it was "sizeable." Given that each table sat ten persons, I did count the number of tables in the center, and it was relatively easy to estimate the attendance was between 300 and 400 people.

The "Meet and Greet" event took place in a center that was part of a church in another affluent suburb, though it was in a building separate from the church. Though Anne and other participants referred to this event as speed dating, the scope of the activity would not technically be called speed dating because people were not matched prior to or at the end of the event. Instead, they sat wherever they chose, mingled as they chose, and any connection between participants was established and followed up individually and without the help of a mediator. Because of the size of the group, one had to stand in line to enter. The cost was four dollars to attend, and it was paid at the entrance. The fee included a buffet dinner. Those who were hungry remained in the buffet line, and others simply roamed the hall or sat at tables. Each round table had a lit candle, a white tablecloth, and seated ten participants. Rarely was a table wholly occupied. Most tables varied from four to six people at a table, and occasionally, one could see fully occupied tables. It was clear that people at these tables had some familiarity with one another. Also, the occupied tables were often toward the front of the center, while those tables with as few as two or three people were at the back. People walked around and socialized. It did appear that women were more likely to sit, and men were more likely to be the persons walking around. However, it was clear that many people knew one another, and I wondered if this was because they attended regularly or because they were part of a group or members of the church. It also appeared to me that many people attended with a friend (again, mostly women). I did not engage in any formal attempt to determine the accuracy of these observations, and in this case, I was unable to speak with the director, who was clearly part of the church.

The "Meet and Greet" event began a short while later as the director welcomed everyone and made some brief comments. He described other activities offered by the church and offered a brief homily (no more than ten minutes) on some themes (e.g., establishing relationships, divorce). Frequently, this occurred while people were still at the buffet table, and many participants remained engaged with each other while he was speaking, though the volume in the hall moderated. The director acknowledged this event as a relatively new addition to the church's offerings and stated it was a very successful one that drew people from a number of suburbs and even the city. I wondered whether it was part of the church's mission as an attempt to proselytize new members.

I attended this event three times to understand its size and how the event might have been adapted to approximate Anne's description of it as speed dating. The size of the group did not vary significantly during my visits. This may have been because of the time of year (this was spring), and without a formal analysis, it isn't possible to know whether attendance was typically this substantial. Nevertheless, I could see how Anne had arrived at her conclusion that the size of the "Meet and Greet" event indicated there was a significant number of people who enjoyed help in meeting people. The range of participants was also significant, but this was not a place where people in their 20s convened. My guess was that the age range was people in their 30s through their 50s.

Unlike other explicit speed-dating activities with limited group size and a restrictive format, this "Meet and Greet" event may well have drawn participants for various reasons. In my brief encounters, I met someone who was new to the area, having moved because of her job. I also met people who participated in multiple activities offered by the church, and this was just one of them. They liked the social life created by these activities. I met divorced people who found it easier to engage with others like themselves in a church-sponsored environment. During one of my visits, I sat at a table where a woman who seemed to be about my age (around 40) was sitting alone. I introduced myself and began to engage in small talk as I learned that we both played tennis, but after a couple of minutes, she conveyed that she was there to meet men and not women, and she would appreciate it if I would leave the table.

Just as Anne had mentioned, men stood against the wall in the back of the center and gazed on the scene. A few of them then strolled around the tables and, without speaking to anyone, brazenly looked as though they were scanning women from head to toe, assessing different women as their eyes traveled up and down the length of the woman's body. While only a few men did this, the way they acted, and the fact that they did not speak at all except to the chosen woman, made the impression a negative one for many of us. One of the women with whom I sat found this aspect of the Meet and Greet "revolting" and compared it to her experiences at a dance studio.

[Anne] I just hate it when men do that. It makes me feel as though I'm back in the meat market ... in the bars and dance studios where you get ten thousand feels as you try to squeeze your way to where you want to be. You know those places? There's one downtown, close to Navy Pier. There are four floors and on each floor is a different type of music so people can go to the floor that's playing the music they like. Anyway, it doesn't matter what floor you go to because just trying to move around, it's so crowded that when you walk through, you get a thousand different hands on you, feeling you, pinching you ... you know, just everything. It makes me feel like I need a shower when I get home. Having these guys walking around here and sizing us up makes me feel the same way ... it's revolting.... I thought I got out of that scene ... it just seems like anywhere you go, there's always some like them [nods in the direction of the men standing against the wall and walking in between the tables].

The Differences Between Online and Offline Impression Management

From the number of speed-dating events that could be found year after year, it was clear these activities served a purpose. What wasn't clear was how impression management in online personal advertising, the behaviors used by participants to control how others perceive them, differed from speed-dating situations where people who engaged in speed dating were also advertising an abbreviated self in a circumscribed time and space but with the advantage of being face to face. I asked each of the ten women who engaged in speed dating how they modified their self-presentations and what were the benefits of speed dating? Also, did it work? While my limited observations do not allow me to infer anything about speed dating or its participants, I offer them simply as descriptive of the variations in speed dating that accommodate different demographics and interests—and in the case of the Meet and Greet, as part of a broadly defined religious experience for some, a church setting that provided a safe opportunity for unattached people to *meet and mate.*

> I began by coming to the Meet and Greet, and then I did some other activities. The people were nice, and I enjoyed myself. I started to attend service because some of the people I met were members of the church, and they seemed like really good people. I've been going to the services for a while. Not all of the time, but I do go.

Much like online dating, there are multiple variations, event sizes, and types of participants who relied on speed dating to create additional opportunities to meet and mate. Most of these conversations preceded FaceTime, WhatsApp, and even some dating apps, where the visual evaluation could happen immediately. None of the ten women I interviewed believed they engaged in impression management differently when meeting people in person versus online. Still, all of them acknowledged that in-person dates generated more self-consciousness and anxiety. They did not perceive a significant difference between the two types of activities, nor did they believe they altered their performance of identity in these different contexts.

> [Sheryl] I think they're a lot alike [online and speed dating], and I approach them in the same way. It's better than just hanging out in bars where you wait for someone to come over to you and hope he's not a jerk. With this, you have more control. You can choose to continue talking with someone

you meet online, and you can choose which men you want to meet in speed dating. In the beginning, I was uncomfortable with it because it was new, and I didn't know what to expect, but now, I like it. I feel like I have more say about things, and I'm not just hanging out at bars waiting.

[Laura] I do think more about how to dress, my makeup, when I know I'm going to meet someone. But that is about the only difference. It's not the same, but … you don't have the problem of worrying about whether you look good enough when you're online, but eventually, you do because if you decide to meet or FaceTime, you still end up dealing with the same issues you deal with in any dating situation. I really don't think I do anything differently, but I'm sure I worry more when I'm meeting someone in person. The good thing about it [speed dating] is it's shorter than a real date; if you don't like each other, you're off the hook in four or five minutes.

Early research on online dating suggested that the lack of restraints and anxiety generated from face-to-face meetings often allowed participants to interact more freely, resulted in substantive conversations and allowed more meaningful relationships to develop. This suggested that without the constraints of traditional and in-person dating, where participants responded to superficial aspects of dates that prevented them from looking beyond the physical, ad placers who dated online were better able to assess relevant characteristics of the person.

However, more recent speed-dating research has argued that people were able to make accurate assessments about potential dates within the first minute of the date.[18] In this research, "thin-slicing," a brief excerpt of behavior as a sample of the "behavioral stream," could result in adequate decision-making. Researchers found that daters were able to make adequate judgments in a brief encounter.[19] For example, in one study, researchers found accurate assessments of racial bias by Black participants,[20] and in another study, daters could make accurate assessments about homophobia.

Matchmaker, Matchmaker, Make Me a Match

In many respects, and much in the way that Operation Match worked, speed dating was about matchmaking. Developed in the mid–1960s, the early attempts of Operation Match were to use science to create matches between people interested in finding a romantic partner.[21] Francesca Beauman described Operation Match as one of the early versions of computerized matchmaking that sought a dominantly White population of men (and, to a lesser extent, women) to validate its use.[22]

Operation Match was one of several precursors to both speed dating and online services such as eHarmony, where predominantly heterosexual White people were matched based on a significant number of variables. Other than the email addresses received at the end of the session, speed dating was less bound to technology, but it was still a matchmaking service.

I do not have an adequate sample of speed daters to allow me to offer more than anecdotal information about the differences between how relationships progress online versus in speed dating. As one participant shared:

> I've done both, but I did online dating before I did speed dating. I think because it was new and I didn't know how things worked, I was very cautious about everything. So, I would have to say that I took more time online to get to know the person before meeting him in person. But the truth is that you don't really know anything about the guy you want to go out with from a speed date, so I realize now that what I've just said doesn't really make sense [laughs]. I guess I count on the place [speed dating] to be the filter, and I don't really know that I should or that it is, but that's probably why I'm more willing to trust the speed dating situation and not the online stuff so much. I don't know.

It is important to remember that the Internet is not a generic space. The site context and its structure shape the interactions and variations in relationships and how they progress online. In early research of online dating, scholars argued that letter writing, telephone conversations, and email allowed people to take their time, and these forms of communication facilitated substantive interactions compared to many of the modern modes of dating. Scholars later found that the transition from online to offline meetings occurred rapidly, perhaps not as rapidly as in speed dating but more quickly than was once presumed.[23]

Still, despite its similarities and its differences, speed dating differed from traditional dating. It was a structured matchmaking event that guided and delimited participants in the dating process and provided protective mechanisms for women and men. It could easily be engaged with friends and in a location known to participants. Each of these aspects of speed dating served as the basis for establishing thin trust for participants. Participants also had some control over who they met, so long as the selected date reciprocated their interest and responded to them.

In almost every interview I conducted, women described one of the benefits of personal advertising as instilling a sense of control in the dating process. In speed dating, even when s/he did not reciprocate interest, the ad placer was spared the humiliation of being rejected publicly. Also, advocates of speed dating suggested that while looks remained important, other self-presentation skills were more valuable than looks for successful matches.

7

Serendipity
in Personal Advertising

*Couples Yoga, Couples Massage
and Adult Dating "Classes"*

Beyond the world of online websites, matchmaking services, and dating apps were other services designed to help people meet and mate in person. I first learned about several of them through interviews with my participants in the Chicago area. Of the women with whom I spoke, 20 of them had engaged in at least one of these activities that serendipitously became part of personal advertising, meaning an activity that was not originally created as a dating activity but was engaged in by people who were either looking for a date or even as a first date. Learning to trust strangers is not only a feature of online dating, but in modern society fit also becomes relevant in face-to-face activities and activities where ad placers meet strangers early in the dating process.

So, how did participating in couples yoga, couples massage, and adult classes fall under the rubric of personal advertising? For those who engaged in these activities, the requirements were like online dating and speed dating. People were not what we assume to be "couples." Instead, they were relative strangers who were meeting each other for the first or possibly second time and therefore required to present and market the self in a circumscribed place or time. There was also a mediator, who often was also a stranger to the participant. This occurred in several ways. Participants could transition from online encounters to an in-person or face-to-face meeting. They could also have been meeting at a class designed for this purpose (such as Mix and Match or Speed Dating Boot Camp, a class that served as both instruction and opportunity to meet potential mates). A third way in which this occurred was the instructor, who created a course, such as couples yoga, shifted his/her focus to offer an event or "class" for singles looking to partner. While these dating activities mirrored traditional dating activities in that they offered cues and nonverbal behavior typically associated with traditional dating, they also differed because the date evolved either from an online format and interaction or offline registration without the traditional filters available in traditional dates and with participants often strangers to one another. The "couple" might have attended only one time, or they could have attended more than once (*if* the class met regularly). One couples yoga event was a single class advertised as a unique way to meet someone and where yoga poses were presented on the brochure (e.g., Valentine's Night Couples Yoga). This provided another illustration of the intersection of romance with commerce. Two types of activities fell into this classification—couples yoga and couples massage. Though relatively small in number (eight women had engaged in couples yoga, five women in couples massage, and 11 participated in an adult dating class), these women signaled participation in other types of dating activities that can be placed in personal advertising.

Based on my research of these activities, couples yoga and couples massage were not originally intended to serve as part of personal advertising (as explicitly a dating activity) or at least not by the persons with whom I spoke in the Chicago area. Nor were most of these activities marketed as dating activities but rather as an activity for persons already in a relationship. Generic descriptions of some sites could be interpreted as open to the idea of dating—"take your relationship to the next level," "build intimacy and trust," "allows people to better relate to one another," "allows couples to play, relax and deepen their relationship," "learn the strength and sensitivity of your partner," and "cultivate connection and intimacy." At the time that I learned about this form of yoga, an online search of couples yoga revealed specializations, including Black couples yoga, intimate couples yoga, sensual couples yoga, and reunion yoga. Some sites were explicit about this activity as a dating opportunity. One site stated, "It can also be a magical way to get to know someone new in your life!"

Couples Yoga

Couples yoga was also known as partner yoga,[1] double yoga or acro yoga. Couples yoga was described as having multiple purposes. The primary purpose appeared to be to help couples relax, communicate, and use somatic-based techniques to enhance well-being. Another use of couples yoga was therapy. As a therapeutic approach, sites claimed couples yoga addressed conflict, anxiety, and tension by releasing hormones that enhanced well-being and built trust. In therapeutic sessions, couples were taught to synchronize their breathing, engage in poses designed to help partners to connect better, encourage trust and communication. The stated outcome was to help partners build trust and thereby strengthen their relationship. Couples yoga was recognized as a way to slow down the nervous system and encourage partners to be proactive instead of reactive.[2]

Another site claimed that partner yoga helped to build relationships—as partners shared the pose, they were required to work together to sustain the pose; thus, yoga helped them communicate, rely on each other, and enhance their relationship. Another site suggested that partner yoga encouraged fun, playfulness, and laughter. It was not unusual to see couples yoga marketed as a "scientifically-backed approach" that could decrease stress and "enhance sexual intimacy, improve relationship satisfaction, and cultivate compassion." As a marketing tool, one website embedded the potential of yoga within science—"We bring healthy couples practical tips and life-changing ideas to deepen the capacity for intimacy based on science."

I refer to them as part of the serendipity of personal advertising where activities became part of the mix of in-person dating that also involved mediators, strangers, and marketing the self. When one of my participants mentioned couples yoga as something in which she engaged on a first date, I asked a friend of mine who owned a yoga studio whether she offered couples yoga and who attended it. Beth, the owner of Namaste (a pseudonym), began her couples yoga to help couples and to increase her class offerings. In the process, she became aware that some people used couples yoga as a dating activity.

> [Beth] Some of the women in my classes complained about wanting their husbands and partners to get into it [yoga] with them. That's when I started thinking seriously about it ... but I had no experience, so I had to learn more before I could offer it. It really is different from Hatha or Bhakti. But it really took off. I have two classes and could probably add more if I wanted to.... So, yeah, some are married, some are couples, but you know, not married, and yeah, I've had a few come in on a date who barely knew each other. But, it's fun, and everyone is relaxed. It's not that easy for everyone so we have a lot of fun and laugh a lot and people seem to enjoy it.

Couples yoga involved married and cohabiting people, friends, people who had been dating for a while, people who had been dating only briefly, and people who met in the class. A look at couples yoga activities online suggested an assumption of people who were already in a relationship, but the truth is that couples yoga merely required two people. (This could involve a teacher and her/his student or simply two friends.) Mandy, a couples yoga instructor, described how her business evolved to include couples yoga and special events at Christmastime and Valentine's Day.

[Mandy] The only requirement of couples yoga is that you need two people. I created the class ... or I should say I *added* the class, I didn't create it ... but I added it thinking of couples, with the idea that this could be a period of time away from the kids where they can focus on one another and just learn to relax, tune into their bodies, and each other. You know, something that was both emotionally and physically satisfying.

It probably is the majority of people who come to the class on a regular basis anyway, you know, married ... especially because of where we are, [a suburb known as predominantly family-oriented] but then again, it doesn't really make a difference, so long as people are interested in yoga and are able to work together. I think it can be good ... you know, beneficial for everyone. I offer a Valentine's Day event that is fun. We have a little wine, and we socialize a bit before the session. That's how I learned about people who are dating. The first time I had it, I had two couples who barely knew each other. One couple was meeting for the first time ... at the yoga session. And I started thinking about it. We do have single people who live in Forest Hills [a pseudonym], so I decided to offer it again, but I also decided to try to pull in those people, you know, who may not have someone and who probably need something like this just as much as parents. It's still mostly married couples, but I do get folks who are hooking up here at the studio.

Patti, a yoga instructor, focused almost exclusively on couples.

[Patti] To me, it's therapy ... exercise ... meditation ... it's about well-being. Of course, all yoga is about these things. I specialize in partner yoga. Once I began offering it, I didn't want to go back to Hatha. There's just something great about working with couples and helping them to find a way to communicate and improve their relationships ... to get to a place they didn't know they could. And it's not just about marital or sexual relationships, ... it's also about friendships ... and people moving into relationships, people meeting for the first time.

I've had a lot of people who are not married participate. Some are dating; some are friends; some have just met. I encourage people to come to my classes even without partners, and if the numbers don't match up, I am their partner. I will do private yoga sessions if a couple doesn't feel comfortable in a group setting. That is another way I meet people who are dating and who've just met. I do think that in some situations the guy believes it makes him look more sensitive, and, of course, that impresses women [laughs], but they also enjoy it. In partner yoga, you do touch one another; that's the point. I'm convinced that's the appeal. And I honestly believe we lack that experience too often. Believe it or not, even married people often don't touch one another. And touch is so important ... so necessary. Partner yoga gives people an opportunity to touch each other without worrying about the issues of sexual inappropriateness.... Maybe it makes things a bit easier.

Though the niche it occupies may be a relatively small one, couples yoga served those people who wanted to connect with another person and were open to trying new ways to do it. Another couples yoga class was recommended by one of my participants who had participated with a friend (who eventually became her romantic partner), laughter yoga for couples. I had never heard of laughter yoga, let alone laughter yoga for couples, but I looked it up, contacted the session leader, and attended a session. The laughter yoga sessions (and laughter yoga for couples) were held in one of the conference rooms of a Unitarian church. Laughter yoga combined laughter exercises with (pranayama) breathing techniques. Like other health-related activities, laughter yoga was offered in sessions, laughter yoga clubs, senior facilities, and workshops for corporations and businesses. According to my source, it was free and typically run by a volunteer facilitator. Like many other activities, laughter yoga was situated within the science of health benefits to laughter. These could be found on the website.

Laughter Yoga is both preventive and therapeutic. It is like aerobic exercise and the best cardio workout. It is like a breathing exercise for those suffering from bronchitis and asthma. Laughter Yoga releases endorphins which are natural pain killers that can help those suffering from arthritis, spondylitis, chronic migraine headaches, chronic pains, fibromyalgia, autoimmune and chronic inflammatory diseases. It unwinds the adverse effects of stress and strengthens your immune system. If you laugh every day, you will not fall sick easily. If you have chronic health conditions like heart disease, Hypertension, Diabetes, Depression, Anxiety, Panic attacks, and even Cancer, you will heal much faster. Laughter Yoga increases oxygen to your body and brain and makes you feel healthy and energetic. It is a great exercise for team-building peak performance, creativity, and emotional intelligence.[3] Laughter Yoga's site also lists a book by neuroscientist Robert Provine, *Laughter: A Scientific Investigation*.

Though there is little empirical evidence to support these claims, those who appreciated alternative health therapies or who engaged in yoga were likely to appreciate the social and emotional benefits of a couples yoga session even if they were not entirely sure of the veracity of its health-related claims. Started by Dr. Madan Kataria, laughter yoga was predicated on the assumption that laughter has positive benefits for the body. It was argued to strengthen our immune system, increase energy and accelerate recovery from chronic illness. Though used by therapists and healthcare workers, research on the benefits of laughter was limited to having therapeutic utility as opposed to positive physiological outcomes.[4] By combining laughter exercises with yoga exercises, the argument was that overall well-being was improved. Like laughter yoga, laughter yoga for couples was less common than other yoga classes.

Nevertheless, the advertisement of laughter yoga for couples was like those of other yoga classes, offering to help participants create a "positive emotional climate and a sense of connection between two people." The website stated that "Laughter plays a big role in mating. Men like women who laugh heartily in their presence."[5] The site also encouraged partners and defined the term broadly to include "friends, life partner, teenage child." And although it did not explicitly encourage people looking for a mate, it offered couples the opportunity to book a private session. It was the private session in which my ad placer had participated that led me to observe a laughter yoga for couples session.

I arrived at the church and followed the signs to the room where the session would take place. There were three couples who had arrived earlier, and as we engaged in casual conversation, I learned that one of the couples was new to the activity. The leader arrived about five minutes later and explained how he had become a fan of laughter yoga. A middle-aged man whose job was graphic design was neither a yoga instructor nor even a therapist. Instead, he was an interested local who had become hooked on the concept of laughter yoga and had decided to start a laughter yoga club. He later decided that it would be nice to offer a session for couples because he had been reading about the value of laughter yoga to relationships. There was no fee for participation and minimal structure to the session. We introduced ourselves and why we were attending. I explained the research, how I had happened upon laughter yoga for couples, and asked if it was okay for me to observe the session. Despite being the "extra" person, I was welcomed and invited to participate.

What followed was literally an hour of laughter and basic yoga poses, sometimes done individually, sometimes together. We played follow the leader, with the instructor serving as the pied piper, dancing and gesturing (waving our arms). We also remained stationary with our partners (my partner was the instructor), with music playing lightly in the background. We were given tips to help initiate laughter (funniest memory, a movie scene, and other ideas to change our frame of mind from the issues of the day to a lighter disposition, presumably to open us to what followed). Often laughter was generated by our limited abilities to do a pose. However, we also engaged in laughter exercises and literally laughed. The instructor always began the sequence of laughter with variations of laughter from a resounding "ho ho ho" type of laughter to a silly giggle, and inevitably what began as an exercise of forced laughter resulted in genuine laughter. Although I admit feeling foolish throughout the session, I, too, laughed. What began as an artificial or forced effort to laugh grew into genuine and robust laughter that exhausted everyone by the end of the session.

I remained after the session to ask the instructor whether he had participants who used laughter yoga for couples as a dating activity. He said that he had another session where a couple met for a date and that one of his fellow instructors had mentioned this happening at his sessions but that he had only one couple meet at the session.

> [Instructor] You were surprised that you could laugh, weren't you? Once you do and you learn to let go and enjoy yourself, it is a lot of fun. Did you enjoy yourself? That's what we want. That's why I do it anyway. I want people to relax and just have fun. I'm a strong believer that laughter is healthy. And we don't laugh enough anymore. So, if I can do something that contributes just a little, even if it's just one day out of the week … if I can do that for folks, I feel it's worth it.

Whether it's Black couples yoga, laughter yoga for couples, or any of the titles used to market couples yoga, this activity has become one of many that targets, results in, or accepts its role as part of personal advertising. There is even a website that targets singles who like yoga—Yoga Partner for Singles,[6] which is an online dating site that matches persons interested in yoga. The first arranged date is a couples yoga date!

Couples Massage

Another dating activity marketed for "couples" is partner or couples massage. Like couples yoga, participation in this activity as a date (with a stranger) was revealed in five interviews. Albeit not many women in my research had participated in couples massage to meet someone, when first I learned about it, I regarded it as a very unusual activity to meet a stranger for the first time. And since two of the women who I interviewed knew other women who had done the same thing, I decided to search the Internet for this activity and speak with a few massage therapists (Reba, Rick, Jessie, Scott, and Maria—pseudonyms). I knew two of the therapists. Two of the five therapists I spoke with did have clients who met each other at the session and explicitly referred to them as a first date or having just met. In fact, these two therapists advertised couples massage to meet someone and as an alternative to the traditional date. They both began by promoting couples massage as "something that married people can do for a change and to relax together" and eventually evolved to promoting it as a dating activity.

> [Scott] I've offered couples massage for a while now. When I first began, it was with the idea that couples could have a time to get away from the kids ... from the daily grind of life, and just be into each other ... just relax with each other. So, I guess you could say I had a more traditional approach to couples massage. I hadn't thought about the fact that I'm in an area of the city that has changed a lot over the years. There are a lot of single people now, and they hook up in a number of ways. My class is one of them, and I'm okay with that. In fact, I changed the wording of the class to be more inclusive.
>
> [Reba] I accept people. We all have experiences that bring us to different places in our lives. I lived in California for so long, and I worked there as a therapist.... I think maybe living there as long as I did, and of course my own journey, I learned to be open ... we all have different pathways, and we bring our own energies to situations. I have a woman.... I've worked with her for a while now ... who said she felt safe in our sessions, and so when she was going to meet this man for the first time, she wanted to bring him here [Reba's studio] where she would feel comfortable. I was so touched. If being here can help them in their journey, I'm happy. I was so touched that she would think of me and of this space as one where she could do that. Eventually, I decided to open a regular session for couples, you know, anyone who wanted to have the experience with someone else. It's been great.

Rick also offered couples massage, but he was surprised to find a couple who was using the class as a date.

> [Rick] We started the couples thing because my wife and I are massage therapists, and we've led couples' classes before at a couple of places here in Evanston, so when we decided to start our own place, it was just part of what we've been doing for a long time. What I really didn't expect was to have people come and not really know each other.... I just never thought about it. They were meeting here, you know. I approach couples massage in a therapeutic way, and so it wasn't something I adapted to right away. I'm still not sure that I have, but I do have a business to run, and this is part of it.

Couples massage has been used as part of holistic medical treatment and supplemental to Western medical treatment. It has been used therapeutically to enhance partners well-being, as part of marriage counseling and infertility treatment,[7] to reduce lower back pain and a few other medical issues.[8] Even partners chair massage has emerged as helpful in alleviating anxiety for pregnant women.[9] Indeed, traditionally regarded as an alternative therapy, massage has increasingly been incorporated into Western medical practice and is even covered by some insurance companies. Studies have supported couples massage as having positive benefits for both those who give the massage as well as for those who receive it. An extensive review of the evidence-based literature on massage that included experimental studies found massage effective for the management of nausea (oncology, palliative care, and obstetrics), chronic lower back pain, and delayed onset of muscle soreness, stress reduction in critical care patients, symptom management and quality of life for patients with terminal illnesses (HIV, multiple sclerosis, and cancer).[10] As far back as 1887, massage was considered part of basic nursing skills, and turn-of-the-century nursing texts revealed that massage was part of the nursing curriculum taught in nursing schools. Back massages, specifically, have continued to be part of nursing care, and only in the past few decades have they been replaced by analgesics and other demands on nurses' time.[11]

Given the multiple benefits to massage, it should not be too surprising that couples massage was promoted as supportive of emotional well-being and good for a relationship. It was also an activity marketed as a new way for couples to break out of old habits: as something new, a way to reconnect, an opportunity to increase affection, encourage intimacy, lower anxiety, and create quality time. It was not uncommon to see couples massage on the Internet advertised as a dating activity with a variety of promotional statements made to couples who had been together for many years as well as to those who were meeting for the first time.

"You will not be disturbed with calls, texts, or any other notifications that might distract you from your partner. It helps you to come out of your self-centered lifestyle" [Ditto app].
"Couples Massage can be a unique way to have a date."
"Couples Massage can help you learn new things about one another."
"Couples Massage is an off-beat way to celebrate love with your partner."
"When you get a great massage, your body releases oxytocin, the "love hormone" that creates a sense of affection and love. When you get a Couples Massage, that means love is literally in the air (and the bloodstream)."

7. Serendipity in Personal Advertising

"The [spa name] experience is all about the ambience.... Time ceases to exist as you experience health and beauty rituals from all around the Mediterranean and beyond."

There was even an app designed to help couples reconnect or "take your relationship to the next level," with couples massage as just one of the many recommendations offered on this relationship-advice app (Ditto app). Couples massage could occur at a spa, a therapist's studio, or in the privacy of a couple's home. For new couples or people on a first date, it was offered as a way to try new things and as "a unique way to have a date." Some sites even offered the female-happy-ending massage, though whether this was part of a couple's activity and who provided the happy ending was unclear.

Couples massage essentially consisted of two persons, two massage tables, and (depending on the location) two therapists, one for each person, or if offered privately in the home, one therapist split her/his time between the couple. Often, the activity included candle lighting, aromatherapy, and music, such as one might have in any other massage. If the massage took place at a spa, there was also access to additional amenities, such as a pool, jacuzzi, or sauna. Couples were encouraged to express their preferences and limitations prior to the session so that the therapist could address each person's desires. The obvious goal was for both participants to have a positive experience.

Some exclusive locations offered opportunities to have "unique experiences" that culminated in couples massage. For example, one location offered $780 (per couple) that included different temperature baths, a bar, cheese plate, full body and facial massage, followed by tea (and water, of course). Multiple locations offered variations of these amenities in their fees. A few even provided gift certificates for dinner to follow the massage. Another location offered champagne to its guests, followed by water, tea, cookies, fruit, and nuts. A bubble bath (for two) with more champagne (or water) was followed by a massage with hemp oil.

Most websites framed couples massage as an opportunity for couples to experience total relaxation and an opportunity to reconnect. For those who were dating, advertisements described how couples massage increased the chemicals that produce feelings of happiness, affection, and intimacy. It was relatively easy to make the leap from married or long-term partners to those who simply wanted to try a new way to meet, date, and mate. It was difficult to know whether in competing for clients, the massage studios created the demand or the activities offered

125

were a response to couples' interests. Likely, it was a combination of the two. Still, each of the therapists with whom I spoke indicated that they were responding to people who elected to try couples massage as a first date, a special date (birthday or Valentine's Day), or as part of dating in an existing relationship. The therapists claimed to have broadened their promotion of the class after realizing there were people in couples massage who may not be in a relationship.

The cost of couples massage ranged from $65 to $780. One of my participants, who met her date on the Internet and subsequently agreed to try this activity as a first date, went to an exclusive location for their massage. Although she thought it was wonderful, the date ended poorly when her date complained about the event as an enormous waste of money.

> [Linda] Here, I actually enjoyed the whole thing, and I was touched that he had suggested it. I mean, at first, I was sort of weirded out, but then I thought, it took a real effort to come up with something that was different. We really connected … or at least I thought we did [online] … until we got out of there. Then, all he could do was complain about what a rip-off it was and what a waste of money, you know … so, all of the good feelings I had about it … and him, just evaporated. I mean, he should've known what it cost, so why do it if you're just going to complain about the money, you know? He didn't even ask me if I enjoyed it.

Another feature of couples massage that created unease for one woman was the alcohol offered as part of the experience. A look at multiple websites that feature couples massage as a dating event shows that several places offer wine, champagne, or some type of alcoholic beverage as part of the experience.

> [Elaine] We were offered wine when we got there. A small glass. I thought it was a nice touch and didn't think much beyond that. It was a very nice place, well-appointed, a good aesthetic. But when we entered the room, there was an open bottle of wine … so, it was more. That was excessive. Water is the drink recommended for massage. I would've expected cucumber water or water with fruit but not more wine. Also, I didn't really know this guy, so getting a massage was okay. I was cool with that, but getting drunk while getting a massage, that was not cool.

Part of the advice given to those who engage in couples massage, besides the recommendation to arrive early to allow time to relax, was also to minimize talking to avoid distracting from the experience. To Sheryl, this made it more difficult to relax and enjoy the experience.

> [Barbara] I am a talker. Even when I get a massage by myself, I usually end up talking with my therapist. I mean, we don't talk about climate change or

anything like that, you know. We just talk about enjoyable things, like what movie we've seen or silly stuff, you know. But lying there next to someone I hardly knew, and I admit I was nervous … talking would've helped me to relax, but I didn't want to break the rules, so I didn't. I didn't enjoy it.

[MaryAnne] I tried it. It's no big deal to me. I'm 58 years old, I've had 12 children … yes, 12 children. And when they were grown, I fell in love with a woman. So, I guess you could say my life is not exactly what you might expect. It was not what I expected, but there it is. I'm also a massage therapist. So, I can tell you that it's a great way to relax and just be with your partner. I love it. We both love it. And we're trying to make time to do it on a regular basis.

Perhaps one of the most important bits of advice that websites provided to the public was that participants should first be certain they were comfortable with this intimate activity to avoid an awkward moment. Beverly learned this by agreeing to a first date with a man she had met on the Internet.

[Beverly] It's strange because I am the first person to try things. I mean, I really am regarded as "out there" by my friends. I'll try anything once. So, I did not expect to have trouble with getting a [couples] massage. And it wasn't like we were complete strangers. We had been communicating for a while on the email. We'd seen each other's profiles. And yet…. I don't know why, but it was just too uncomfortable to be lying naked next to someone you had just seen for the first time, minutes before. I thought it was going to be exciting, you know? It was intimate but not intimate, supposed to be relaxing, but not so relaxing. We went out to eat afterward, and everything turned out okay, but it's probably not something I would recommend to anyone.

For the most part, it was not undressing (which is done in another room) or the intimacy of the couples massage that bothered participants. Rather, it was other features of the experience, the alcohol, the inability to speak, or what they learned about their dates during their sessions. It is possible that the problems offered were merely substitutes for being nervous.

Adult Classes and Dating Activities

Aside from online profiles, a more common way for people to meet was through structured dating activities and adult classes. These classes and dating activities are just one of the multiple categories of classes that comprise what scholars refer to as "learning across the life course." Learning across the life course is an expansive view of education as occurring in multiple contexts (schools, work, and leisure activities) and involving people of all ages. Life course education can increase work skills, athletic skills, language skills, and it can improve social and emotional well-being. As part of adult education, activities spanned many categories of learning: art, business, technology, performing arts (such as dance), investing, personal growth and life skills, real estate, language, and many more areas of interest. In the case of personal advertising, classes that focused on dating, intimacy, and sex were also offered in life course learning programs across the country. They included classes that focused on basic instructions to help the shy and uncertain meet members of the opposite sex, teach participants how to better engage in sexual practices and uncommon sexual behaviors: "How to Flirt," "Sensual Self Care," "Meet Your Mate," "The Highs and Woes of Internet Dating," "Love Passion and Your Pelvic Floor," "Blow His Mind: Fellatio Workshop," and "How to Meet and Connect with Women: Bootcamp." There was even a course on bondage and domination ("Introduction to Bondage and Domination: S&M an Introduction")[12] where singles and couples were introduced to the use of handcuffs, floggers, crops, and other tools of bondage and "incorporated into your life in a healthy, safe manner to enhance your personal relationships expand self-esteem and broaden your lovemaking horizons." Described as a "sex and dating class," all genders and sexual orientations were welcomed, and the course was described as learning a safe way to explore other sides of one's personality. Most of the dating classes were explicit about welcoming singles, couples, friends, gay, straight, and curious. In fact, it is easy to understand how single persons looking for dates could be found in the classes, given the inclusive promotion and nonjudgmental descriptions of the courses.

These classes were run by life and relationship coaches, therapists, sexperts, and certified sex educators. Most of these classes were one-time events, and classes ranged from one to three hours. They were often set in different locations, such as a restaurant or a center. Mix and Match was referred to as a "provocative social gathering." Each class was geared toward a particular age group (e.g., 25–39). There were even classes on couples massage. Classes ranged from $50 to $100. Classes on bondage and domination were advertised for singles and couples. Adult dating classes could be a single class or multiple classes that offered overviews of a topic or intense boot camps and ranged from cheap to slightly more expensive (e.g., $25 to $3,000).

Eleven of the women with whom I spoke had tried one or more

classes as part of their efforts to meet men. Just as with any instruction, the courses (and their titles) changed frequently. Most of them described participating in classes focused on meeting people or some version of speed dating. Other activities in which a few women engaged were classes created to help singles and couples (either marital, cohabiting, or newly dating) to enhance their sex lives. They consisted of participants who either met as strangers or who engaged in the activity as a first face-to-face date (an extension from meeting online).

For example, Denise had taken a class on the use of "Sex Toys" with the goal of meeting someone. Jane had taken a course on "Meet and Mate," which was a prior version of "Talk to Anyone Anytime," geared toward helping singles to learn how to engage in conversation with strangers successfully and to maintain the conversation. Like most of the adult dating classes, the "Sex Toys" class was described as open to singles, couples, and all sexual orientations. A friend had persuaded Denise to take the class with her, having heard that this was a class where they could meet men, as she explained:

> [Denise] A friend of mine wanted to take this class. She [the friend] heard that all types of people took the class and that it was fun. I've gone to a couple of sex toy parties, but they were only women, you know, as the guests, usually friends of mine. Someone would stand at the front of the room and show you the different toys, and then we lined up if we wanted to buy one. It was fun. And I sure learned a few things about my friends! Anyway, the class was supposed to be men and women, and the "instructor" was supposed to do the same thing, you know, tell us about the different toys. Only this one included items that were for both men and women. We met at this sex toy shop in the near north side, and there was a small room where they had the "class." There were only about 12 or 13 of us. I was hoping there would be more. It sort of allows you to hide better when there are more, you know, if something embarrasses you. But with only 12 of us, you couldn't do that. There were five or six men there, but I think only one or two looked as if they were alone, I'm not sure. I think I was too embarrassed really to try to get into the whole thing. I thought it would be okay because it was like she said, "we wouldn't know anyone and so who cares what they think of you if you don't like them," but I just wasn't able to get comfortable ... especially when she [the instructor] asked if anyone had questions. She was showing us the stuff and explaining how it worked. Then asking if anyone had questions.... It's one thing when you're with your friends, but I wasn't comfortable.

Another class was called "Safari Flirting." Annette had taken this class and enjoyed it a great deal. Because of her enthusiasm and perception that this class did have positive outcomes, I decided to observe one of the "Safari Flirting" classes. Like the "Sex Toys" class, the context for safari flirting was a similar section of Chicago that attracted singles. A set of vintage clothing stores, record and CD stores, along with funky restaurants and bars, provided the setting for the class. The format of safari flirting was simple. Participants were asked to meet at a particular restaurant/bar where participants were served a drink followed by the instructor's introduction and request that participants tell their name and why they were in the class. The instructor described "flirting" (as a social behavior that used conversation and body language to communicate interest in a deeper relationship to the person playfully) and offered tips on how to flirt. He repeatedly stated the goal was to have fun.

The focus was on advice: focus on a particular person, have an opening line (e.g., compliments were recommended); determine whether you want her/his name and contact information; and if you don't, have an exit line and move onto the next person. The advice also included what *not* to do: don't make overtly sexual comments; don't be overbearing; don't ignore the signals sent by the person with whom you flirt.

Once advice on flirting was concluded, participants were directed to a shopping section and another bar, where the class reconvened for "evaluation" and feedback. The class I observed had 16 male and female participants, with most participants (appearing to be) in their late 20s to mid–30s. The class was nearly equally divided between the sexes. Participants went their separate ways. I stayed with the instructor, who browsed from store to store, always at a distance. When the group came together at the end, women were more likely to offer their assessments. It appeared that the men had less trouble flirting. The women confirmed my impressions by describing their difficulty approaching men.

> I had a lot of fun. It wasn't so much learning to flirt as being forced to do it. I think we all flirt naturally, but maybe we don't think about it. This [class] forced me to think about it. It was fun, and the people were nice. I'm going on a date [with one of the guys in the class], so I guess it worked! [laughs].

Of course, the purpose of the class was not to produce results by having each person return with someone's name and phone number. Rather, its purpose was to help people who wanted to find romance a way to feel more comfortable initiating dialogue.

"Thin Slices of Life": Trust Created Online and Offline

Whether it was speed dating, dating apps, or offline activities, participation in personal advertising illustrated how our societal shifts, based on digital platforms and interactions, promoted behavior that involved trusting strangers. In addition to the behaviors mentioned in Chapter 5 (use of online commercial activities like HomeExchange, Airbnb, Uber, and other commercial enterprises), there were important implications for attitudes and behaviors that were not limited to resource exchanges and economic transactions online. Interactions stimulated online, searches for "things to do," could result in participation in offline activities as women placed themselves in trust situations that were unthinkable 40 years ago. Ad placers engaged in these activities with minimal or no prior knowledge of the persons with whom they engaged. They did not meet through family, friends, or church. Instead, a paid mediator or platform facilitated the activity, whether through a website, in a yoga or adult education class, or through a dating app. The increased attention by technology companies to the efficiency of communication and the explosion of information through social media are what made personal advertising possible, both online and offline.

Social media platforms enabled users to develop relationships with one another, albeit limited, and these interactions were imbued with some degree of trust. Online rating systems, combined with offline friendships and other indirect affirmations of sites and activities, resonated with ad placers. While it is difficult to assess the social impact of participation in the digital economy, we do know that approximately 40 percent of the population uses online platforms, and it is likely that those who engaged in personal advertising were part of this population. Developing trust in these interactions may well have led people to develop trust more easily in dating activities.

If user trust in a platform could lead other users to trust in that platform, it could positively impact that platform. But what about dating classes and couples yoga and massage? Perhaps people who engaged in these activities were more active members in the digital economy who could more easily develop trust. A yoga studio or day spa recommended by someone in one's neighborhood, or a place where the ad placer was already a participant, became the source for trust-building, along with ratings (provided by a website, Yelp, or other rating platforms). These were some of the mechanisms that helped participants reduce risk and engage in trusting strangers.

A woman attended a speed dating event with a friend or because someone she knew (and already trusted) recommended the activity. In this situation, the friend served as the source of trust. Once the ad placer observed 400 people at the event, she used this information to build on that trust and further reduce uncertainty. Subsequently, a decision evolved that because these people were strangers congregating in a known community center with a minister, the activity was less risky. What 40 years ago would have generated greater distrust (that everyone was unknown to the participant) may have lessened the risk of embarrassment, failure, or physical risk since no one would judge her, or at least no one she knew or cared about. The fact that the event was frequented by hundreds of people encouraged her to think that if these people were engaging in this activity, it must be okay. The trust was in the behavior—the rating, the interaction, the recommendation, the participation in a speed dating activity, not in a particular person.

Some women engaged in an activity with someone they met online or someone they met at the activity. For other women, online interactions were their source of trust-building. For some, it was the reputation of the center that sponsored the class/activity. Each of these served as the building blocks for trust. Each of these trust-building situations was accountability-based, with assessments of risk being dynamic, always subject to change. Women who became ad placers and who participated in face-to-face dating activities such as safari flirting or couples massage, first assessed that either the risk was minimal or the provider/activity would meet their needs (i.e., the benefit outweighed the risk). If the attitude was to simply have fun with minimal expectations of hooking up with someone, the emotional or social-psychological risk was minimal.

Some ad placers may have relied on generalized and distributive trust, hoping it would evolve to relational or "thick" trust. Some were happy to have the experience and did not expect it to evolve into a relationship. Ad placers were tasked with the challenge to build trust, and women in these studies revealed how their personal advertising activities were constructed, planned, and engaged with friends who supported their participation. Perhaps these worlds did not intersect, but the ad placer's existing trust relations were critical to her participation.

Two elements drove trust situations: uncertainty and vulnerability. Ad placers used several tools to decide when to place trust. One woman used an interview schedule, and several relied on friends. A few women discussed the reputations of dating activities, such as eHarmony, or the location of a speed dating activity. All of these women used online dating and were under the age of 60. Participation on the Internet was a part of engaging in distributive trust. Another reminder from our trust experts is that while connections (generalized trust) can be built relatively easily online, trust frequently fades over time as interactions continue. This was quite common among ad placers. As more information about the respondent was acquired, ad placers often ended interactions. There were also the limits of a sharing economy grounded in digital trust-building.[13] One might argue that the phenomenon of personal advertising supports Putnam's thesis that "thin trust" situations are what increasingly characterize modern society.[14]

8

Dating Apps

Finding Love Just Around the Corner

Beth Bailey wrote about the impact of industrialization and technology and how it changed the shape of American courtship in the early twentieth century.[1] The telephone was one of the inventions that modified communication and interaction between the sexes. This happened again in the 1980s when the telephone industry was deregulated.[2] During this period, deregulation combined with technological advances in telecommunications to once again modify exchanges between the sexes. In the 1980s, one of these modifications included the 900 number, known as *fantasy lines*.[3] In this billion-dollar industry, women engaged in "vocal pornography" to satisfy the fantasies of male callers. In the 1980s, prior to FaceTime and WhatsApp, telephones precluded visual interaction and, therefore, promoted fantasies. Analogous to personal advertising, one of the features of fantasy lines that attracted men was its anonymity. This, combined with the lack of visual cues, allowed participants to be imaginative and to create their preferred person with whom to share the fantasy experience. Kira Hall characterized "Dial-a-porn" as a unique mixture of public and private discourse.[4] Like women ad placers, women who worked for fantasy line businesses described the sense of control they had in "accessing men's minds" and regarded the job as empowering to their everyday cross-sex interactions. Hall attributed part of the growth of this phenomenon to fear of the AIDS epidemic and the interest in safe sex.

Just as the telephone excluded the visual and paved the way for fantasy, so too did personal advertising, particularly the advent of online dating. In both situations, the anonymity that telephones and the Internet provided enabled less self-conscious interactions between participants. Whereas earlier communications scholars argued that the telephone restricted individual expression, the emergence of cell phone technology resulted in a metamorphosis in the function and use of the telephone, shifting it from a business and home device to a personal device. And as the AT&T salesman said to me five years ago, the telephone ultimately became a multifaceted device.

About five years ago, when I was purchasing a cell phone for my oldest son, the AT&T attendant quoted the price at $600. I had only recently upgraded from my outdated flip phone and was literally in shock as I said, "My god, it's only a phone!" to which the salesperson, also a young man not much older than my son, responded, "Oh no, ma'am. It's so much more than a phone. It's a camera, a computer, and a television altogether." Indeed, cell phones now have a multimodal capacity for communication and are used for location-based dating, also known as satellite, mobile, and GPS dating. In location-based dating, smartphone technology is linked to apps to engage in connecting with others for the purposes of friendship, romance, or sexual encounters. (Apps is simply shorthand for application software that can run on any smartphone device.)

It was in the first decade of the twenty-first century that dating apps became popular. Unlike dating websites, which could involve a lengthy survey of personality characteristics used to match participants and that could be more costly depending on one's level of membership, dating apps were relatively easy to use and provided almost instant gratification by providing profiles and even matches with users quickly. Users of dating apps created profiles in which they shared personal information with other users. This information generally consisted of photographs, brief descriptions and, on some apps, personal interests. Users swiped or scrolled through the app and selected or "liked" persons based on characteristics which they "filtered" such as interests and the proximity of matches.[5] Once two people chose each other, a "match" was made, and the pair was able to communicate in a chat room. They may or may not have agreed to meet. Dating apps were easy and affordable and typically opened to a wide variety of people. Dating apps used GPS (global positioning system) technology to locate and send information about the proximity of users, and matches facilitated mobile intimacy.[6] These apps helped strangers arrange hookups focused on friendship, romance, serious relationships, or casual sex. Used predominantly by a young or queer segment of the population, the popularity of dating apps has grown and now crosses more demographics. Like online dating, dating apps have become ubiquitous, and the use of dating apps is also a normative way to meet and mate with others anywhere and anytime.

The earliest dating apps emerged between 2003 and 2005 and quickly established themselves as a new tool by which young people could connect (e.g., Skout, PlentyofFish, MeetMoi, Zoosk, and Assisted Serendipity). In 2006, approximately 3,000,000 users were logging into dating apps. By 2012, the number and use of dating apps exploded. Also in 2012, we saw Tinder, which became the dominant dating app and continues to be so today. In fact, Tinder became a global phenomenon with more than 50,000,000 global users in 196 countries and more than 9,000,000,000 matches.[7] Tinder's website stated it was "the biggest and flyest party in the world for singles—it's about time you showed up" and "Whether you're looking for love, need a date today, or just want to chat: We've got something for local singles everywhere." Along with Tinder, some of the more popular dating apps have included:

Bumble: Launched in 2014, Bumble's unique feature was that only women could make the first contact with matched male users. This app allowed for romantic connections or those simply looking to make friends. Bumble advertised that "On *Bumble*, women make the first move. We're leveling the playing field and changing the dynamics of dating. We believe relationships should begin with respect and equality," undoubtedly, appealing to many women app users.[8]

Hinge: Launched in 2012, Hinge used the slogan, "the relationship app that promotes long-term connections between users." Hinge allowed users to filter matches based on traits. Designed to reduce ghosting, ending communication with a partner without warning or response to the partner's inquiries, Hinge had a "Your Turn" feature to remind the user to continue the conversation. Hinge stated it is the "Dating app designed to be deleted.... Meet people who want to get off dating apps, too."[9]

CoffeeMeetsBagel. Launched in 2012, CoffeeMeetsBagel was created by three sisters and launched in New York City. Shortly thereafter, it was launched in San Francisco and Boston. This app feature included limiting the number of profiles users could interact with each day and offering icebreaker information for matches. CoffeeMeetsBagel also launched virtual speed dating in response to the pandemic. This app competed against Tinder by stating that it was "The original anti-swiping app," with a subheader that stated, "meet better people, go on better dates." "We create meaningful connections that spark hearts and inspire people to share themselves authentically and enthusiastically."[10]

Happn. Launched in 2014, Happn served 10,000,000 users two years later. Happn claimed to "provide you with people with whom you have crossed paths," arguing that "Since you've crossed paths with this person, there is a good chance the other person works or lives nearby, or has the same after-work lifestyle as you." The claim was that Happn made it feel more personal than Tinder.

Grindr. Launched in 2009, Grindr served gay, bi, trans, and queer people. It was the largest and most popular mobile app for gay people in the world. By 2014, Grindr averaged more than 5,000,000 monthly users worldwide. "From social issues to original content, we're continuing to blaze innovative paths with a meaningful impact for our community. At *Grindr*, we've created a safe space where you can discover, navigate, and get zero feet away from the queer world around you."[11]

OkCupid. Launched in 2004, OkCupid was one of the earlier apps that provided online dating, friendship, and social networking. Originally designed to get users to focus less on physical traits, for those who wanted to date, OkCupid allowed users to design their own filters to connect with only those who matched [their filters]. OkCupid popularized the concept of "sapiosexuality," meaning romance or sexual attraction based on intellectual rather than physical traits but removed that identity in 2019.[12] OkCupid stated that it was "the first dating app to introduce 22 gender and 13 orientation options. It was called "revolutionary." We called it "about time" and "the only dating app with thousands of questions—on everything from climate change to cilantro—that match you on what matters."[13]

Like websites and speed-dating sites, dating apps have attempted to carve a niche in the romance industry by targeting groups, advertising their unique features, and offering new features over time.

Amourfactory: "Love comes in various ways, and you can find the right way here."
Charmdate: "Meet attractive singles from Russia and Ukraine."
Loveaholics: "Choose an active dating lifestyle."
UniformDating: "Find out what's underneath a uniform!"
AsiaMe: "International dating with Asian women."
BeNaughty: "Have fun tonight."

A few modeled themselves after dating websites and included romantic personality tests or personality profiles that allowed them to claim they generated scientific-based matches. Tinder allowed people to see photos of others but offered little demographic information and user preferences. OkCupid operated as a matchmaking service and allowed users to filter who they saw based on answers to a variety of questions about politics, religion, and other topics. According to scholars who have compared the websites, Tinder drew people who were interested in casual sex (it had a reputation of being a hookup site), OkCupid attracted people who were looking for serious relationships, and PlentyofFish fell somewhere in between the other two.[14]

And like other personal advertising activities, mobile dating involved a process. Tinder revolutionized the ease with which one could engage in location-based dating by selecting Facebook photos and a brief self-description in the text along with the "swipe" (akin to turning a page). Once a profile was created, the user selected her interests (men, women, or both), the proximity of the "other," and the acceptable age range. The user then swiped left on those she did not like and swiped right for those she did like. If the person who was swiped also swiped the user, a match was made. Those matched were then allowed to chat within the app.[15] In this form of personal advertising the mediator was not a person such as in speed dating, but rather technology.

No doubt, because of Tinder's popularity, other apps advertised themselves as "anti-swipe" and tried to promote their differences with Tinder. Apps like Hinge and Bumble took issue with Tinder's approach and claimed to offer more personal and safer opportunities to meet and mate. Research examined who was likely to use specific apps and supported earlier applications of how context mattered. For example, there was some indication that anxious and insecure people were more likely to use dating apps.[16] Also, scholars examined the different uses of dating apps and found that it was just as important to understand the significance of social space in the motivation to use dating apps by diverse populations as the importance of geographic space.[17] Several of the ad placers with whom I spoke between 2008 to 2015 also used dating apps, though they were among the younger women (mostly in their 20s). Most of these women used only one dating app (Tinder), but a few tried different apps (PlentyofFish).

> [Karen] I tried PlentyofFish and then Tinder. I like Tinder. It's fun to see who you attract. I don't limit myself to one thing. I try different things, and I like the fact that it's easy and quick. It just depends on my mood at the time. When I don't want to spend a lot of time on it, I use the app and see what happens. It works. It takes time to use websites, and sometimes I just don't want to spend the time.

The features of dating apps regarded as the key to its popularity were relative ease, low cost, and the proximity of potential mates. Proximity and speed were what set dating apps apart from other forms of personal advertising. Dating apps also have been regarded as lowest on the hierarchy of modes of communication that result in intimacy, with a telephone conversation, texting, and email regarded as more conducive to establishing connections and relationships. The difficulty in *doing identity* for ad placers when using dating apps was because the format relied heavily on superficial features (photographs) and comparatively more limited information made available before making a connection. Most people using the apps wanted fast connections. Though the use of dating apps was regarded as unthinkable to most of my older participants, these tradeoffs were considered acceptable by ad placers who used them. App users were not concerned about the lack of information.

> [Sue] I do use Tinder. I don't see the difference between going online and Tinder. Well, actually, I do. Tinder is better. You can get on and get matched so fast. And you get more matches than when you're online. It's a lot easier. I just put my photo up there, and that's pretty much it.

Collapsed Contexts, Profiles, Doing Identity and Dating Apps

Whether the ad placer used dating websites, speed dating, or dating apps, she had to engage identity performance in a circumscribed place, space, and time and often with mediators who were also strangers. *Doing identity* in any personal advertising activity was vital to connecting with the desired person. With dating apps the focus was on the intersection of technology (the smartphone) and intimacy (location-based dating) within *collapsed contexts*.

Because of the structure of digital dating—limited information and the implicit emphasis on physical attractiveness (photos)—users had to adapt and find ways to present identity through technology which served as a virtual mediator. In some respects, the features of apps that attracted users were also what generated more effort to present themselves to potential mates.

Collapsed contexts is the conceptual understanding of how the public and private, professional, and personal, and multiple selves and contexts merge or overlap through digital media. In these contexts, different people, information, and norms meet.[18] In such contexts, the boundaries of separation become blurred. This reality created difficulty for participants to frame their messages targeted to members or sub-groups in that context, in this case, dating apps. The assumption was that collapsed contexts affected how people performed identity and disclosed information..[19] This could also have made it more challenging to establish trust.

However, ad placers who used dating apps described it as an "experiment," "fun," and something to pass the time, suggesting they did not take it seriously or that it was not problematic. Still, each admitted the added effort in developing her profile to assure elicited responses from men. And though the processes involved in dating apps also appeared to be accelerated, women spent a fair amount of time developing their presentations, particularly their visual presentation. Despite the fact that doing identity using a dating app occurred in a collapsed context, the time spent on something that appeared casual and for a fast connection was substantial. Even more interesting was that the time spent on the app was incongruous with the normative purpose of apps to provide instantaneous connections.

> [Laurie] I found it is easier to use a dating app than some websites where you have to complete a survey … and they're not short either. I decided to try Tinder. I pretty much just use it now. I want to say it was easier because technically it was, but it was also more difficult because the website pretty much forced me to think about things I did not think about. It [the website] sort of does the work for you. Or it forces you to do the work, but it also helps structure the work, and you think more about what you want and, really, who you are. With Tinder, it's fast, but all you have is your photograph because you can't really say much on an app. So, I'm not sure I would enjoy the app if I had not done the online dating first.

Some scholars have found that less attractive users were more likely to augment identity with misinformation about other features of the self. Because the objective was to transition to a face-to-face meeting, ad placers with whom I spoke said they did not try to deceive. In fact, they maintained it was not possible to be deceptive because this form of connecting relied so heavily on the visual, and deception would result in rejection.

> [Carmen] Not a chance. I don't want any surprises, and I don't want to see that surprised look on anyone's face. You know, like they thought they were getting Salma Hayak and then be all disappointed and stuff.

Just as they had placed personal ads online by first reading others' ads, participants who used dating apps also looked at other people's profiles and how information was presented. They described "molding" a profile on Tinder as an "evolving process" of learning how to present themselves visually and succinctly, stating that it was far more difficult than online websites. Unlike online dating, the women with whom I spoke expressed more casual attitudes about dating apps, how and why they used them. This aligned with several studies of online dating that found more variation in the motivations for using dating apps when compared to dating websites. And yet users did not view this activity as revolutionary or novel. Instead, they saw it as ordinary.[20]

One feature of identity performance on a dating app was that of marketing the self as a product as several women described the "market," and certainly the apps assisted users to brand themselves by offering suggestions for creating a profile. The profile was not as dependent on text, such as those found in dating websites, but it was still essential to success in dating apps.

> [Marta] After doing my profiles online [on the website], I learned how to market myself. It wasn't that difficult to figure out how to present a more generic picture, you know, one that would get the most attention. On the one hand, I do want an attractive man to see it and to get to know him. I don't want just anyone, but I DO want to be as open as possible ... to cast a wide net.
>
> [Penny] I have a good body, and I use it to stand out in the crowd. I make certain my photograph will catch their attention. I show my assets.

Dating App Courtship

The adjective "speed" in speed dating suggested the format for finding someone. However, speed dating and the process of finding a match were described as protracted activities when compared to the use of dating apps. Ostensibly, the purpose of dating online or face to face was to develop an intimate relationship with someone. Prolonged dating with one person, or courtship, was generally assumed to lead to a more enduring relationship. Women who engaged in speed dating characterized it as both a "lark" and with the intention of finding a mate and establishing a relationship. At the time of my studies, those who used dating apps were also women who dated online, either before or during their use of dating apps. There was substantial evidence that suggested these populations were not generally the same and that as we became more reliant on smartphones, our romantic practices shifted. Dating apps were now used by a broader (though still younger) segment of the population. Estimates were that by 2020, approximately 30 percent of 18–29 year olds in the U.S. used dating apps.[21]

> [Carmen] I have dated, you know, the old-fashioned way. I've gone on blind dates ... those are the worst, the ones your friends promise you you'll like, and then you realize they fixed you up because of some reason of their own, a favor to their boyfriend or something. I tried websites. I've done speed dating, dating apps, other stuff. It's fun. Why not try different things? You only go around once, and I don't intend to go like my mother. Whatever they come up with next, I'll try that too.

Some scholars and journalists have argued that we are undergoing a dramatic transformation of dating, romance, and relationships and that modern courtship and enduring relationships have been transformed into a "commodified game."[22] In *Liquid Love*, Zygmunt Bauman argued that courtship and romantic relationships had been liquefied by technology and the individualization of society.[23] Bauman believed that innovations like dating apps transformed romance and intimate relationships into a type of entertainment and commodification of people, where, like everything else, relationships became disposable. If the user did not like the date/mate, they could always return to the marketplace and find another. According to Bauman, these transformations changed the way we valued and interacted with people.[24] Others were more optimistic about the digital transformation of intimacy.[25] They suggested that dating apps, and technology in general, did not erode ideals of romantic love, monogamy, and sustained relationships. Instead, as with other forms of personal advertising, dating apps augmented modern courtship and sexual relationships. People still wanted to date. They still wanted and expected fidelity. They wanted their relationships to endure. And though technology assisted in finding dates and mates, it did not obviate the need for trust.

Trust and Dating Apps

The central dilemma of personal advertising was how to establish trust, particularly to women. As described in Chapter 5, trust relationships have changed due to technology and the rise of the sharing economy. Still, with each innovation, participants in this economy must manage trust. Because of the risky nature of dating apps, researchers have focused on which personality characteristics predisposed people to use dating apps but found little to suggest that personality traits were significant.[26] These findings required us to explain trust behaviors in the use of dating apps since users had to develop some level of trust prior to connecting, or at least that is what has been assumed. One woman used Facebook to locate the (matched) person's profile. This strategy established the veracity of self-presentation along with providing a check on attractiveness (matching the person's photos on Facebook to those uploaded on the app).

> [Sheryl] I did check him out on Facebook, I have to admit. I wasn't that sure about what I was doing ... using an app. I'm still not sure I will do it again. But I wanted to be sure that he was who he said he was, and that made me feel better. I checked out his photographs. I don't even know what I was looking for, but I think just any sign that made me uneasy, anything that said ... "don't do this."

Other ad placers described using the app in much the same way as they had online websites, connecting with matches but trying to prolong their exchanges as long as they could before the meeting. This resulted in losing matches whose motivations may have been different from theirs.

> [Sheryl] I spend as much time as I can without being too extreme. I have friends who don't really hesitate. They told me just to be sure to choose a public place and a good time to meet, and things would be alright. One of my friends does this frequently, but it never felt right to me.

Still, others found a middle ground by using a more condensed but limited time frame in which they sought to build trust prior to meeting a match.

> [Marta] I typically spend some time, at least a week or maybe even two, before I will meet someone. I want to feel like I have gotten to know him, to be sure I want to meet him in person.

The notion of distributional trust and the ease with which participants in the sharing economy move into digital exchanges was highlighted in the use of dating apps. A dating expert from *Crime Watch Daily* engaged in an undercover experiment to see how trusting women were in using dating apps. After creating a profile on Tinder and without revealing anything about himself, Chris Powers was able to match with 100 women, several of whom offered him their home address immediately and either agreed to come to his hotel room or to have him come to their home. The degree of trust among these women, two of whom Powers interviewed, was substantial, and they did not have concerns.[27]

Most of the women who used dating apps in my studies were relatively unconcerned about safety.

[Karen] Here is how I see it. If I'm meeting men who are living in the same neighborhood or hanging out in the same neighborhood, I know we at least have that in common. If you live or hang out around here, you have to be a certain kind of person because this is a neighborhood where there are a lot of college educated people in the arts. People who like to go bowling and drink beer are not going to be hanging around here. This is a particular kind of place.

Annette's analogy of dating apps and meeting men at bars or parties mitigated her concerns about the risks involved with apps.

[Annette] I look at it this way. Just because I hook up with some guy at a bar and I'm with my friends doesn't mean I know who he is any more than I do with an app. The only difference is that I'm with my friends. So, maybe one of them will know the guy, but if they don't, I think it's the same thing. You're taking the same chance as you do on an app.

Though they had heard about dangerous incidents, they did not believe anything would happen to them. One example of how dating apps attempted to support the development of distributional trust was a dating app, the Grade. Created in 2015, the Grade was yet another female-friendly dating app designed to hold users responsible by having users grade their match. The Grade's peer review allowed users to anonymously grade each other. The app had an algorithm that assigned letter grades to users based on profile quality, responsiveness, and peer reviews (from "A+" to "F"). It also advertised that "With the Grade, our goal is #NoMoreCreeps." As in a classroom, users who received a grade of "D" or "F" received a warning along with instructions on how to improve their app etiquette. If a user failed to change his behavior or continued to receive an F, he was "expelled." Though users who were expelled could appeal these decisions, there was no assurance they would succeed. The explicit focus of the Grade was to create accountability and satisfy the female user. In keeping with the dynamic nature of digital dating, grades were recalculated every ten minutes. And just as HomeExchange, Uber, and other online services relied on user ratings, the Grade advertised, "Nobody makes a big decision without checking reviews—restaurants, TVs, shoes—so why would you make a decision about your love life without doing the same?" Though the Grade was an excellent example of accountability of users, dating apps, it was never terribly successful, and few other apps have modeled after the Grade.

Possibly women's trust in dating apps is the result of the optimism of youth with participation in the sharing economy. Young people tend to have more optimistic views of the world, and though they may have read or heard about incidents that happened on dating apps, these women did not believe that anything bad could really happen to them. Each of the women was also an active Internet user. Though I did not explicitly inquire about their specific activities on the Internet, surveys of online behavior consistently supported the pervasive use of the Internet by millennials and Generation Z. It is fair to assume they participated in the sharing economy, but I do not know that for certain. These two factors may provide a partial explanation for participation and trust in dating apps.

Lying, Catfishing and Posting: Deviance, Deception and Dating Apps

As with any innovation, dating apps provided opportunities and presented risks. Possibly because of the format of dating apps, where technology was the primary mediator and dating apps remained relatively unregulated, the risks were substantial. Fake profiles, sexual predators, financial cons, cyberbullying, discrimination, even health concerns emerged as hooking up with strangers for casual sex resulted in increased sexually transmitted diseases and crimes.[28] Meeting strangers armed with minimal information placed participants at risk. GPS technology, the feature of dating apps that conveyed the distance between two users, enabled an individual to monitor others, and, thus, an offender was able to use this information to prey on his/her victims. Few dating apps provided substantial safety mechanisms for users, except Bumble, Hornet, and Tinder.[29]

Bumble provided women with the opportunity to be the first to send a message, and matches formed because mutual swipes expired after 24 hours. And though the man had the option to extend the window another 24 hours, if the woman still did not respond to the man, the match would permanently expire. In this way, Bumble assured that matches were always up-to-date and gave women more control over the men with whom they communicated. However, the app did use Facebook to provide users' age, job, education and, most importantly, a location that was available to all users. Tinder used Facebook accounts to set up a user's profile. Users answered questions about sexual orientation, age, and the preferred distance to hook up with a match. Facebook was regarded as safe, and the link between the two allowed participants to verify the identity of users. Nevertheless, Tinder also allowed known sex offenders to use the app. The feature that makes Tinder (and all dating apps) unique is geolocation tracking, which allows users always to know who is nearby. The convenience of apps, at the same time, invited danger when a disreputable person used this information for illicit purposes.

My participants talked about the "downside" of dating apps and not only knew about the risks, but each one had also experienced some form of online harassment. They could describe the different types of risks and understood that a significant number of women had bad experiences with dating apps. Yet, they did not associate the risks or danger as something personal or something that could happen to them.

> [Penny] I've seen things on social media and heard things, and I know it happens. I guess I just don't think it's going to happen to me. I don't take it personally.
>
> [Carmen] It's like going to the movies, to those horror movies, you know, like *Saw*, where you see it, and you know it's happening, but then you leave the movie, and you forget about it. You know, it's never going to happen to you. I guess that's how I think of it. I know shit happens, but I don't think it's going to be me that it happens to.

Although dating apps were not created to serve offenders, nor did they intend to promote deviant or criminal behavior, both types of behavior occurred, and some argued they gave rise to a new type of offender, a *digital age offender*. The claim was that digital crimes had increased exponentially within the past four years.[30] Dating app companies could not be legally compelled to remove or block sexual offenders from their platforms nor did they screen users for criminal backgrounds.[31] Added to this was the lack of reporting on criminal behavior linked to dating apps and online dating. Most dating apps offered advice to engage in protective behavior, such as the recommendation to meet in a public place, refrain from going to a stranger's apartment too quickly and inform friends about the location and time of the date or meeting. Apps also provided opportunities to report inappropriate behavior and may even have removed someone from the app. However, self-protection was the primary approach to safety, and there was no way to ensure that participants followed the advice. Bumble's dating app promoted itself as safer because it put women in charge of making the first connection. Deviant and criminal behavior occurred in the world of dating apps, and the onus was typically on the user.

The Pew Research Center found that a significant number of women claimed to have been harassed online and that 41 percent of

8. Dating Apps

18–29 year olds had unfriended or blocked someone who made them uncomfortable online.[32] In 2011, Match.com began screening U.S. members against a database of known sex offenders when a woman claimed to have been raped by someone using the site and sued the company. At least some speculated that the use of geolocation was part of the problem. One reporter declared that by using dating apps, women were engaging in a dangerous game of "romantic Russian roulette." By trusting strangers and placing themselves in dangerous situations, women were subjected, minimally to harassment and possibly to serious crimes such as rape, abduction (sex trafficking), and even murder. Though the data was (and continues to be) imprecise, it was fair to speculate that because of the source of these criminal activities, many criminal activities were likely to have been under-reported. Skout once marketed its app as having two communities: an adult community and a teen community of users. It claimed to restrict users to each community according to age-appropriate groups. Members could only communicate with peers close to their age. In 2011, to provide assurance that members were secure, the app claimed, "we ban over 40,000 devices each month for violations," though just how secure participants might have felt knowing the company's need to ban this number of devices regularly is anybody's guess. Skout was forced to shut down its teen hub after three U.S. rape cases occurred with men who used the app to target children. One was a 12-year-old girl. This claim, designed to assure users, suggested a fair amount of inappropriate behavior occurred on Skout and likely other app sites. Bumble was undoubtedly created as a response to concerns about risks.

In 2019, reporters described the reality that sex offenders could be found on all dating apps, including Tinder. They began with a story about a woman who found her mate on PlentyofFish in 2016. The woman had engaged in online dating for years but found a man who claimed he wanted someone to marry. PlentyofFish did not verify whether users told the truth about their criminal histories. Rather, it requested that customers sign a statement that they had not been convicted of a sex offense and accepted customers' signatures. What the woman did not know was that the person with whom she was matched was a dangerous registered sex offender. He raped her. PlentyofFish was one of 45 dating apps owned by Match Group, a Dallas-based corporation that dominated the dating industry and owned Tinder. The Match Group first agreed to screen for registered sex offenders in 2011 when Carole Markin had been connected with a six-time convicted rapist who raped her on their second date. These measures were only taken when members subscribed, not when they used the free version of an app.

It is not surprising that women were predominantly the victims of harassment and gender abuse online or even rape and murder because this was the reality for women offline. Dating violence and harassment of women have long been known to occur, and some might argue they have even been normalized.[33] Pressure has been mounting to regulate digital platforms, and dating apps were among those companies. A few dating apps have already strengthened their security, though the added measures do little to avoid much of what happens on the apps. In the future, other technological changes may assist in creating security measures for dating, such as augmented reality. Some project that augmented reality could provide a way to assess a person's dating profile by allowing people to simply point their phone at the person and learn if that person has a record as a sex offender.

A house subcommittee investigated popular dating services Bumble, Grindr, the Meet Group, and Match Group, which owned Tinder, Match.com, and OkCupid. The targets of the investigation by the U.S. House Oversight and Reform Subcommittee on Economic and Consumer Policy were Tinder and Bumble for allegedly allowing minors and sex offenders to use their services.[34] Other suggestions were to have the National Sex Offender Registry updated and to track the digital footprint of sexual offenders and allow dating apps and other social media to block them from participating.[35]

> Our concern about the underage use of dating apps is heightened by reports that many popular free dating apps permit registered sex offenders to use them, while paid versions of these same apps screen out registered sex offenders," Rep. Raja Krishnamoorthi, the Illinois Democrat who heads the subcommittee, said in a statement. "Protection from sexual predators should not be a luxury confined to paying customers."[36]

In *Alone Together*, Sheryl Turkle described the effects of technology on human behavior and insisted that we began with an illusion that technology would give us control, but we ended up being controlled by technology.[37] She also assessed how computers and digital devices changed what we do and how we think. Like Bauman, Turkle believed that virtual relationships and digital connections were displacing enduring relationships in favor of transient ones. Several scholars emphasized the unintended but negative aspects of technology as they suggested that we relied on technology to mediate human relations and the digital environment. They concluded that the digital environment encouraged us to be narcissistic and to address other people as either potential matches or as problems that can be managed or "deleted." Regardless of the type of hookup or relationship in which participants were interested, the use of dating apps necessarily involved identity performance and, to some extent, what one scholar called "selling the self" and "buying the other" as participants increasingly engaged in relationship tourism and shopping for mates. Despite an abundance of research on mediated intimacy, we still do not have a firm grasp on the implications of personal advertising and specifically the trajectory of connections made using dating apps.

Where Do We Go from Here?

The use of mobile dating apps has exploded in the twenty-first century, and they have already become part of the mainstream way to meet and mate. The features marketed by mobile dating services—time, ease, and proximity, align perfectly with a society that values individuality, autonomy, and the ability to do things quickly. Despite the risks and negative experiences with dating apps, the women in my interviews maintained the perception of increased options and greater freedom to engage those options. In addition to convenience, location-based dating allowed participants to connect with several men. Dating apps offered even more opportunities to fantasize about anonymous others and enhanced one's self-esteem by examining the number of "matches" they achieved.

One can question the priorities of dating apps—location and proximity (over commonalities), but ad placers explained how they used location as a proxy for other similarities. They assumed that if they and their "matches" also lived in the same area or frequented the same restaurant or bar that she and he had something in common. They may have assumed that if they were in the same neighborhood that they were from the same social class. In other words, geographic proximity was used as ground zero for "commonalities." As one interviewee stated, it was not that different from meeting a stranger at a bar or restaurant and "hitting it off." No one questioned whether the "match" was transient and simply passing through their neighborhood, bar or restaurant.

It is also easy to wonder why users were not more concerned about the flow of information on dating apps that put them at greater risk. Most of my interviewees did not dwell on the negative aspects of dating apps or at least not the danger and possibilities of encountering criminal behavior. Instead, their concerns focused on identity performance within this context and whether they would secure multiple matches from which to choose. Alyssa Murphy suggested that the relative ease of being able to engage on dating apps when a user decided, and possibly from her couch at home, created a false sense of comfort and safety that was transmitted in interactions on the app.[38]

An empirical response to the plethora of journalistic and scholarly articles that suggested modern technology was tearing apart our society and creating social isolation found that contrary to this position, only 25 percent of participants used dating apps explicitly for sexual hookups. The majority used them to find dates to pursue a more enduring relationship. And while enduring may not mean the golden wedding anniversary our parents and grandparents celebrated, it still referred to something beyond a one-night stand. Most of those surveyed (71 percent) said they would prefer to find love through a traditional face-to-face encounter.[39]

Another feature of dating apps that was important was when and how they were used. Vicky shared with me that she valued the dating app she used because it helped her at a particularly important juncture in her life.

> My husband left me for another woman, and I was pretty messed up. I cried a lot, and it really affected my self-esteem. I didn't feel like I was worth anything or that any man would want me. I'm embarrassed to admit it, but I started on Tinder before we even got the divorce finalized. A friend of mine convinced me, and I didn't take it seriously at first. I wasn't even interested in a relationship. It was just something to do ... about getting my confidence back. Knowing someone would be interested in me. Having sex ... it worked. It feels good when you get a lot of matches, but it also ... and I know this is going to sound like high drama, but it gave me my confidence back ... knowing someone wanted me.

While the relationship between the use of dating apps and health concerns has been examined, particularly with respect to the spread of sexually transmitted diseases such as AIDS, the impact on well-being has not. Self-esteem, empowerment, and a sense of control over one's life—sexual health and self-care are also important aspects of overall health. Some research has addressed the positive outcomes of the use of dating apps. Indeed, broadening one's sexual network can be a positive outcome if sexual activity is safe.

Even with all the caveats, it is not only appropriate, but it is also necessary that our dating and courtship practices mirror our modern society. It is reasonable to expect that people who live in complex, technologically advanced, and highly mobile societies should also appreciate the tools that enable them to pursue their desires and meet their needs. It is also reasonable to assume that in modern societies where inequalities and disparities between groups have grown and many people feel disempowered, a tool that provides a sense of control over an essential element of one's life and expands one's network of intimacy would be valued. In an era of terrorism, school shootings, natural disasters, and pandemics, people remain risk-averse. But even if they try to minimize risk and are not accepting of risk, it is possible that they are becoming accustomed to it. Within this worldview, it may be that relative to some of these other issues, the use of a dating app and the possibility of encountering cyberstalking are viewed as no riskier than shopping online or going to school. For most Americans, the global pandemic in 2020 changed everything.

9

Personal Advertising
in the Age of Covid-19

It is not possible to write about the increase of personal advertising, trust, and other issues without addressing the coronavirus (Covid-19) pandemic and its impact on these activities. The work that was done with participants in these studies predated the pandemic (1998–2015). I do not have data that I have acquired past the year 2015, and therefore, I cannot claim to know what has happened to speed dating and other face-to-face dating activities, but as a sociologist, I do believe it is possible to provide informed speculation about these activities. What follows is based largely on information from the Pew Research Center, newspaper articles, and experts' perspectives on what is happening now in the world of personal advertising, or at least dating websites and dating apps.

It should also be clarified that the Pew research data, while comprehensive and offering insights into the changes that have occurred in the past ten years, was gathered prior to the pandemic. I include the Pew studies because these surveys informed my interviews with the women who were willing to speak with me about their experiences. My primary sources of data were interviews, content analyses, and observations of face-to-face activities. These data do not provide the broader picture captured by carefully constructed surveys, and it is always preferable to have as much data as possible to understand an issue and to capture the broader perspective of the phenomenon.

Pew Survey on Dating: What Have We Learned?

The Pew Research Center developed its Pew Internet & American Life Project in the fall of 2005. The project was led by Dr. Phillip Morgan from Duke University and Dr. Seth Sanders from the University of

Maryland. These researchers wanted to understand the impact of technology on dating, relationship formation, and family change. The first of these surveys, conducted in 2005, discovered that most singles found it difficult to meet people where they lived, but 61 percent of singles did not use the Internet or dating websites at that time.[1] Approximately 11 percent of singles (one in ten) had used a dating website to meet people. It is not surprising that those who had tried a dating website were younger (18–29 years old). The most popular dating sites were Yahoo Personals and Match.com, and most users reported positive experiences with the activity. Other sites included MarketRange Inc., Spark Networks, MATE1.com, TRUE.com, eHarmony.com, LOVE@AOL, ZenconTechnologies Dating Sites, and LOVEHAPPENS.com. Another feature we learned about persons who used online dating websites in 2005 was that they tended to have more liberal attitudes. A follow-up survey in 2006 found the public split in its assessment of online dating, with 44 percent who agreed that using the Internet was a good way to meet people and 44 percent who disagreed with that assessment. Regardless of their perspective about its utility, most Internet users did not regard online dating as an act of desperate or unattractive people. One commonality between users of dating websites during 2005–2006 and 2019 is the perception that these sites provided more opportunities for people to be disingenuous. In 2006, the majority of users believed that people lied about their marital status. In 2019, the majority of users believed that people inflated their profiles (particularly with regard to their attractiveness).

In 2019, the form of the American Life Project changed, partially due to the changes in society; that is, people no longer responded to telephone surveys in the same way they had in the past (2005, 2013, and 2015). The 2019 survey was conducted online using a probability sample. The October 2019 survey provided one of the most current and comprehensive analyses of dating. The Pew Research Center found that 32 percent of married adults met through social networks of friends and family, 18 percent through work, 17 percent school, 12 percent online, 8 percent at a bar or restaurant, 5 percent at a place of worship, and 8 percent elsewhere.

One of the most interesting findings from the Pew survey was that nearly half of Americans surveyed believed that dating was harder today than it was ten years ago (47 percent), particularly women (55 percent women vs. 39 percent men).[2] Women claimed it was more difficult to find someone to date, and their primary reason for this assessment was the perceived increased risk involved in dating. Other reasons that dating was perceived as harder today include technology (12 percent), the impersonal nature of dates (10 percent), the increasingly casual nature of dating (9 percent), and gender roles (8 percent).[3] These tended to be younger singles. Those who had been in their relationship less than three years were just as likely to have met their partner online as through other support networks. In much the same way that the women in my studies responded, most persons in the Pew survey (67 percent) did not regard their dating life as "going well." More than half of the women had experienced some form of harassment while on a date. This included pressure to have sex (33 percent). Another interesting finding was that nearly half of current singles were not interested in dating, given their priorities.

The Pew Director of Technology and Internet Research, Monica Anderson, stated there had been a clear increase in the number of people using online dating sites and dating apps.[4] In 2013, Pew survey data found that 11 percent of adults had used a dating site or app, and just 3 percent reported they had entered into a long-term relationship or marriage through either of these dating modes. By 2019, these numbers had changed significantly as three in ten adults (30 percent) claimed to have used a dating app or website, and 12 percent had married someone they met through online dating. Internet dating was the third most popular means of meeting a long-term partner. And half of the 18–34 year olds had used a dating app. At least 71 percent of online daters responded that it was very important for them to see a photograph of the person responding to the advertisement. And among online daters 50 and older, it was also important that the person's profile include her/his race or ethnicity.

Pew data allowed us to see the increase in the use of online dating and dating apps in the past 15 years. Whereas some of the earliest data on online dating indicated that the primary placers of personal advertisements were in their late 20s to late 30s, currently, it is the younger population (18–29 year olds) who are the primary users of online dating and dating apps; most of these persons reported that it was relatively easy for them to find compatible dates/mates through this process.[5] There does not seem to be a distinction between White ethnics, African Americans, and Latinos, though it is not clear whether the survey examined certain behaviors with respect to race and ethnicity. It is also important to acknowledge that the response of meeting online did not mean that everyone met through a dating app or website. Rather, the majority of those who met their partner online did meet through a dating website or dating app (61 percent). Still, others met through a social media site (21 percent), online discussion forum (10 percent), texting or messaging app (3 percent), or online gaming (3 percent).[6] And although the stigma of online dating has diminished, nearly half of those surveyed still regard it as unsafe, though these were more likely to be persons who had never taken part in these activities. The way people interpreted their experiences with online dating varied by socioeconomic factors, such as education and income. Persons with more education (a bachelor's or advanced degree) were more likely to interpret their experience positively compared with persons with a high school diploma or less.[7] Similarly, those who earned $75,000 or more per year were more likely to interpret their experience with online dating positively compared to those who earned less than $30,000 (70 percent vs. 44 percent).

Some of the highlights from this latest Pew survey indicated that about 47 percent of online daters (meaning all age groups) described their online experiences negatively, and nearly 71 percent of those surveyed believed it was common for people online to lie about themselves to make themselves appear more desirable. Finally, though relatively few respondents indicated they were subjected to serious threats or harm, most women who dated online had experiences of harassment, rude or unwanted attention, including touching.

Merging Survey Insights with My Interviews

The picture provided by these surveys and the interviews I gathered is a growing use of technology to establish relationships and openness, by at least younger women, to experiment with ways to date. Along with entrepreneurial modes of matchmaking (couples yoga), those looking to find a mate or long-term relationship are engaging in online dating and matchmaking sites. Typically, we assume that the growth of an industry is related to how well its agents meet the needs or demands of clients. And though the romance industry has clearly expanded, dating websites, activities, pills, and gimmicks also become defunct, eliminated by the market. One example is PerfectMatch.com, a dating website which once boasted that it was the largest dating website in the country and was linked to multiple celebrity events (e.g., it served as the site on which Diane Lane and John Cusack met in the romantic comedy *Must Love Dogs*).

Another example is Just Eye Contact, a version of speed dating that relied upon silently looking into a prospective date's eyes instead of verbal exchanges. With the variety of websites, dating apps, and matchmaking activities available, it is easy to assume these are the "supply" responding to demand and that they are successful. Yet, the Pew surveys conducted across 15 years[8] and the women I interviewed conducted across 17 years suggest that most users of these activities did not claim success. If anything, they were somewhat disappointed. And apparently, women at least regarded dating as more challenging today than it was ten years ago, despite the technology that allows us to optimize the male-to-female ratio at our favorite gathering place, coffee shop, or restaurant. Supposedly, women have more control over their lives, and the women in my interviews at least talked at length about the ongoing appeal of dating online or dating apps as offering more control over the dating situation. Connections were made, but much like traditional dating, which has its problems, twenty-first-century dating (with and without technology) has its own dilemmas—online harassment, deception, failed in-person meetings, and the added risk of meeting strangers found through a virtual mediator. This reality is often linked to the fact that online dating is the process of trying to build trust in a sharing economy where strangers are less accountable to ad placers and, therefore, perhaps more willing to violate norms. It is possible for dissatisfied clients to review and evaluate a website or dating activity on the Internet (and sometimes on the dating website). Participants have also filed complaints with the Better Business Bureau. But unlike eBay, Amazon.com, Uber, or other commercial platforms in the sharing economy, it is nearly impossible to hold individuals accountable in online dating. And now, thanks to Covid-19, those who are interested in dating and establishing intimate relationships also must contend with an ongoing pandemic.

Distance Dating: A Return to Courtship

The onset of the coronavirus (Covid-19) upended everyone's life, and singles were no exception. In fact, for those who were unattached but looking for a mate and for those who were newly dating when the pandemic hit, social distancing was as challenging as the issues parents, elders, and families were navigating. As journalists and scholars pointed out, millennials and Gen Zers were navigating a part of their lives that was critical to the formation of all types of healthy relationships, including intimacy. And though data revealed the satisfaction of a segment of the singles population who elected to remain single or who were pursuing relationships, it remains to be seen what the long-term impact of social distancing will have on people who live alone. Did living alone through a pandemic result in being lonely?

Relationship experts argue there was a silver lining to the pandemic as people were forced to take a step back and engage with others beyond the superficial connections that often characterized online dating. Some have suggested that having multiple connections could be too much for people who cannot handle too many choices without faltering. Freedom and an excessive number of choices could devolve into being distracted by always chasing opportunities for the next hookup instead of paying attention to the existing one. As an older person, I liken this to the introduction of cell phones and the call-waiting feature, where one could find people attending to every ring of the phone, even when they were supposed to be engaged in a meeting. Many of us can recall a meeting in which we have participated where colleagues were texting or checking their email instead of paying attention to the meeting. I know I am guilty of that as well. Unless the interruption was an emergency or a child in need of her parent, I was often irritated when a friend or colleague used her call-waiting feature to juggle multiple calls while she also interacted with me. Technology has provided us with more ways to connect and with new types of connections, but these connections have not always translated into meaningful interactions. We were too often distracted and afraid we would miss something. In the meantime, we were ignoring the person or group with whom we were supposed to be engaged. According to some, the pandemic forced people to slow down and invest more in interactions instead of the fast-food approach to connecting and dating, where people are connected but not tuned in, and it's easier to dispose of someone to connect with another person.

According to Rachel Wolfe, being at home alone, and in some cases without a job, resulted in singles being more active on dating apps, particularly in cities hardest hit by the virus.[9] Wolfe cited the dating app Bumble as her example, which reported a 21 percent user increase in Seattle, a 23 percent increase in New York City, and a 26 percent user increase in San Francisco. Use of Bumble's video chat feature was reported to have increased by 93 percent, with chats averaging 29 minutes. In fact, the pandemic has given dating apps a boost. According to Melissa Hobley, OkCupid's chief marketing officer, a city's lockdown resulted in a huge boon for the service (a 700 percent increase).[10] This was also the case for other dating apps.[11]

Several dating apps created ways to allow daters to meet for a virtual date, video chat, icebreaker games, and suggestions for virtual dates. CoffeeMeetsBagel's "Virtual Date Nudge" provided a prompt for daters to select from among several options such as a virtual tour of a museum, cooking together over a video, game night, or even blind dates (where cartoons obscure each person's profile while they talk). The ad placer responded, and the other person with whom she was chatting was alerted. Some app creators claimed the pandemic forced them to rethink how to facilitate a meeting to encourage prolonged virtual interactions that were more substantive before an in-person date. Such activities were intended to serve as a prelude to FaceTiming, Zooming, and video connections, which in turn served as the prelude to face-to-face meetings. Obviously, the primary motivation for these services to innovate was likely commerce, but multiple journalistic accounts suggested that users were responding favorably to these changes. Even without gimmicks or modifications, users found that time at home has translated into a different mode of getting to know potential mates, even when the source was an online website or dating app. The fear of contracting the coronavirus caused daters to find the time to get to know a potential mate instead of quickly moving on to the next one.

Post-Pandemic Dating: Moving Forward from the Past

The Kinsey Institute Anthropologist and Match.com adviser, Helen Fisher, stated that the coronavirus resulted in slowing the courtship process and causing people to rethink their objectives.[12] At the same time, it accelerated the trust process by encouraging people to engage in more meaningful discussions. And it has taken issues of sex and money out of the equation, allowing people to avoid navigating who pays the bill on a date or whether to have sex without first getting to know someone. And though the women I interviewed associated personal advertising with expanding their opportunities and choices, Fisher pointed to research that suggested human beings cannot handle too many choices, referring to this as the "paradox of choice" where our short-term memory cannot handle more than five to nine choices. Fisher also noted that "the human brain is soft-wired to attach to a partner slowly," whereas romantic love could be achieved rapidly but that enduring relationships (i.e., long-term relationships and marriage) are "built for slow love."

The acceleration of trust-building described in Chapter 5 was also described in several articles devoted to the coronavirus (Covid-19) and its impact on online dating. Experts described distance dating and the reflexivity generated by the pandemic as linked to working harder at getting to know someone, spending more time with them, and sharing relationship objectives. One dating app, *WooPlus*, hired a polling group to conduct a survey of 2,000 Americans about the outcomes of Covid-19 and found that most of their respondents (63 percent) believed the pandemic permanently changed the way we date and mate.[13] Thirty percent believed that post-pandemic, people would be more likely to use dating apps, and 38 percent believed virtual dating forces daters to "take things more slowly." Finally, respondents believed that the pandemic both facilitated and accelerated reaching "the comfort zone" with a partner (57 percent).[14] Some of the indicators of the comfort zone included:

Sleep in the same bed	48%
Meet their family	38%
Leave the door open when I use the bathroom	37%
Tell them a deep secret	36%
Shower at their place	36%
Call each other pet names	34%
Don't wear makeup in front of them	32%
Have them meet my family	32%
Talk about a future together	29%

Source: SWNS, 2020.

If Helen Fisher is correct, the women with whom I spoke and the singles responding in the dating surveys may have *wanted* the array of potential mates from which to choose, but they may not be hardwired to successfully manage multiple opportunities. It may be that personal advertising, which depends on distributive trust, is an evolving structure that may be better suited to those singles who use online dating as part of their social life and who are content with casual relationships. According to Pew, this is a significant segment of the population who date online. Once the pandemic has been successfully managed, we will see whether those who once participated without a commitment to creating long-term relationships continue to be satisfied with casual encounters. It will also be interesting to examine whether face-to-face dating activities survive the pandemic and how they manage in the "new normal." One thing is certain. Just as we have witnessed the multiple modes that have developed to meet the human need to date, mate, and relate in the past two decades, and particularly during the pandemic, we are sure to see new and provocative innovations because we are human, and we need to connect to each other.

Appendix: Methods

When I first began to pursue personal advertisements as a scholarly project in 1996, it was not my plan to engage in four separate data-gathering efforts. Rather, as an assistant professor, I planned the typical trajectory of creating my "pilot" study and then producing a more extensive Internet survey of participants. My plan met with such resistance from senior colleagues that I almost abandoned the study. I had been told that no one had yet figured out how to address the multiple issues of validity and reliability with Internet research or how to guarantee anonymity to participants on an Internet study. There were no formal guidelines for internal review boards to assess a study. I'm sure there were other statements that I no longer remember. It was my time at Stanford University's Center for the Advanced Study of the Behavioral Sciences when senior colleagues encouraged me to continue the research.

There were several reasons I changed my original research plan and that personal advertising held my interest over the years. No one had interviewed participants to understand ad placers' phenomenology of this experience (see list of sociological studies of personal ads). I also found that several of my other research interests intersected with the topic of personal advertising (identity, trust, race relations, and intersectionality). I became interested in the interdisciplinary scholarship on *trust* and issues of trust that are fundamental to personal advertising. My broader interests in identity and race motivated me to target a particular population of ad placers because no person of color had responded to my first effort and even less attention had been given to race in personal advertising. Finally, the changing character of personal advertising kept drawing me back to explore how technology and dating innovations impacted ad placers. As I pursued each project, I also read the literature on trust, intersectionality, race and dating, and interracial dating. What evolved over the years were four projects, each expanding some element of personal ad placements and, ultimately, what I refer to as personal advertising.

Appendix: Methods

I also modified my original goal to research both men's and women's participation in personal advertising. While I had no difficulty acquiring participants in the first project, my second project did not result in men responding to my solicitations. Both because women appeared to be more responsive and because I regarded a gendered view of this activity as entirely appropriate, I modified the subsequent projects to focus exclusively on women. The exception to this was the content analysis presented in the first chapter (men and women who advertised across centuries in the *Matrimonial News* and *Social Connections*).

Personal advertising held my attention over the years because of how it has continued to evolve—the shift from print to online, the proliferation of matchmaking services, other dating activities, and the growth of this industry into a $2,000,000,000-a-year industry. Undoubtedly, there are those who will take issue with how I collapse these activities online and offline under one header, but I suggest the common thread is their explicit purpose of helping persons to meet and mate under unique conditions: there is no prior connection to the persons they meet, a paid mediator is part of the process, and ad placers must advertise themselves to engage in these activities in often limited ways, and participation required some modicum of trust and performance of identity. The seemingly obvious answers to what gave rise to personal advertising were absent during the 1990s and even the first decade of the twenty-first century. Even now, less attention is given to the structural contexts and cultural transformations that generate these activities. The focus on interviews was designed to fill a gap and explore identity and how it was managed in different contexts and situations. I was also interested in the phenomenology of ad placers and how they experienced this new form of courtship.

When I began this research, I was 37 and divorced. That was 24 years ago, and I am now remarried and the mother of two teenage sons. One of the questions I have been asked during my presentations on this topic is whether I engaged in personal advertising. The answer is no, but I did participate in a couples laughter yoga session and a speed tennis session. Both of these activities were part of my research observations; however, participant-observer was not part of my study design. I do have several friends and colleagues who have engaged in personal advertising. It was even suggested by a colleague that I engage the research as a participant-observer or by placing my personal advertisement and subsequently engaging in an autoethnographic account of my experiences. However, I could not anticipate how I would avoid ethical dilemmas that might occur, and so I decided against it. Instead, I acquired internal review from my universities, solicited participants through advertisements and flyers that stated my goals explicitly, and signed the same consent forms that my participants signed. Although attitudes have changed since I began this work, and many of my participants in the last two studies were unconcerned about these promises, I used pseudonyms throughout the manuscript to assure the confidentiality and anonymity I promised to my participants.

I see myself as a successful cultural straddler, a feminist, and a researcher of contemporary inequality. Nevertheless, I recognize my identities may have inadvertently influenced this work, and I've done my best to engage this work reflexively, conscientiously, and ethically. I worked with three research assistants over the years who assisted in the coding and analyses of the text of personal ads and at least one set of interviews. The following describes, with modest variation, the format for each research method used in these studies. Though I have named each major city where these studies were conducted (Boston and Chicago), I have used pseudonyms for ad placers and advertising contexts.

In my first project, I made the mistake of providing my home telephone number to responders. At that time, I assumed that the stigma attached to placing personal ads would result in a limited number of responses to my solicitation for participants. I was wrong. I left home for a week, and when I returned, I had more than 300 responses to my solicitation. This was in 1997. I admit I did not receive the same response to my solicitations in Chicago as I had in Boston. Because I used the same approach and similarly worded solicitations, I'm left to wonder about the role of regional context.

Content Analyses of Newspaper Contexts, Dating Apps, and Dating Activities

Comparison of Three East Coast Newspapers (1998)

The first study involved content analysis of three New England newspapers to understand how the context of the newspaper impacted ad placement. First, my research assistant and I independently engaged in an exploratory analysis of the newspapers and their personal

Appendix: Methods

advertisement contexts (*Tribune*, the *Idealist,* and the *Mirror*). We then compared our notes and impressions, developed a coding template, and recorded our impressions of the newspapers. We each looked for dominant or modal characteristics, how newspapers defined the parameters of participation, and delimited "who" could participate. Ad placement specifications for each newspaper were presented in the form of codes, categories of advertisers, limitations, and costs. These codes framed the written discourse within ads, reduced ambiguity, and allowed shared construction of meaning. Each newspaper offered customer assistance for ad placers in order to generate the optimal advertisement. Supplementary to the codes was the varying amount of space offered by each newspaper (i.e., the number of lines of text) within which the ad placer had to capture the reader's attention and evoke a response from the reader. These specifications were also accompanied by an explicit statement or set of guidelines dealing with issues of liability, such as minimum age for advertising, or in the *Tribune*'s case, the requirement that advertisers be "only persons seeking long-term monogamous relationships." To varying degrees, each newspaper's vocabulary of codes, restrictions, guidelines, and customer service representatives participated in shaping the personal advertisers' construction of identity and the possibilities for interaction.

I selected a sample from each newspaper at two points in time (second week of the month in the fall and again in the spring). Personal ads were placed monthly. Interpretation of these codes and demographics were interpreted by running some simple statistics. (We had coded the material into a text analysis program called NUDIST.) [Note: In two years, this program name would become NVIVO.] Demographic information on ad placers from each newspaper was coded (i.e., gender and age) and entered into a file to calculate descriptive statistics such as frequencies, means, and cross-tabulations. To compare gender differences with respect to desired attributes by advertisers, cross-tabulations of gender and a single attribute (desired/not desired) were calculated. Additionally, cross-tabulations were also performed with variables collapsed as synthetic indices of such items as physical factors, personality factors, and financial factors.[1] Prior to these calculations, however, a 20 percent random sample of the ads in each category (i.e., men, women) were independently coded, and reliability coefficients were calculated for the selected coded attributes. These descriptive statistics allowed me to address questions such as what characteristics define individuals placing personal ads and how these populations of advertisers vary across newspapers. Codes and materials were compared across newspapers, and analysis was supplemented by interviews to provide a deeper understanding of newspaper parameters, services provided by newspapers to assist personal ad placers, and how the context and parameters of newspapers impacted ad placement. For example, we compared the categories of ad placers defined by the newspaper with the average number of ad placers who identified as gay or bisexual. In this way, we could assess differences between newspapers (e.g., Men Seeking Men or Men Seeking Women and one newspaper that offered no specific categories for ad placers).

Matrimonial News (1887)— *Social Connections* (1997)

In trying to provide a perspective of how the content of personal ads has shifted over time, I conducted a comparative analysis of personal ads placed in the *Matrimonial News* in the nineteenth century with those placed in *Social Connections* 100 years later (with the help of my research assistant). I examined one month of personal advertisements placed by men and women in the dedicated newspaper, the *Matrimonial News* (June). I compared them with a month of personal advertisements placed in a twentieth-century newspaper that contracted with *Social Connections* (June), a newspaper's personal advertisement section. To allow a comparative analysis of the two sets of advertisements, only personal ads placed by men and women seeking partners of the opposite sex in *Social Connections* were included in this analysis. This resulted in an inventory of characteristics sought by each set of ad placers.

I used the same process of looking at descriptive information as in the earlier examination, focusing again on gender and age. NUD-IST allowed me to make basic comparisons between desired characteristics. However, due to language use and modifications, more time was spent with my research assistant comparing our interpretations of the text.

Subsequently, we looked for desired exchanges of traits by gender, along with patterns found in the personal ads. We also discovered that even though men and women in the nineteenth century were assumed to be looking for a marriage partner, a significant number of men and women ad placers were explicit about looking for fun, more than one partner, and activities other than marriage.

Appendix: Methods

African American Personal Advertisements (2004)

This project focused on 52 personal advertisements placed by African American and Latina women in a local Chicago newspaper, *The City*. *The City* was chosen because personal ads had been placed in it for more than 25 years, and the format of the paper encouraged a range of responses from people with a variety of relationship objectives (i.e., restrictions on ad placers were minimal, and the available codes were suggestive of a variety of possible associations). Personal ads were extrapolated for the newspaper at two time points in the spring of 2004 (i.e., two months apart). Only those women whose identification included "Black," "Hispanic," or "Asian" were included in the sample.

I chose to use a framework of intersectionality to analyze these advertisements. I focused on discursive patterns in the sample of 52 personal ads placed by African American women and Latinas. Discourse strategies refer to linguistic and sociocultural practices of ad placers to express meaning to the reader of the ad. The ads were pre-coded (i.e., BFPNS "Black Female Professional Nonsmoker"), and the focus of interpretation was the intersectionality of interests emphasized by participants through the use of phrase tokens. Phrase tokens are meaningful and written linguistic expressions. In this case, they reflect both the parameters of the advertising venue and the "identity talk" of ad placers where intersecting markers of identity are made explicit, and patterns about master categories are revealed. We ultimately produced a coding scheme that focused on three master categories—gender, race, and class—to standardize the coding process.[2] The markers of race, class, and gender were chosen based on recent studies of race in personal ads and an attempt to complicate these examinations by looking at the intersection of these axes.

Because I believed that the experiences of women of color might be qualitatively different from the White women who comprise the majority of participants in these studies, I wanted to explore their experiences. The analysis is grounded in the assumption that the intersection of race, sex, and class produces qualitatively different experiences for women who engage in personal advertising beyond the explanatory power of any single master category or marker.

A first read of the advertisements focused on the preferences of women of color. Results were similar to other studies of personal ads and focused on master categories, as African American women tended to seek racial homogamy while Latina women expressed openness to dating racial/ethnic others. Because personal ads were pre-coded, the focus of interpretation was the intersectionality of interests and attempts by participants to present complex identities through the use of phrase tokens as women chose to exist in society. Phrase tokens represent the unit for coding and analyzing the ad placer's meaning regarding race, class, and what she desired in the responder.[3] Phrase tokens in the texts of personal ads illustrate the intersectionality of identities in personal advertising, the ad placer's perceptions of how ad readers react to her information and, ultimately, her effort to attract a particular or ideal "other."

The initial coding scheme focused on two master categories (race and social class) to standardize the coding process. A subsequent coding focused on other "mutually constitutive relations among social identities."[4] However, the goal was to interpret participants' discursive strategies in personal advertising as a configuration of identity in which intersecting markers of identity were made explicit, as opposed to discrete traits presented about the self or desired in others. Because of the collapsed contexts, each ad consisted of no more than two phrase tokens. The analysis focuses on the sociocultural circumstances in which identity and personal preferences and goals are expressed.

"Loving-the-One-You're-Near": A Comparison of Dating Apps

By 2011, it had become clear that dating apps were emerging as the latest innovation in personal advertising. Multiple news outlets focused on the relatively new phenomenon called location-based, satellite, and/or GPS dating—now simply referred to generically as dating apps. As the media editor for the *Journal of Humanity & Society*, I had not been successful in securing the next issue's article. Therefore, I decided to draw from my work on personal advertising by comparing a number of known dating apps (at that time). Content analysis was also used for this exploratory examination of six dating apps: Grindr, Skout, PlentyofFish, MeetMoi, Zoosk, and Assisted Serendipity. I compared the year that each of the apps was created, cost, eligibility, security provided to users, the stated purpose of the app, and how each app marketed some unique feature to users. At the time, the news outlets that featured dating apps (*CNN*, *The New Yorker*, *The New York Times*, and National Public Radio) were asking whether dating apps were taking the place of online dating and suggesting that security concerns of women had yet to be allayed.

Appendix: Methods

Interviews

Personal Advertisers and a Comparison of Three East Coast Newspapers (1998)

Three east coast newspaper editors and six of their customer service representatives (two from each newspaper) were interviewed. These newspapers served an area with a large city (Boston), a mid-size town (i.e., 150,000), and several smaller surrounding towns (10,000–35,000). The newspapers were generally regarded as conservative (*Tribune*), liberal (the *Idealist*), and progressive (the *Mirror*).

Interviews were also conducted with 32 ad placers (16 women and 16 men) in the Boston area. Interviews were arranged by placing an advertisement in each of the newspapers (with the permission of the editors), and persons who had advertised in at least one of these newspapers were selected according to how they assisted in completing the following cells: (1) Women Seeking Men, (2) Women Seeking Women, (3) Men Seeking Women, and (4) Men Seeking Men. My advertisement solicited men and women ad placers and offered two options for interviews: face to face or telephone. I received a large number of responses to my ad, and therefore, I took the first 32 persons who responded to my call. Since the newspapers were within a 50-mile radius of each other, some ad placers had advertised in more than one of these newspapers at one time or another, and some advertised in one or more of the newspapers simultaneously. The advertising strategy for interview participants does produce a self-selection bias; however, the anonymity of the Personals and the confidentiality provided to customers by the newspaper left little alternative other than snowball or convenience sampling. All of the persons who responded were White ethnic. Only two ad placers requested interviews by telephone. Interviews were semi-structured and ranged from 45 minutes to an hour and a half. They included questions on motivations for ad placement, the processes involved in personal advertisement construction and presentation of identity, the risks and strategies used to select persons for dates, and the meanings ascribed to advertising along with its success. Interviews were tape-recorded and transcribed.

2004 Women of Color Ad Placers (14 participants)

Interviews were conducted during this same year. The number of print ads placed by women of color in *The City* newspaper was significant, and so I assumed it would be easy to solicit interviews with women of color from this venue. I was wrong. A personal ad was placed in the newspaper to facilitate interviewing women locally. Though there was minimal overlap between print ads and interview analysis, I hoped that drawing both samples locally would assist in maintaining some degree of isomorphism between the two sets of narratives. Although it was clear that between 2004 and 2015 both groups of women were participating in online dating, I was unable to solicit a large number of participants for interviews. My best guess about why these numbers were so small (a total of 27 from 2004 through 2015) was that other than 2004, I did not concentrate on drawing women of color into the first study. Possibly, I may not have produced a compelling solicitation, or there may have been a lack of trust in such a study by members of these communities. In addition to the advertisement in the newspaper, I also solicited in one local newspaper, one magazine, and one weekly reader.

This project involved a set of interviews with women of color who engaged in online and/or print personal advertisements and other related activities. The number of women who responded to my solicitation was 25, but only women of color who had engaged in print and online advertising were chosen. This did limit my selection, but it cannot account for my failure to solicit more women of color.

Despite the greater difficulty in obtaining responses for interviews, the interviews were longer than prior interviews, ranging from one hour to an hour and a half. A few participants had also used It's Just Lunch, Speed Dating, or eHarmony. The interview questions were the same as those in the prior study, with two exceptions. First, women were asked about the difference in the creation of their profiles/ads online versus in print. Second, women were also asked how/if race impacted their experiences. This group of women was also asked to provide their age, job, and sexual orientation.

2008 (20 participants) and 2014–2015 Research Studies (22 participants)

I had more ambitious goals for the last two sets of interviews because of the large number of online dating sites, an increasing number of dedicated websites, and the increasing use of dating apps. Before these interviews, hardly anyone had mentioned using dating apps, and I wanted to gain an understanding of women's experience with dating apps and the other activities available to them to meet and mate. Once I learned about participation in yoga classes as a date, I began to ask about these and other activities. Again, I used the same approaches to solicit participants with increased use of

Appendix: Methods

flyers placed at certain locations and with the help of my friend who owned Namaste (a pseudonym). I even tried finding participants who engaged in couples massage by leaving flyers describing my study with the proprietors of a few day spas and a couple of friends, both massage therapists. In truth, the advertisements in the newspaper and online were more successful than flyers left at businesses, and my connections to women generally came through participants and the newspaper advertisement rather than the flyers. The number of women of color who responded between 2008 and 2014–2015 was small (a total of 13 in a large city with a significant population of African Americans and Latinos); consequently, the majority of my participants are White women.

   The core interview remained the same but added questions about their experiences with different types of activities, how their identities were modified and presented in each of them. How did ad placers experience doing identity in speed dating versus dating online? Were some activities more appealing than others, riskier than others, and how did participants build trust and navigate the risk?

Interview Analysis

   The most important source of information in this study is the qualitative interview. Qualitative interviews were particularly valuable given my goal to take a deep dive into identity, the intersection of identities, the impact of contexts on identity performance, and the processes involved in personal advertising. Although I used semi-structured interviews, I attempted to engage participants in a conversational style. The process involved asking questions, recording the answers, and following up with prompts. The interview process corroborated and contrasted initial assumptions and findings and enhanced the study by providing vivid and in-depth narratives and anecdotes about what it's like to engage in personal advertising. Interviews were typically completed in one session, with several participants offering to speak with me again if I needed more information. The interviews were either tape-recorded or digitally recorded and transcribed into a word processor. I took measures to protect the anonymity and confidentiality of my participants. I was the only person to contact them, and I did not reveal the names of persons who recommended the other people with whom I spoke unless authorized to do so (e.g., yoga instructor). I provided each participant with a written statement about the study, their confidentiality and anonymity, and my obligations. I signed the sheet and left it with the participant. I provided verbal and written assurance along with the reminder that they could withdraw or refuse to respond to any question. Interviews took place at a location chosen by the participant (coffee shop, a café, her apartment, and rarely in my office).

Although the manuscript uses many direct quotes, I do not anticipate that any participant could be identified. Nevertheless, participants were informed that while every effort would be made to maintain confidentiality, along with how I would try to achieve this, there was still a remote possibility that they might be identified indirectly. Participants acknowledged that they understood and agreed to proceed with the project. Over time, I used the interview protocol as a guide to ensure I asked each participant the same questions, but the order of the questions changed according to the conversation. I included all of the questions despite changing the order; however, I allowed the conversation to proceed as directed by the participant.

In addition to recruiting and interviewing ad placers, I used a snowball technique to identify additional persons who might have information about personal advertising, particularly when new information emerged, such as a woman who participated in couples massage on a first date. These persons included business owners and activity directors who provided services and activities or classes in personal advertising. I did not engage in formal interviews with them, but I did take notes.

Dating Activities, Observations and Informal Conversations

Formal interviews, content analyses of print or online personal ads, websites, collected flyers, brochures, and newspapers comprise the core of this book. The idea was to obtain as much background and understanding as possible to identify and refine the themes that ultimately laid the foundation for subsequent interviews. These documents augment other sources of information and provide the context and the background for understanding these activities. They are often the beginning of understanding. Also, I engaged in scores of informal conversations with a variety of people associated with personal advertising. With the permission of the appropriate people (participants, activity directors), I also observed several activities. My very limited experience with some of the activities also limits what I can say about how people engage or how it becomes a dating business. Still, I hope some insight is gained from Chapters 6, 7, and 8. The use of multiple sources for analysis allowed me to address a broader range of historical, psychological, and behavioral issues. According to Yin, one of the advantages of using multiple sources of information or "data" is in the development of converging lines of inquiry.[5] It enhances the reality presented and provides a much more convincing (and genuine) study.

The locations of the study, the strategies used to solicit participants for interviews, and the manner in which I found activities to examine undoubtedly produced a self-selection and site bias; however, the anonymity of outlets for personal advertising, the confidentiality provided to participants by online and offline sites, and the desire to solicit in-depth interviews with participants promoted the use of convenience sampling. The two locations of data acquisition are the Boston and Chicago areas, but the document acquisition and analyses extended beyond these areas to multiple localities across the country. Pseudonyms were assigned to participants, business owners, professionals (massage therapists), and even to businesses, with the exception of the dating sites, the laughter yoga, safari flirting, and coffee mating. Interviews were transcribed and analyzed as an iterative analytic process of induction and deduction to understand participants' experiences and perspectives.

By organizing the transcripts using the interview protocol and ongoing familiarity with the literature, I was able to look for patterns. Some responses reinforced some perceptions but contradicted others. The grounded theory that is so common to analysis of qualitative interview data helped to refine and connect ideas. This approach consists of collecting data (interviews), identifying categories, connecting the categories, and forming a theory that explains the process.[6] It is an iterative and comparative process where interviews and other data (observations, documents, informal conversations) contribute to the refining of an argument. Quite literally, the frameworks and explanations regarding personal advertising have been an ongoing process, not simply because of the methodology but also because of the dynamic character of personal advertising, most recently because of the Covid-19 pandemic.

Observations of Activities

In addition to the content analyses of newspapers and websites, I observed a number of activities (with the approval of the activity leader and/or participants). These included coffee mating, speed dating at a community center, a church, and a high school, couples yoga and a laughter yoga for couples session, and safari flirting. Each activity was observed at least one time, but I have continued to search these activities on the Internet over the years. I also participated in a speed tennis event at the invitation of the director. Though I worried about the effects of participating in these events, I did not want to offend the instructor or the participants. The groups were small and responded positively to the instructor's invitation, and I concluded it would be better to participate than to be seen as aloof. This was also the case with the tennis speed dating event, where the group was larger (approximately 23 participants) but had an uneven number. My participation enabled the instructor to fill the courts.

I write about these experiences as one who observed and participated. I also engaged in informal discussions with activity directors, massage therapists who offered couples massage, and yoga instructors who led "couples yoga" activities. And while the discussions did not involve structured interviews, participants gave informed consent, and I would often sit in my car and write notes about these conversations after we met. A few of the persons with whom I spoke casually were also friends (yoga instructor and a massage therapist), which made it possible to have multiple conversations about the topic. Besides the informal aspects of these projects, I continued to read the literature, gather information on personal advertising activities both in the Chicago area and on the Internet. Even in Houston, I have searched information on local activities comparable to those mentioned in this book. And it is not surprising to me that I found several similar activities in different regions of the country.

Limitations

My research is located in two places, the Boston, Massachusetts, and Chicago, Illinois, metropolitan areas. I do not have large numbers of personal advertisements in any of my content analyses, nor do I have a random or national sample of people who engage in personal advertising. Added to this, my participants are the result of convenience samples and placing ads in certain areas. Instead, I have two regional samples. I even acknowledge that I probably came across the activities I write about because of the places where I solicited participants (neighborhoods in the city with large numbers of singles). I came across other locations through interviews, friends, local news, and Internet outlets. My only caveat is that these activities were also found in suburban neighborhoods, and the face-to-face activities (speed dating, classes) could be found across the country along with dating websites and matchmaking services. Some activities and websites no longer exist, such as Just Eye Contact, PerfectMatch.com, and coffee mating, though others have taken their place.

I confess that I tend to view this endeavor as one project, shifting in scope and attention but extended over time. However, I recognize that it is actually four small projects at four different moments in time (n=16 women [of 32]; n=14; n=20; n=22), and the book relies heavily on these interviews. My insights into the modern form of dating and mating emerge from these interviews.

Because I elected to focus exclusively on women (with exceptions to the content analyses), I am unable to say much about men's participation in personal advertising. My initial study does provide some indication of the differences between men's and women's approaches to engaging in personal advertising and how they craft and present their identities, though I do not write about that in this book. I make no apologies for focusing on women, but I recognize the value of comparative analysis to offer greater insights into the connections, differences, successes, and failures of these approaches for both genders.

Another issue some might take with this work is my use of the term *Personal Advertising* to encompass dating online and in person. I admit that most of these activities were engaged in by couples whose relationships were formed in a more traditional manner. What was surprising to me, however, was that strangers did use couples yoga, mix and mate class, safari flirting, and even couples massage as a first date, with someone they met on the Internet, informally, or that same evening at a day spa or massage therapist's studio. These women also pointed to other women they knew who did the same things. The fact that a significant number of "adult classes" are structured similarly encouraged me to believe these women are not atypical. Once I spoke with the persons who created and ran these activities, I was convinced that collapsing these dating activities into *Personal Advertising* was appropriate. I leave the decision to you, the reader.

Sociological Studies
of Personal Ads

Ansari, Aziz, and Eric Klinenberg. *Modern Romance: An Investigation.* New York: Penguin, 2015.

Feliciano, Cynthia, Belinda Robnett, and Golnaz Komaie. "Gendered Racial Exclusion Among White Internet Daters." *Social Science Research* 38, no. 1 (2009): 39–54.

Feliciano, Cynthia, Rennie Lee, and Belinda Robnett. "Racial Boundaries Among Latinos: Evidence From Internet Daters' Racial Preferences." *Social Problems* 58, no. 2 (2011): 189–212.

Gonzalez, Marti Hope, and Sarah A. Meyers. "Your Mother Would Like Me: Self-Presentation in the Personal Ads of Heterosexual and Homosexual Men and Women." *Personality and Social Psychology Bulletin* 19, no. 2 (1993): 131–142.

Goode, Erich. "Gender and Courtship Entitlement: Responses to Personal Ads." *Sex Roles* 34, no. 3–4 (1996): 141–169.

Hollander, Paul. *Extravagant Expectations: New Ways to Find Romantic Love in America.* Chicago: Ivan R. Dee, 2011.

Hwang, Chin Wei. "Who Are People Willing to Date? Ethnic and Gender Patterns in Online Dating." *Race and Social Problems* 5, no. 1 (2013): 28–40.

Montini, T., and B. Obrero. "Personal Relationship Ads: An Informal Balancing Act." *Sociological Perspectives* 33, no. 3 (1990): 327–339.

Phua, Voon Chin. "Sex and Sexuality in Men's Personal Advertisements." *Men and Masculinities* 5 (2002): 178–191.

Phua, Voon Chin, and Allison Caras. "Personal Brand in Online Advertisements: Comparing White and Brazilian Male Sex Workers." *Sociological Focus* 41, no. 3 (2008): 238–255.

Phua, Voon Chin, and Gayle Kaufman. "The Crossroads of Race and Sexuality: Date Selection Among Men in Internet Personals Ads." *Journal of Family Issues* 24, no. 8 (2003): 981–994.

Turkle, Sheryl. *Alone Together: Why We Expect More from Technology and Less from Each Other.* New York: Basic Books, 2017.

Wilson, Shauna B., William D. McIntosh, and Salvatore P. Insana II. "Dating Across Race: An Examination of African American Internet Personal Advertisements." *Journal of Black Studies* 37, no. 6 (2007): 964–982.

Yancey, George, and Sherelyn Yancey. "Interracial Dating: Evidence from Personal Advertisements." *Journal of Family Issues* 19, no. 3 (1998): 334–348.

Chapter Notes

Introduction

1. Beth L. Bailey, *From Front Porch to Back Seat: Courtship in Twentieth-Century America* (Baltimore: Johns Hopkins University Press, 1988).

2. Kathy Bogle, *Hooking Up: Sex, Dating and Relationships on Campus* (New York: New York University Press, 2008); Michael Kimmel, "Hooking Up: Sex in Guyland," in *Guyland: The Perilous World Where Boys Become Men* (New York: Harper, 2009), 190–216.

3. Stephanie Coontz, *Marriage, A History: From Obedience to Intimacy or How Love Conquered Marriage* (New York: Viking Books, 2005); Ellen K. Rothman, *Hands and Hearts: A History of Courtship in America* (New York: Basic Books, 1984); Meredith F. Small, *What's Love Got to Do with It? The Evolution of Human Mating* (New York: Anchor Books, 1995).

4. Aaron Smith and Maeve Duggan, *Online Dating & Relationships* (Washington, D.C.: Pew Research Center, 2013), accessed November 2, 2020, https://www.pewresearch.org/internet/2013/10/21/-online-dating-relationships/.

5. Monica Anderson, Emily A. Vogels and Erica Turner, *The Virtues and Downsides of Online Dating* (Washington, D.C.: Pew Research Center, 2020), accessed August 31, 2020, https://www.pewresearch.org/internet/2020/02/06/-the-virtues-and-downsides-of-online-dating.

6. Naomi Gerstel, *A Fact Sheet Prepared for the Council on Contemporary Families in Honor of Unmarried and Singles Week,* September 18–24, 2011.

7. Erick Klinenberg, *Going Solo: The Extraordinary Rise and Surprising Appeal of Living Alone* (New York: Penguin, 2012).

8. Ellen McCarthy, "Marriage-Minded Do Better Online Than at Bars, Survey Claims," *The Washington Post*, April 25, 2010.

9. For exceptions, see Marti Hope Gonzalez and Sarah A. Meyers, "Your Mother Would Like Me: Self-Presentation in the Personal Ads of Heterosexual and Homosexual Men and Women," *Personality and Social Psychology Bulletin* 19, no. 2 (1993): 131–142; Erich Goode, "Gender and Courtship Entitlement: Responses to Personal Ads," *Sex Roles* 34 no. 3–4 (1996): 141–169; Elizabeth Jagger, "Marketing the Self, Buying Another: Dating in a Post Modern, Consumer Society," *Sociology* 34, no. 4 (1998): 759–814; T. Montini and B. Obrero, "Personal Relationship Ads: An Informal Balancing Act," *Sociological Perspectives* 33, no. 3 (1990): 327–339.

10. Meredith Child, Katherine Graff Low, Cheryl McDonnell McCormick, and Andrew Cocciarella, "Personal Advertisements of Male-to-Female Transsexuals, Homosexual Men, and Heterosexuals," *Sex Roles* 34 (1996): 447–455; K. Deaux and R. Hanna, "Courtship in the Personals Column: The Influence of Gender and Sexual Orientation," *Sex Roles* 11 (1984): 363–375; Katelyn Y.A. McKenna, Amie S. Green, and Marci E.J. Gleason, "Relationship Formation on the Internet: What's the Big Attraction?," *Journal of Social Issues* 58, no. 1 (2002): 9–31; Voon Chin Phua, "Sex and Sexuality in Men's Personal

Advertisements," *Men and Masculinities* 5 (2002): 178–191; Voon Chin Phua and Gayle Kaufman, "The Crossroads of Race and Sexuality: Date Selection Among Men in Internet Personals Ads," *Journal of Family Issues* 24, no. 8 (2003): 981–994; Jane E. Smith, V. Ann Waldorf, and David L. Trembath, "Single White Male Looking for Thin, Very Attractive...," *Sex Roles* 23 (1990): 675–685; George Yancey and Sherelyn Yancey, "Interracial Dating: Evidence From Personal Advertisements," *Journal of Family Issues* 19, no. 3 (1998): 334–348.

11. Cynthia Feliciano, Rennie Lee, and Belinda Robnett, "Racial Boundaries Among Latinos: Evidence from Internet Daters' Racial Preferences," *Social Problems* 58, no. 2 (2011): 189–212; Cynthia Feliciano, Belinda Robnett, and Golnaz Komaie, "Gendered Racial Exclusion Among White Internet Daters," *Social Science Research* 38, no. 1 (2009): 39–54; Neal A. Lester and Maureen Daly Goggin, *Racialized Politics of Desire in Personal Ads* (Lanham, MD: Lexington Books, 2007); Belinda Robnett and Cynthia Feliciano, "Patterns of Racial-Ethnic Exclusion by Internet Daters," *Social Forces* 89 (2011): 807–828.

12. Traci L. Anderson and Tara M. Emmers-Sommer, "Predictors of Relationship Satisfaction in Online Romantic Relationships," *Communication Studies* 57, no. 2 (2006). doi: 10.1080/10510970600666834; McKenna, Green and Gleason, "Relationship Formation," pp. 9–31.

13. Daniel McFarland, Dan Jurafsky, and Craig Rawlings, "Making the Connections: Social Bonding in Courtship Situations," *American Journal of Sociology* 115, no. 6 (2013): 1596–1649; Rajesh Ranganath, Dan Jurafsky, and Daniel A. McFarland, "Detecting Friendly, Flirtatious, Awkward, and Assertive Speech in Speed-Dates," *Computer Speech and Language* 27, no. 1 (2013): 89–115.

14. Jeremy Rifkin, *The Age of Access: The New Culture of Hypercapitalism, Where All of Life Is a Paid-for Experience* (New York: J.P. Tarcher/Putnam, 2001).

15. Pamela Paxton, "Trust in Decline?" *Contexts* 4, no. 1 (2005): 40–46; Robert D. Putnam, *Bowling Alone: The Collapse and Revival of American Community* (New York: Simon & Schuster, 2000).

16. Anderson, Vogels and Turner, "The Virtues and Downsides of Online Dating."

Chapter 1

1. Pamela A. Quiroz, "From Mail Order and Picture Brides, Lonely Hearts and Social Clubs, to eHarmony, 'Just Lunch,' Speed Dating, and Coffee Mating: The Evolution of Personal Advertising," in *Dynamics and Interconnections in Popular Culture*, edited by Ray B. Brown and Ben Urish, pp. 114–129. (Newcastle upon Tyne: Cambridge Scholars Publishing, 2013). Published with the permission of Cambridge Scholars Publishing.

2. Marcia Zug, *Buying a Bride: An Engaging History of Mail Order Matches* (New York: New York University Press, 2016).

3. Francesca Beauman, *From Personal Ads to Swiping Right: A Story of America Looking for Love* (New York: Pegasus Books, 2020).

4. Chris Enss, *Hearts West: True Stories of Mail-Order Brides on the Frontier* (Guilford, CT: Globe Pequot Press, 2005).

5. Beauman, *From Personal Ads to Swiping Right.*

6. Zug, *Buying a Bride.*

7. Personal communications with L. Henelson, University of Kansas, October 18, 2001.

8. Catherine Lee, *Prostitutes and Picture Brides: Chinese and Japanese Immigration, Settlement, and American Nation-building, 1870–1920*, Faculty Working Paper 70 (San Diego: University of California, The Center for Comparative Immigration Studies, 2003).

9. Jeffrey L. Pasley, "Politics, Citizenship, and Collective Action in Nineteenth-Century America: A Response to Stuart Blumin and Michael Schudson," *Communication Review* 4 (2000): 39–54.

10. Cathy Luchetti, *"I Do!": Courtship, Love and Marriage on the American Frontier: A Glimpse at America's*

Romantic Past Through Photographs, Diaries, and Journals, 1715–1915 (New York: Crown Trade Paperbacks, 1996).

11. *Ibid.*

12. *Ibid.*

13. Lesley Poling-Kempes, *The Harvey Girls: Women Who Opened the West* (New York: Marlowe, 1994).

14. Coontz, *Marriage, A History*; Arland Thornton and Linda Young-DeMarco, "Four Decades of Trends in Attitudes Toward Family Issues in the United States: The 1960s through the 1990s," *Journal of Marriage and Family* 63 (2001): 1009–1037.

15. Sociologist Georg Simmel defined "social types" as repeated behaviors, the consequence of social situations that produce habitual ways of thinking and acting. These behaviors and thoughts reinforce one another and become self-sustaining, thus forming social types. For analyses of modern personal ads, see Bolig, Stein, and McKenry; Cameron, Oskamp, and Sparks; Child et al.; Gonzalez and Meyers; Goode; Harrison and Saeed; Lynn and Shurgot; Smith, Waldorf, and Trembath.

16. Enss, *Hearts West.*

17. Personal ads, see Bolig, Stein, and McKenry; Cameron, Oskamp, and Sparks; Child et al.; Gonzalez and Meyers; Goode; Harrison and Saeed; Lynn and Shurgot; Smith, Waldorf, and Trembath.

18. For analyses of "means" in modern ads, see Simon Davis; Harrison and Saeed; Rajecki, Bledsoe, and Rasmussen; Willis and Carlson.

19. Women did live together in marriage-like arrangements called "Boston marriages"; however, there is no indication that these arrangements occurred through personal advertisements placed in newspapers or magazines.

20. Other newspaper personals in 1997 included transvestites, bisexuals, transsexuals, and even married couples who sought friendship, sexual activity, or ongoing relationships, with one personals section called "Anything Goes."

21. Beth L. Bailey, "From 'Bundling' to 'Hooking Up': Teaching the History of American Courtship," *Organization of American Historians Magazine of History* 18, no. 4 (2004): 3–4.

22. Francesca Beauman, *Matrimony Inc.* (New York: Pegasus Books, 2020).

23. Yaacov Deyo and Sue Deyo, *Speed Dating: The Smarter, Faster Way to Lasting Love* (New York: HarperCollins, 2002).

24. Just Eye Contact, accessed October 2008, http://www.justeyecontact.com.

25. John Cockburn, *Lonely Hearts: Looking for Love Among the Small Ads* (London: Simon & Schuster, 1988).

26. Beauman, *Matrimony Inc.*

Chapter 2

1. ExtenZe, accessed March 27, 2011, www.extendzeforlife.com.

2. For exceptions, see Elizabeth C. Hirschman, "People as Products: Analysis of a Complex Marketing Exchange," *Journal of Marketing* 51 (1987): 98–108; Jagger, "Marketing the Self," 759–814.

3. McCarthy, "Marriage-Minded Do Better Online"; eHarmony, accessed November 27, 2008, www.eharmony.com/harrisinteractivepoll.

4. Rifkin, *The Age of Access.*

5. Vivian Zelizer, *The Purchase of Intimacy* (Princeton: Princeton University Press, 2005).

6. Jagger, "Marketing the Self," 759–814.

7. These include but are not limited to Catherine Cameron, Stuart Oskamp, and William Sparks, "Courtship American Style: Newspaper Ads," *The Family Coordinator* 26 (1977): 27–31; Simon Davis, "Men as Success Objects and Women as Sex Objects: A Study of Personal Advertisements," *Sex Roles* 23 (1990): 43–51; Marti Hope Gonzalez and Sarah A. Meyers, "Your Mother Would Like Me: Self-Presentation in the Personal Ads of Heterosexual and Homosexual Men and Women," *Personality and Social Psychology Bulletin* 19, no. 2 (1993): 131–142; Albert A. Harrison and Laila Saeed, "Let's Make a Deal: An Analysis of Revelations and Stipulations in Lonely Hearts Advertisements," *Journal of Personality*

and Social Psychology 35 (1977): 257–264; Elizabeth Jagger, "Is Thirty the New Sixty? Dating, Age and Gender in a Postmodern, Consumer Society," *Sociology* 39 no. 1 (2005): 89–106; Richard Koestner and Ladd Wheeler, "Self-Presentation in Personal Advertisements: The Influence of Implicit Notions of Attraction and Role Expectations," *Journal of Social and Personal Relationships* 5, no. 2 (1988): 149–160; Michael Lynn and Barbara A. Shurgot, "Responses to Lonely Hearts Advertisements: Effects of Reported Physical Attractiveness, Physique, and Coloration," *Personality and Social Psychology Bulletin* 10, no. 3 (1984): 349–357; Frank N. Willis and Roger A. Carlson, "Singles Ads: Gender, Social Class, and Time," *Sex Roles* 29 (1993): 387–404.

8. For exceptions, see Debra L. Merskin and Mara Huberlie, "Companionship in the Classifieds: The Adoption of Personal Advertisements by Daily Newspapers," *Journalism and Mass Communication Quarterly* 73, no. 1 (1996): 219–229; Susan Steinfirst and Barbara B. Moran, "The New Mating Game: Matchmaking Via the Personal Columns in the 1980s," *Journal of Popular Culture* 22, no. 4 (1989): 129–139.

9. Mary Riege Laner and G.W. Levi Kamel, "Media Mating I: Newspaper 'Personals' Ads of Homosexual Men," *Journal of Homosexuality* 3, no. 2 (1977): 149–162; Merskin and Huberlie, "Companionship in the Classifieds," 219–229; Phua, "Sex and Sexuality in Men's Personal Advertisements," 178–191.

10. Bargh and McKenna, "The Internet and Social Life," 573–590; McKenna, Green, and Gleason, "Relationship Formation on the Internet," 9–31; Monica Whitty and Adrian Carr, *Cyberspace Romance: The Psychology of Online Relationships* (New York: Palgrave, 2006).

11. Susan Frohlick, *hypermainstream* as cited in McCarthy, "Marriage-Minded Do Better Online Than at Bars, Survey Claims.".

12. eHarmony, accessed November 4, 2020, www.eharmony.com.

13. "eHarmony's 10 Anniversary Celebration!" accessed November 4, 2020, https://www.eharmony.com/dating-advice/using-eharmony/eharmonys-10-anniversary-celebration/.

14. eHarmony, "Singles & Desirability Study," accessed December 2, 2020, https://www.eharmony.com/desirability-study.

15. eHarmony, "12 Great Reasons to Use Video Date from eHarmony," accessed November 4, 2020, https://www.eharmony.com.au/dating-advice/dating/videodate-12-great-reasons.

16. The Right Stuff Dating, accessed November 4, 2020, www.rightstuffdating.com.

17. Daniele Nicole DeVoss, "From the BBS to the Web: Tracing the Spaces of Online Romance," in *Online Matchmaking*, edited by Monica Whitty, Andrea J. Baker, and James A. Inman (New York: Palgrave, 2007).

18. Naughty Meetings, accessed November 4, 2020, www.naughtymeetings.com.

19. Though recently the app has had to eliminate its teen community due to a case of sexual abuse, the app still advertises as having two communities, a teen community and an adult community, each with different minimum age limits, 13 years old and 18 years old, respectively.

20. Lauren Silverman, "Smartphone Apps Help More Singles Find the Boy (or Girl) Next Door," accessed November 4, 2020, http://www.npr.org/blogs/alltechconsidered/2012/08/20/159365445/smartphone-apps-help-more-singles-find-the-boy-or-girl-next-door.

21. Zelizer, *The Purchase of Intimacy.*

Chapter 3

1. Stuart Hall and Paul Du Gay, *Questions of Cultural Identity* (Thousand Oaks: Sage, 1996).

2. Candace West and D.H. Zimmerman, "Doing Gender," *Gender & Society* 1 (1987): 125–151.

3. Anthony Giddens, *The Transformation of Intimacy: Sexuality, Love & Eroticism in Modern Societies* (Palo Alto: Stanford University Press, 1992).

4. Linda Duits, *Multi-Girl-Culture: An Ethnography of Doing Identity* (Amsterdam: Amsterdam University Press, 2008).

5. Sheldon Stryker, "Identity Salience and Role Performance: The Relevance of Symbolic Interaction Theory for Family Research," in *Social Psychology and the Self-Concept*, edited by Morris Rosenberg and Howard B. Kaplan (Arlington Heights, IL: Harlan Davidson, 1982), 200–208; p. 203.

6. Emile J. Pin and Jamie Turndorf, "Staging One's Self," in *Life as Theater: A Dramaturgical Sourcebook* (New Brunswick: Aldine Transaction, 2009), 163–182.

7. Douglas L. Anderton, Richard E. Barrett, and Donald J. Bogue, *The Population of the United States*, third edition (New York: Free Press, 1997).

8. Anthony Cilluffo and D'Vera Cohn, "6 Demographic Trends Shaping the U.S. and the World in 2019," Pew Research Center, https://www.pewresearch.org/fact-tank/2019/04/11/-6-demographic-trends-shaping-the-u-s-and-the-world-in-2019/.

9. Stryker, "Identity Salience and Role Performance," 200–208.

10. Katelyn McKenna, Amie S. Green, and Marcie E. J. Gleason, "Formation of Relation on the Internet: What's the Big Attraction?" *The Journal of Social Issues* 58, no. 1 (2002): 9–31.

Chapter 4

1. Portions of this chapter appeared in a much earlier form in Pamela A. Quiroz, "Women of Color Participating in Personal Advertising: Dating, Mating and Relating in a 'Post' Racist, Sexist, and Modern Society," in *Notions of Family: Intersectional Perspectives* (*Advances in Gender Research*), Vol. 17, eds. Marla Kohlman, Dana Balsink Krieg, and Bette Dickerson, 49–66 (Emerald Publishing). Reproduced with permission from Emerald Publishing Limited.

2. Colleen Poulin and Virginia Rutter, "How Color Blind Is Love? Interracial Dating: Facts and Puzzles," Council on Contemporary Families, 2011, accessed September 19, 2011, www.contemporaryfamilies.org/marriage-partnership-divorce/how-color-blind-is-love; Jenny Davis, "Race and Online Dating," Council on Contemporary Families, Unconventional Wisdom, Vol. 6, 2014, accessed May 8, 2015, http://contemporaryfamilies.org/-unconventional-wisdom-6/; Celeste Curington, Lin Ken-Hou, and Jennifer Lundquist, "Dating Partners Don't Always Prefer 'Their Own Kind': Some Multiracial Daters Get Bonus Points in the Dating Game," Council on Contemporary Families, accessed July 20, 2019, http://www.contemporaryfamilies.org/-multiracisl-dating-brief-report; Shauna B. Wilson, William D. McIntosh, and Salvatore P. Insana II, "Dating Across Race: An Examination of African American Internet Personal Advertisements," *Journal of Black Studies* 37, no. 6 (2007): 964–982.

3. Yancey and Yancey, "Interracial Dating," 334–348.

4. Saleem Alhabash, Kayla Hales, Jong-Hwan Baek, and Hyun Jung Oh, "Effects of Race, Visual Anonymity, and Social Category Salience on Online Dating Outcomes," *Computers in Human Behavior* 35 (2014): 22–32; Chin Wei Hwang, "Who Are People Willing to Date? Ethnic and Gender Patterns in Online Dating," *Race and Social Problems* 5, no. 1 (2013): 28–40; Kimberly K. Barsamian, Katherine Spencer, and Jack Glaser, "Online Prejudice and Discrimination: From Dating to Hating," in *The Social Net: Understanding Our Behavior Online*, edited by Yair Amichai-Hamburger, 201–219 (Oxford: Oxford University Press, 2013).

5. Cynthia Feliciano, Rennie Lee, and Belinda Robnett, "Racial Boundaries Among Latinos: Evidence from Internet Daters' Racial Preferences," *Social Problems* 58, no. 2 (2011): 189–212.

6. Gerald A. Mendelsohn, Lindsay Shaw Taylor, Andrew T. Fiore, and Coye Cheshire, "Black/White Dating Online: Interracial Courtship in the 21st Century," *Psychology of Popular Media Culture* 3, no. 1 (2014): 2–18; Celeste

Notes—Chapter 4

Vaughan Curington, Ken-Hou Lin, and Jennifer Hickes Lundquist, "Positioning Multiraciality in Cyberspace: Treatment of Multiracial Daters in an Online Dating Website," *American Sociological Review* 80, no. 4 (2015): 764–788.

7. See Jennifer Hickes Lundquist and Celeste Vaughan Curington, "Love Me Tinder, Love Me Sweet," *Contexts* 18, no. 4 (2019): 22–27.

8. Yancey and Yancey, "Interracial Dating," 334–348.

9. D.L. Blackwell and D.T. Lichter, "Homogamy Among Dating, Cohabiting and Married Couples," *Sociological Quarterly* 45, no. 4 (2004): 719–737; Phua and Kaufman, "The Crossroads of Race and Sexuality," 981–994.

10. Robnett and Feliciano, "Patterns of Racial-Ethnic Exclusion by Internet Daters," 807–828.

11. Kimberlé Crenshaw, "Mapping the Margins: Identity Politics, Intersectionality and Violence Against Women," *Stanford Law Review* 43, no. 6 (1991): 1241–1299; Patricia Hill Collins, *Black Feminist Thought: Knowledge, Consciousness, and the Politics of Empowerment* (New York: Routledge, 2000).

12. Phua, "Sex and Sexuality in Men's Personal Advertisements," 178–191.

13. Media scholar Dana Boyd suggests that such codes force people to "mentally over-generalize" resulting in conjuring stereotypes that must be overcome. Less obvious is how coding frames provided by personal advertising venues (i.e., print and online) personify the hegemonic domain of language, profiles, images, tastes, and values, and implicitly reproduce the cultural sphere of influence, even as they shape the interpersonal domain. See Danah Boyd, *It's Complicated: The Social Lives of Networked Teens* (New Haven: Yale University Press, 2015).

14. Bogle, *Hooking Up*.

15. Neal A. Lester and Maureen Daly Goggin, *Racialized Politics of Desire in Personal Ads* (Lanham, MD: Lexington Books, 2007).

16. Warner, "A Best Practices Guide to Intersectional Approaches in Psychological Research," 454–463.

17. All but one of the women advertised in print media and on the Internet; several had used a matchmaking service or other personal advertising activity (12) but only a few used dating apps (6), suggesting that populations of ad placers are not mutually exclusive.

18. Paul Hollander, *Extravagant Expectations: New Ways to Find Romantic Love in America* (Chicago: Ivan R. Dee, 2011); Leon Kass, "The End of Courtship," *The Public Interest* 126 (1997): 39–49.

19. Warner, "A Best Practices Guide to Intersectional Approaches in Psychological Research," 454–463.

20. See Kass, "The End of Courtship," 39–49, or Hollander, *Extravagant Expectations*.

21. Ann Swidler, "Culture in Action: Symbols and Strategies," *American Sociological Review* 51, no. 2 (1986): 273–286.

22. Virginia Rutter is co-author or co-editor of *Families as They Really Are*, second edition, *The Gender of Sexuality, and The Love Test*, and numerous review articles and chapters. She writes and researches topics related to sexuality in more- and less-committed relationships, divorce, family policy, infidelity, feminism, and inequality. See Colleen Poulin and Virgina Rutter, "How Color Blind Is Love? Interracial Dating: Facts and Puzzles," Council on Contemporary Families, 2011, accessed September 19, 2011, www.contemporaryfamilies. org/marriage-partnership-divorce/how-color-blind-is-love.

23. *Post gay*, see Amin Ghaziani, "Post-Gay Collective Identity Construction," *Social Problems* 58, no. 1 (2011): 99–125; races *post racial*, see Eduardo Bonilla-Silva, *White Supremacy and Racism in the Post-Civil Rights Era* (Boulder: Lynne Reinner, 2001); genders *post feminist*, see Susan Faludi, *Backlash: The Undeclared War Against American Women* (New York: Crown, 2006), and Angela McRobbie, "Post Feminism and Popular Culture," *Feminist Media Studies* 4, no. 3 (2004): 255–264.

Chapter 5

1. Pamela Paxton, "Is Social Capital Declining in the United States?" *American Journal of Sociology* 105, no. 1 (1999): 88–127; Pamela Paxton, "Trust in Decline?" *Contexts* 4, no. 1 (2005): 40–46.

2. Robert D. Putnam, *Bowling Alone: The Collapse and Revival of American Community* (New York: Simon & Schuster, 2000).

3. Everett C. Ladd, "The Data Just Don't Show Erosion of America's Social Capital," *The Public Perspective*, June/July 1996: 1–22.

4. See also Robert Edward and Michael W. Foley, "Much Ado About Social Capital," *Contemporary Sociology* 30, no. 3 (2001): 227–230; Paxton, "Is Social Capital Declining in the United States?" 88–127; John Wilson, "Dr. Putnam's Social Lubricant," *Contemporary Sociology* 30, no. 3 (2001): 225–227.

5. Robert J. Samuelson, "'Bowling Alone' Is Bunk," *The Washington Post*, April 10, 1996, 1–22.

6. Putnam, *Bowling Alone: The Collapse and Revival of American Community*.

7. James S. Coleman, *Power and the Structure of Society* (New York: W.W. Norton, 1974).

8. Susan Shapiro, *Wayward Capitalists: Targets of the Securities and Exchange Commission* (New Haven: Yale University Press, 1984).

9. Dalton Conley, *Elsewhere USA: How We Got from the Company Man, Family Dinners, and the Affluent Society to the Home Office, BlackBerry Moms, and Economic Anxiety* (New York: Vintage, 2010); Eric Klinenberg, *Going Solo: The Extraordinary Rise and Surprising Appeal of Living Alone* (New York: Penguin, 2012).

10. Putnam, *Bowling Alone: The Collapse and Revival of American Community*; Bert Useem, "Solidarity Model, Breakdown Model, and the Boston Antibusing Movement," *American Sociological Review* 45 (1980): 357–369.

11. Paolo Parigi and Warner Henson II, "Social Isolation in America," *Annual Review of Sociology* 40 (2014): 153–171.

12. Claude S. Fischer and Greggor Mattson, "Is America Fragmenting?" *Annual Review of Sociology* 35, no. 1 (2009): 435–455.

13. Rachel Botsman, *Who Can You Trust? How Technology Brings Us Together and Why It Might Drive Us Apart* (New York: PublicAffairs, 2018), Kindle.

14. Paolo Parigi and Rachel Gong, "From Grassroots to Digital Ties: A Case Study of a Political Consumerism Movement," *Journal of Consumer Culture* 14, no. 2 (2014): 236–253.

15. Jaana Räisänen, Arto Ojala, and Tero Tapio Tuovinen, "Building Trust in the Sharing Economy: Current Approaches and Future Considerations," *Journal of Cleaner Production* 279 (2021): 1–30. https://doi.org/10.1016/j.jclepro.2020.123724.

16. Rachel Botsman, *Who Can You Trust?*

17. Clifton B. Parker, "Interpersonal Trust Erodes Over Time in the Online World, Experts Say," https://phys.org/news/2015-03-interpersonal-erodes-online-world-experts.html, March 19, 2015.

18. Paolo Parigi and Karen Cook, "Trust and Relationships in the Sharing Economy," *Contexts* 14, no. 1 (2015): 18–19.

19. Russell Hardin, "Distrust: Manifestations and Management," in *Distrust*, ed. Russell Hardin (New York: Russell Sage Foundation, 2004), 3–33.

Chapter 6

1. Olay Muurlink and Cristina Poyatos Matas, "From Romance to Rocket Science: Speed Dating in Higher Education," *Higher Education Research & Development* 30, no. 6 (2011): 751–764.

2. John Tierney, "Romantic Revulsion in the New Century: Flaw-o-matic 2.0," *The New York Times*, April 10, 2007.

3. Brooke Donald, "New Stanford Research On Speed Dating Examines What Makes Couples 'Click' in Four Minutes," May 2013, https://news.stanford.edu/news/2013/may/

Notes—Chapter 6

jurafsky-mcfarland-dating-050613.html; Eli Finkel and Paul W. Eastwick, "Speed Dating," *Current Directions of Psychological Science* 17, no. 3 (2008): 193–195; Eli Finkel, Paul W. Eastwick, and Jacob Matthews, "Speed-Dating as an Invaluable Tool for Studying Romantic Attraction: A Methodological Primer," *Personal Relationships* 14, no. 1 (2007): 149–166; Mairan Houser, Sean M. Horan, and Lisa A. Furler, "Dating in the Fast Lane: How Communication Predicts Speed-Dating Success," *Journal of Social and Personal Relationships* 25, no. 5 (2008): 749–768; Neil Korobov, "Mate-Preference Talk in Speed-Dating Conversations," *Research on Language and Social Interaction* 44, no. 2 (2011): 186–209.

4. Raymond Fisman, Sheena S. Iyengar, Emir Kamenica, and Itimar Simonson, "Gender Differences in Mate Selection: Evidence from a Speed Dating Experiment," *The Quarterly Journal of Economics* (May 2006): 673–697; Raymond Fisman, Sheena S. Iyengar, Emir Kamenica, and Itimar Simonson, "Racial Preferences in Dating," *The Review of Economic Studies* 75, no. 1 (2008): 117–132.

5. Andrew Chang, Haley E. Kragness, Wei Tsou, Dan J. Bosnyak, Anja Thiede, and Laurel J. Trainor, "Body Sway Predicts Romantic Interest in Speed Dating," *Social Cognitive and Affective Neuroscience* (2020): 1–8; M.J. McClure and J.E. Lydon, "Anxiety Doesn't Become You: How Attachment Anxiety Compromises Relational Opportunities," *Journal of Personality and Social Psychology* 106, no. 1 (2014): 89–111; D. McFarland and Dan Jurafsky, "Making the Connection: Social Bonding in Courtship Situations," *American Journal of Sociology* 118, no. 6 (2013): 1596–1649.

6. M.D. Back, L. Penke, S.C. Penke, S. Schmukle, K. Sasche, P. Borkenau, and J.B. Asendorpf, "Why Mate Choices Are Not as Reciprocal as We Assume: The Role of Personality, Flirting and Physical Attractiveness," *European Journal of Personality* 25 (2011): 120–132; M.D. Back, L. Penke, S. Schmukle, and J.B. Asendorpf, "Knowing Your Own Mate Value: Sex-Specific of Personality Effects on The

Accuracy of Expected Mate Choices," *Psychological Science* 22 (2011): 984–989; Jens B. Asendorpf, Lars Penke, and Mitja D. Back, "From Dating to Mating and Relating: Predictors of Initial and Long-Term Outcomes of Speed-Dating in a Community Sample," *European Journal of Personality* 25 (2011): 16–30.

7. Susanne Fuchs and Tamara Rathcke, "Laugh Is in the Air? Physiological Analysis of Laughter as a Correlate of Attraction During Speed Dating," Laughter Workshop Conference, Paris, August 2018. https://www.researchgate.net/publication/327177342.

8. Elizabeth Stokoe, "'Have You Been Married, or...?': Eliciting and Accounting for Relationship Histories in Speed-Dating Interaction," *Research on Language and Social Interaction* 43, no. 3 (2010): 260–282.

9. Matthew M. Hollander and Jason Turowetz, "So, Why Did You Decide to Do This? Soliciting and Formulating Motives for Speed Dating," *Discourse and Sociology* 24, no. 6 (2013): 701–724.

10. Back, Penke, Schmukle, and Asendorpf, "Knowing Your Own Mate Value," 984–989.

11. Emanuel Jauk, Aljoscha C. Neubauer, Thomas Mairunteregger, Stephanie Pemp, Katherina P. Sieber, and John F. Rauthmann, "How Alluring Are Dark Personalities? The Dark Triad and Attractiveness in Speed Dating," *European Journal of Personality* 30 (2016): 125–138.

12. Paul W. Eastwick and Eli J. Finkel, "Speed Dating: A Powerful and Flexible Paradigm for Studying Romantic Relationship Interaction," in *Handbook of Relationship Initiation* (New York: Taylor & Francis, 2008), 217–234.

13. *Ibid.*

14. Mairan Houser, Sean M. Horan, and Lisa A. Furler, "Predicting Relational Outcomes: An Investigation of Thin Slice Judgments in Speed Dating," *Human Communication* 10, no. 2 (2007): 69–81.

15. Jeff A. Larson and William Tsitsos, "Speed Dating and the Presentation of Self: A Teaching Exercise in Impression Management and Formation," *Teaching Sociology* 41, no. 3 (2013): 307–313.

184

16. Christian Jarrett, "Why Meeting Another's Gaze Is So Powerful," BBC, January 8, 2019, http://www.bbc.com/future/article20190108-why-meeting-another's-gaze-is-so-powerful.

17. Barbara Frederickson, "Love Is a Micro-Moment of True Love," blog, 2020, https://www.cram.com/essay/-Love-Is-A-Micro-Moment-Of-True/PKVWLSXKUZ3Q.

18. Jason Turowitz and Matthew M. Hollander, "Assessing the Experience of Speed Dating," *Discourse Studies* 14, no. 5 (2012): 635–658.

19. Houser, Horan, and Furler, "Dating in the Fast Lane," 749–768.

20. Fisman, Iyengar, Kamenica, and Simonson, "Racial Preferences in Dating," 117–132.

21. Francesca Beauman, *Matrimony Inc.: From Personal Ads to Swiping Right, a Story of America Looking for Love* (New York: Pegasus Books, 2020).

22. *Ibid.*

23. Monica Whitty and Adrian Carr, *Cyberspace Romance: The Psychology of Online Relationships* (New York: Palgrave Macmillan, 2006).

Chapter 7

1. Julia Fraga, "Is Partner Yoga the New Couples Therapy?" *Yoga Journal*, September 10, 2020, https://www.yogajournal.com/lifestyle/partner-yoga-for-couples-therapy/.

2. *Ibid.*

3. Laughter Yoga International, www.laughteryoga.org.

4. Shashi K. Agarwal, "Therapeutic Benefits of Laughter," *Medical Science* 12, no. 46 (2014): 19–23; Lynn Erdman, "Laughter Therapy for Patients with Cancer," *Journal of Psychosocial Oncology* 11, no. 4 (2008): 55–67; Mora Ripoll Ramon and Isabel Quintana Casado, "Laughter and Positive Therapies: Modern Approach and Practical Use in Medicine," *Revista de Psiquiatria y Salud Mental* 3, no. 1 (2010): 27–34; Nancy Recker, "Laughter Is Really Good Medicine," The Ohio State University Extension Fact Sheet, 2007, http://ohioline.osu.

edu/; Julia Wilkins and Amy Janel Eisenbraun, "Humor Theories and the Physiological Benefits of Laughter," *Advances in Mind-Body Medicine* 24, no. 2 (2009): 8–12.

5. www.laughteryoga.org

6. *Yoga Partner for Singles* (www.fitness-singles).

7. Sara Darbandi, Mahsa Darbandi, Hamid Reza Khorram Khorshid, and Mohammad Reza Sadeghi, "Yoga Can Improve Assisted Reproduction Technology Outcomes in Couples with Infertility," *Alternative Therapies* 24, no. 4 (2017): 50–55; Nurcan Kirca and Turkan Pasinlioglu, "The Effect of Yoga on Stress Level in Infertile Women," *Perspectives of Psychiatric Care* 55, no. 2 (2019): 319–327.

8. Saravana Kumar, Kate Beaton, and Tricia Hughes, "The Effectiveness of Massage Therapy for the Treatment of Nonspecific Low Back Pain: A Systematic Review of Systematic Reviews," *International Journal of General Medicine* 6 (2013): 733–741; Sayuri M. Naruse and Mark Moss, "Effects of Couples Positive Massage Programme on Wellbeing, Perceived Stress and Coping, and Relation Satisfaction," *Health Psychology and Behavioral Medicine* 7, no. 1 (2019): 328–347; Sayuri M. Naruse, Piers L. Cornelissen and Mark Moss, "'To Give is Better Than To Receive?' Couples Massage Significantly Benefits Both Partners Wellbeing," *Journal of Health Psychology* 25, no. 10–11 (2020): 1576–1586.

9. Thomas Rutledge, "How Meditation Improves Emotional and Physical Health," *Psychology Today*, Sussex Publishers, August 4, 2019, https://www.psychologytoday.com/us/blog/the-healthy-journey/201908/how-meditation-improves-emotional-and-physical-health.

10. Kenneth Ng and Marc Cohen, "The Effectiveness of Massage Therapy: A Summary of Evidence-Based Research," Global Wellness Summit, 2011, https://www.globalwellnesssummit.com/wp-content/uploads/Industry-Research/Australia/2011-AAMT-Research-Report.pdf; Kathryn F. Westman and Cathy Blaisdell, "Many Benefits, Little Risk:

The Use of Massage in Nursing Practice," *American Journal of Nursing* 116, no. 1 (2016): 34–39.

11. Paula Thomas Ruffin, "A History of Massage in Nurse Training School Curricula (1860–1945)," *Journal of Holistic Nursing* 29, no. 1 (2011): 61–67.

12. Discovery Center, *3651 Bondage and Domination, S&M, An Introduction Class*, https://discoverycenter.cc/bondage-class-intro-to-domination-s-m

13. Jessica Santana and Paolo Parigi, "Risk Aversion and Engagement in the Sharing Economy," *Games* 6, no. 4 (2015): 560–573.

14. Robert D. Putnam, *Bowling Alone: The Collapse and Revival of American Community* (New York: Simon & Schuster, 2000).

Chapter 8

1. Beth L. Bailey, "From 'Bundling' to 'Hooking Up': Teaching the History of American Courtship," *Organization of American Historians Magazine of History* 18, no. 4 (2004): 3–4.

2. Beth L. Bailey, *From Front Porch to Back Seat: Courtship in Twentieth-Century America* (Baltimore: Johns Hopkins University Press, 1988).

3. Kira Hall, "Lip Service on the Fantasy Lines," in Kira Hall and Mary Bucholtz, eds., *Gender Articulated: Language and the Socially Constructed Self* (New York: Routledge, 1995), 188–216.

4. *Ibid.*

5. Jesus A. Ramirez Martinez, "Swiping Your Life Away Failing to Find Love Through the Dating Apps" (Master's Theses, California State University, 2018).

6. M.J. Rosenfeld and R.J. Thomas, "Searching for a Mate," *American Sociological Review* 77 (2012): 523–547; E. Timmermans and C. Courtois, "From Swiping to Casual Sex and/or Committed Relationships: Exploring the Experiences of Tinder Users," *The Information Society* 34 (2018): 59–70.

7. Kristi Chin, Robin S. Edelstein, and Philip A. Vernon, "Attached to Dating Apps: Attachment Orientations and Preferences for Dating Apps," *Mobile Media & Communication* 7, no. 1 (2019): 41–59.

8. https://bumble.com.

9. https://hinge.com.

10. https://coffeemeetsbagel.com.

11. https://grindr.com.

12. Wikipedia, *OkCupid*, https://en.wikipedia.org/wiki/OkCupid.

13. *Ibid.*

14. Chin, Edelstein, and Vernon, "Attached to Dating Apps," pp. 41–59; V.R. Sumter, L. Vandenbosch, and L. Ligtenberg, "Love Me Tinder: Untangling Emerging Adults' Motivation for Using the Dating Application Tinder," *Telematics and Informatics* 34 (2017): 67–78; "Tinder vs. Bumble ... Which is better for you?," 2016, https://www.virtualdatingassistants.com/tinder-vs-bumble.

15. Janelle Ward, "Swiping, Matching, Chatting: Self-Presentation and Self-Disclosure on Mobile Dating Apps," *Human IT* 13, no. 2 (2016): 81–95.

16. Jeremy Birnholtz, Colin Fitzpatrick, Mark Handel, and Jed R. Brubaker, "Identity, Identification and Identifiability: The Language of Self-Presentation on a Location-Based Mobile Dating App," in *Mobile HCI: Proceedings of the 16th International Conference on Human-computer Interaction with Mobile Devices & Services*, 2014, pp 3–12. https://dl.acm.org/doi/proceedings/10.1145/2628363.

17. Chin, Edelstein, and Vernon, "Attached to Dating Apps," pp. 41–59.

18. A.E. Marwick and D. Boyd, "I Tweet Honestly, I Tweet Passionately: Twitter Users, Context Collapse and the Imagined Audience," *New Media & Society* 13, no. 1 (2011): 114–133.

19. Teresa Lopez-Gil, Cuihua Shen, Grace A. Benefield, and Nichaolas A. Palomares, "One Size Fits All: Context Collapse, Self-Presentation Strategies and Language Styles on Facebook," *Journal of Computer-Mediated Communication* 23 (2018): 127–145.

20. Danielle Couch and Pranee Liamputtong, "Online Dating and Mating: The Use of the Internet to Meet Sexual Partners," *Qualitative Health Research* 18 (2018): 268–279; Ward, "Swiping, Matching, Chatting," 81–95.

21. Cassandra Alexopolous, Elizabeth Timmermans, Jenna McNallie, "Swiping More, Committing Less: Unraveling the Links Among Dating App Use, Dating App Success, and Intention to Commit Infidelity," *Computers in Human Behavior* 102 (2020): 172–180.

22. Zygmunt Bauman, *Liquid Love: On the Frailty of Human Bonds* (Cambridge: Polity, 2003).

23. *Ibid.*

24. *Ibid.*

25. Mitchell Hobbs, Stephen Owen, and Livia Gerber, "Liquid Love? Dating Apps, Sex Relationships, and the Digital Transformation of Intimacy," *Journal of Sociology* 53, no. 2 (2017): 271–284.

26. Angel Castro, Juan Ramon Barrada, Pedro J. Ramos-Villagrasa, and Elena Fernandez-del-Rio, "Profiling Dating Apps Users: Sociodemographic and Personality Characteristics," *International Journal of Environmental Research and Public Health* 17 (2020): 1–13.

27. Matt Doran, "CWD Investigation: Exploring the Dark Side of Online Dating Sites and Apps," *True Crime Daily*, September 21, 2015, https://truecrimedaily.com/2015/09/21/cwd-investigation-exploring-the-dark-side-of-online-dating-sites-and-apps/.

28. Kath Albury, Jean Burgess, Ben Light, Kane Race, and Rowan Wilken, "Data Cultures of Mobile Dating and Hook-Up Apps: Emerging Issues for Critical Social Science," *Big Data & Society*, July–December 2017: 1–11.

29. Kamarah Pooley and Hayley Boxall, "Mobile Dating Applications and Sexual and Violent Offending," *Trends and Issues in Crime and Criminal Justice* 612 (2020): 1–16.

30. Alyssa Murphy, "Dating Dangerously: Risks Lurking Within Mobile Dating Apps," *Catholic University Journal of Law and Technology* 26, no. 1 (2018): 100–126.

31. C. Cameron, "Sex Offenders on Tinder, Other Dating Apps, Spur Probe by U.S. House Members," Gizmodo, February 2020, https://www.gizmodo.com.au/2020/02/sex-offenders-on-tinder-other-dating-apps-spur-probe-by-house-members/; Hillary Keith Cousins Flynn and Elizabeth Naismith Picciani, "Tinder Lets Known Sex Offenders Use the App. It's Not the Only One," *Columbia Journalism Investigations*, December 2, 2019, https://propublica.org/article/Tindr-lets-known-sex-offenders-use-the-App.-It's-not-the-only-one/.

32. Cassie Werber, "Nobody Knows How Dangerous Online Dating Really Is—And Dating Sites Won't Talk About It," QZ.com, 2017, Retrieved from https://qz.com/890320/nodobdy-knows-how-dangerous-online-dating-really-is-and-dating-sites-wont-talk-about-it/.

33. Rosalie Gillett, "Intimate Intrusions Online: Studying the Normalization of Abuse in Dating Apps," *Women's Studies International Forum* 69 (2018): 212–219.

34. Barbara Ortutay, "U.S. House Subcommittee Investigates Sex Offenders Use of Dating Apps," *Associated Press*, 2020, U.S. House subcommittee investigates sex offenders' use of dating apps | PBS NewsHour.

35. *Ibid.*

36. *Ibid.*

37. Sheryl Turkle, *Alone Together: Why We Expect More from Technology and Less from Each Other* (New York: Basic Books, 2017).

38. Murphy, "Dating Dangerously," pp. 100–126.

39. Hobbs, Owen, and Gerber, "Liquid Love? Dating Apps, Sex Relationships, and the Digital Transformation of Intimacy," pp. 271–284.

Chapter 9

1. Mary Madden and Amanda Lenhart, "Online Dating," Pew Research Center, March 5, 2006, https://www.pewresearch.org/internet/2006/03/05/online-dating/.

2. Amanda Barroso, "Key Takeaways on Americans' Views of and Experiences with Dating and Relationships," Pew Research Center, August 20, 2020, https://www.pewresearch.org/fact-tank/2020/08/20/key-takeaways-on-Americans-views-of-and-experiences-with-dating/.

3. Interestingly, technology also tops

the list of those who believe dating has gotten easier.

4. Monica Anderson Emily A. Vogels, and Erica Turner, "The Virtues and Downsides of Online Dating," Pew Research Center, February 6, 2020, https://www.pewresearch.org/internet/ 2020/02/06/the-viritues-and-downsides-of-online -dating/; see also Monica Anderson, Emily A. Vogels, and Erica Turner, "Users of Online Dating Platforms Experience Both Positive and Negative Aspects of Courtship on the Web," Pew Research Center, February 2, 2020, https://www.Pewresearch.org/Internet/2020/02/06/users-of-online-dating-platforms-experience-both-positive-and-negative-aspects-of-courtship-on-the-web/.

5. *Ibid.* Note: Earlier PEW Research Center studies did not inquire about dating apps.

6. Anna Brown, "A Profile of Single Americans," Pew Research Center, August 20, 2020, https://pewsocial trends.org/2020/08/20a-profile-of-single-americans.

7. Anderson, Vogels, and Turner, "The Virtues and Downsides of Online Dating" and "Users of Online Dating Platforms."

8. Madden and Lenhart, "Online Dating"; Brown, "A Profile of Single Americans"; Barroso, "Key Takeaways on Americans' Views of and Experiences with Dating and Relationships."

9. Rachel Wolfe, "Online Dating in the Coronavirus Era: How to Get with the Game," *The Wall Street Journal*, June 9, 2020, https://www.wsj.com/articles/-online-dating-in-the-coronavirus-era-how-to-get-with-the-game./June 9,2020.

10. Sara Konrath, "What the Pandemic Has Done for Dating," *The Atlantic*, December 31, 2020, https://www.theatlantic.com/ ideas/archive/2020/12/what-pandemic-has-done-dating/617502/.

11. Eliana Dockerman, "The Coronavirus Is Changing How We Date: Experts Think the Shifts May Be Permanent," *TIME* Magazine, April 11, 2020, https://time.com/5819187/dating-coronavirus/.

12. Helen Fisher, "How the Corona Virus Is Changing the Dating Game for the Better," *The New York Times*, May 7, 2020, https://www.nytimes.com/2020/05/07/well/mind/dating-coronavirus-love-relationships.html.

13. SWNS, "Distanced Dating: Sixty Percent of Americans Say the Coronavirus Pandemic Changed the Dating Game for Good," *The U.S. Sun*, November 11, 2020, https://www.the-sun.com/news/1785487/sixty-percent-americans-coronavirus-pandemic-changed-dating/.

14. *Ibid.*

Appendix

1. Simon Davis, "Men as Success Objects and Women as Sex Objects: A Study of Personal Advertisements," *Sex Roles* 23 (1990): 43–51.

2. Roland Tolentino, "Bodies, Letters, Catalogs: Filipinas in Transnational Space," *Social Text* 48, no. 3 (1996): 49–76.

3. Gerald M. Platt and Michael Fraser, "Race and Gender Discourse Strategies: Creating Solidarity and Framing the Civil Rights Movement," *Social Problems* 45, no. 2 (1998): 160–179.

4. Leah R. Warner, "A Best Practices Guide to Intersectional Approaches in Psychological Research," *Sex Roles* 59 (2008): 454–463.

5. R.K. Yin, *Case Study Research: Design and Methods*, fourth edition (Los Angeles: Sage Publications, 2009).

6. J. W. Creswell, *Research Design: Qualitative, Quantitative, and Mixed Methods Approaches*, third edition (Thousand Oaks: Sage, 2008).

Bibliography

Agarwal, Shashi K. "Therapeutic Benefits of Laughter." *Medical Science* 12, no. 46 (2014): 19–23.

Albury, Kath, Jean Burgess, Ben Light, Kane Race, and Rowan Wilken. "Data Cultures of Mobile Dating and Hook-Up Apps: Emerging Issues for Critical Social Science." *Big Data & Society*, July–December 2017: 1–11.

Alexopolous, Cassandra, Elizabeth Timmermans, and Jenna McNallie. "Swiping More, Committing Less: Unraveling the Links Among Dating App Use, Dating App Success, and Intention to Commit Infidelity." *Computers in Human Behavior* 102 (2020): 172–180.

Alhabash, Saleem, Kayla Hales, Jonghwan Baek, and Hyun Jung Oh. "Effects of Race, Visual Anonymity, and Social Category Salience on Online Dating Outcomes." *Computers in Human Behavior* 35 (2014): 22–32.

Anderson, Monica, Emily A. Vogels, and Erica Turner. "Users of Online Dating Platforms Experience Both Positive and Negative Aspects of Courtship on the Web." Washington, D.C.: Pew Research Center, 2020. https://www.Pewresearch.org/Internet/2020/02/06/users-of-online-dating-platforms-experience-both-positive-and-negative-aspects-of-courtship-on-the-web/.

Anderson, Monica, Emily A. Vogels, and Erica Turner. "The Virtues and Downsides of Online Dating." Washington, D.C.: Pew Research Center, 2020. https://www.pewresearch.org/internet/2020/02/06/the-virtues-and-downsides-of-online-dating.

Anderson, Traci L., and Tara M. Emmers-Sommer. "Predictors of Relationship Satisfaction in Online Romantic Relationships." *Communication Studies* 57, no. 2 (2006): 153–172.

Anderton, Douglas L., Richard E. Barrett, and Donald J. Bogue. *The Population of the United States,* third edition. New York: Free Press, 1997.

Ansari, Aziz, and Eric Klinenberg. *Modern Romance: An Investigation.* New York: Penguin, 2015.

Asendorpf, Jens B., Lars Penke, and Mitja D. Back. "From Dating to Mating and Relating: Predictors of Initial and Long-Term Outcomes of Speed-Dating in a Community Sample." *European Journal of Personality* 25 (2011): 16–30.

Back, M.D., L. Penke, S. Schmukle, K. Sasche, P. Borkenau, and J.B. Asendorpf. "Why Mate Choices Are Not as Reciprocal as We Assume: The Role of Personality, Flirting and Physical Attractiveness." *European Journal of Personality* 25 (2011): 120–132.

Back, M.D., L. Penke, S. Schmukle, and J.B. Asendorpf. "Knowing Your Own Mate Value: Sex-Specific of Personality Effects on the Accuracy of Expected Mate Choices." *Psychological Science* 22 (2011): 984–989.

Bailey, Beth L. "From 'Bundling' to 'Hooking Up': Teaching the History of American Courtship." *Organization of American Historians Magazine of History* 18, no. 4 (2004): 3–4.

Bailey, Beth L. *From Front Porch to Back Seat: Courtship in Twentieth-Century America.* Baltimore: Johns Hopkins University Press, 1988.

Bibliography

Bargh, John A., and Katelyn Y. A. McKenna. "The Internet and Social Life." *Annual Review of Psychology* 55 no. 1 (2004): 573–590.

Barroso, Amanda. "Key Takeaways on Americans' Views of and Experiences with Dating and Relationships." Washington, D.C.: Pew Research Center, 2020. https://www.pewresearch.org/fact-tank/2020/08/20/key-takeaways-on-Americans-views-of-and-experiences-with-dating/.

Barsamian, Kimberly K., Katherine Spencer, and Jack Glaser. "Online Prejudice and Discrimination: From Dating to Hating." In *The Social Net: Understanding Our Behavior Online*, edited by Yair Amichai-Hamburger, pp. 201–219. Oxford: Oxford University Press, 2013.

Bauman, Zygmunt. *Liquid Love: On the Frailty of Human Bonds.* Cambridge: Polity, 2003.

Beauman, Francesca. *From Personal Ads to Swiping Right: A Story of America Looking for Love.* New York: Pegasus Books, 2020.

Birnholtz, Jeremy, Colin Fitzpatrick, Mark Handel, and Jed R. Brubaker. "Identity, Identification and Identifiability: The Language of Self-Presentation on a Location-Based Mobile Dating App." In *Mobile HCI: Proceedings of the 16th International Conference on Human-computer Interaction with Mobile Devices & Services,* 2014, pp. 3–12. https://dl.acm.org/doi/proceedings/10.1145/2628363

Blackwell, D.L., and D.T. Lichter. "Homogamy Among Dating, Cohabiting and Married Couples." *Sociological Quarterly* 45 no. 4 (2004): 719–737.

Bogle, Kathy. *Hooking Up: Sex, Dating and Relationships on Campus.* New York: New York University Press, 2008.

Bolig, Rosemary, Peter J. Stein, and Patrick C. McKenry. "The Self-Advertisement Approach to Dating: Male-Female Differences." *Family Relations* 33 (1984): 587–592.

Bonilla-Silva, Eduardo. *White Supremacy and Racism in the Post–Civil Rights Era.* Boulder: Lynne Reinner, 2001.

Botsman, Rachel. *Who Can You Trust? How Technology Brings Us Together and Why It Might Drive Us Apart.* New York: PublicAffairs, 2018, Kindle edition.

Boyd, Danah. *It's Complicated: The Social Lives of Networked Teens.* New Haven: Yale University Press, 2015.

Brown, Anna. "A Profile of Single Americans." Washington, D.C.: Pew Research Center, 2020. https://pewsocialtrends.org/2020/08/20a-profile-of-single-americans.

Cameron, C. "Sex Offenders on Tinder, Other Dating Apps, Spur Probe by U.S. House Members." *Gizmodo,* February 2020. https://www.gizmodo.com.au/2020/02/sex-offenders-on-tinder-other-dating-apps-spur-probe-by-house-members/.

Cameron, Catherine, Stuart Oskamp, and William Sparks. "Courtship American Style: Newspaper Ads." *The Family Coordinator* 26 (1977): 27–31.

Castro Angel, Juan Ramon Barrada, Pedro J. Ramos-Villagrasa, and Elena Fernandez-del-Rio. "Profiling Dating Apps Users: Sociodemographic and Personality Characteristics." *International Journal of Environmental Research and Public Healt,* 17 (2020): 1–13.

Chang, Andrew, Haley E. Kragness, Wei Tsou, Dan J. Bosnyak, Anja Thiede, and Laurel J. Trainor. "Body Sway Predicts Romantic Interest in Speed Dating." *Social Cognitive and Affective Neuroscience* (2020): 1–8.

Cherlin, Andrew. "Demographic Trends in the United States: A Review of Research in the 2000s." *Journal of Marriage and Family* 72 (2010): 403–419.

Child, Meredith, Katherine Graff Low, Cheryl McDonnell McCormick, and Andrew Cocciarella. "Personal Advertisements of Male-to-Female Transsexuals, Homosexual Men, and Heterosexuals." *Sex Roles* 34 (1996): 447–455.

Chin, Kristi, Robin S. Edelstein, and Philip A. Vernon. "Attached to Dating Apps: Attachment Orientations and Preferences for Dating Apps." *Mobile Media & Communication* 7, no. 1 (2019): 41–59.

Bibliography

Cilluffo, Anthony, and D'Vera Cohn. "6 Demographic Trends Shaping the U.S. and the World in 2019." Washington, D.C.: Pew Research Center, 2020. https://www.pewresearch.org/fact-tank/2019/04/11/6-demographic-trends-shaping-the-u-s-and-the-world-in-2019/.

Cockburn, John. *Lonely Hearts: Looking for Love Among the Small Ads.* London: Simon & Schuster, 1988.

Coleman, James S. *Power and the Structure of Society.* New York: W.W. Norton, 1974.

Conley, Dalton. *Elsewhere USA: How We Got from the Company Man, Family Dinners, and the Affluent Society to the Home Office, BlackBerry Moms, and Economic Anxiety.* New York: Vintage, 2010.

Connor, Dylan Shane, and Michael Storper. "The Changing Geography of Social Mobility in the United States." *Proceedings of the National Academy of Sciences,* 2020. www.pnas.org/cgi/doi/10.1073/pnas.2010222117 .

Coontz, Stephanie. *Marriage, A History: From Obedience to Intimacy or How Love Conquered Marriage.* New York: Viking Books, 2005.

Couch, Danielle, and Pranee Liamputtong. "Online Dating and Mating: The Use of the Internet to Meet Sexual Partners." *Qualitative Health Research* 18 (2008): 268–279.

Crenshaw, Kimberlé. "Mapping the Margins: Identity Politics, Intersectionality and Violence Against Women." *Stanford Law Review* 43, no. 6 (1991): 1241–1299.

Creswell, J.W. *Research Design: Qualitative, Quantitative, and Mixed Methods Approaches*, third edition. Thousand Oaks: Sage, 2009.

Curington, Celeste, Lin Ken-Hou, and Jennifer Lundquist. "Dating Partners Don't Always Prefer 'Their Own Kind': Some Multiracial Daters Get Bonus Points in the Dating Game." Austin: Council on Contemporary Families, The University of Texas at Austin, 2015. http://www.contemporaryfamilies.org/multiracisl-dating-brief-report.

Curington, Celeste Vaughan, Ken-Hou Lin, and Jennifer Hickes Lunquist. "Positioning Multiraciality in Cyberspace: Treatment of Multiracial Daters in an Online Dating Website." *American Sociological Review* 80, no. 4 (2015): 764–788.

Darbandi, Sara, Mahsa Darbandi, Hamid Reza Khorram Khorshid, and Mohammad Reza Sadeghi. "Yoga Can Improve Assisted Reproduction Technology Outcomes in Couples with Infertility." *Alternative Therapies* 24, no. 4 (2017): 50–55.

Davis, Jenny. "Race and Online Dating." Austin: Council on Contemporary Families, Unconventional Wisdom, Volume 6, 2014. http://contemporaryfamilies.org/unconventional-wisdom-6/.

Davis, Kathy. "Intersectionality as Buzzword: A Sociology of Science Perspective on What Makes a Feminist Theory Successful." *Feminist Theory* 9, no. 67 (2008): 67–85.

Davis, Simon. "Men as Success Objects and Women as Sex Objects: A Study of Personal Advertisements." *Sex Roles* 23 (1990): 43–51.

Deaux, K., and R. Hanna. "Courtship in the Personals Column: The Influence of Gender and Sexual Orientation." *Sex Roles* 11 (1984): 363–375.

DeVoss, Dànielle Nicole. "From the BBS to the Web: Tracing the Spaces of Online Romance." In *Online Matchmaking,* edited by Monica Whitty, Andrea J. Baker, and James A. Inman. New York: Palgrave, 2007.

Deyo, Yaacov, and Sue Deyo. *Speed Dating: The Smarter, Faster Way to Lasting Love.* New York: HarperCollins, 2002.

Dockerman, Eliana. "The Coronavirus Is Changing How We Date: Experts Think the Shifts May Be Permanent." *TIME* Magazine, April 11, 2020. https://time.com/5819187/dating-coronavirus/.

Donald, Brooke. "New Stanford Research on Speed Dating Examines What Makes Couples 'Click' in Four Minutes." *Stanford News,* May 6, 2013. https://news.stanford.edu/news/2013/may/jurafsky-mcfarland-dating-050613.html.

Doran, Matt. "CWD Investigation:

Bibliography

Exploring the Dark Side of Online Dating Sites and Apps." *True Crime Daily,* September 21, 2015. https://truecrimedaily.com/2015/09/21/cwd-investigation-exploring-the-darkside-of-online-dating-sites-and-apps/.

Duits, Linda. *Multi-Girl-Culture: An Ethnography of Doing Identity.* Amsterdam: Amsterdam University Press, 2008.

Eastwick, Paul W., and Eli J. Finkel. "Speed Dating: A Powerful and Flexible Paradigm for Studying Romantic Relationship Interaction." In *Handbook of Relationship Initiation* (pp. 217–234). New York: Taylor & Francis, 2008.

Edward, Robert, and Michael W. Foley. "Much Ado About Social Capital." *Contemporary Sociology* 30, no. 3 (2001): 227–230.

Enss, Chris. "Branded But Unbroken: Thirty-Two Tenacious Women Who Left Their Mark on the Old West." *True West: History of the American Frontier,* November 4, 2014. www.truewestmagazine.com/branded-but-unbroken/.

Enss, Chris. *Hearts West: True Stories of Mail-Order Brides on the Frontier.* Guilford, CT: Globe Pequot Press, 2005.

Erdman, Lynn. "Laughter Therapy for Patients with Cancer." *Journal of Psychosocial Oncology* 11, no. 4 (2008): 55–67.

Faludi, Susan. *Backlash: The Undeclared War Against American Women.* New York: Crown, 2006. www.susanfaludi.com/backlash-chapter.html.

Feliciano, Cynthia, Belinda Robnett, and Golnaz Komaie. "Gendered Racial Exclusion Among White Internet Daters." *Social Science Research* 38, no. 1 (2009): 39–54.

Feliciano, Cynthia, Rennie Lee, and Belinda Robnett. "Racial Boundaries Among Latinos: Evidence from Internet Daters' Racial Preferences." *Social Problems* 58, no. 2 (2011): 189–212.

Finkel, Eli, and Paul W. Eastwick. "Speed Dating." *Current Directions of Psychological Science* 17, no. 3 (2008): 193–195.

Finkel, Eli, Paul W. Eastwick, and Jacob Matthews. "Speed-Dating as an Invaluable Tool for Studying Romantic Attraction: A Methodological Primer." *Personal Relationships* 14, no. 1 (2007): 149–166.

Fischer, Claude S., and Greggor Mattson. "Is America Fragmenting?" *Annual Review of Sociology* 35, no. 1 (2009): 435–455.

Fisher, Helen. "How the Corona Virus Is Changing the Dating Game for the Better." *The New York Times,* May 7, 2020. https://www.nytimes.com/2020/05/07/well/mind/dating-coronavirus-love-relationships.html.

Fisman, Raymond, Sheena S. Iyengar, Emir Kamenica, and Itimar Simonson. "Gender Differences in Mate Selection: Evidence from a Speed Dating Experiment." *The Quarterly Journal of Economics* May (2006): 673–697.

Fisman, Raymond, Sheena S. Iyengar, Emir Kamenica, and Itimar Simonson. "Racial Preferences in Dating." *The Review of Economic Studies* 75, no. 1 (2008): 117–132.

Flynn, Hillary Keith Cousins, and Elizabeth Naismith Picciani. "Tinder Lets Known Sex Offenders Use the App. It's Not the Only One." *Columbia Journalism Investigations,* December 2, 2019. https://propublic.a.org/article/Tindr-lets-known-sex-offenders-use-the-App.-It's-not-the-only-one/

Fraga, Julie. "Is Partner Yoga the New Couples Therapy?" *Yoga Journal,* September 10, 2020. https://www.yogajournal.com/lifestyle/partner-yoga-for-couples-therapy/.

Frederickson, Barbara. "Love Is a Micro-Moment of True Love." *Cram,* 2020. https://www.cram.com/essay/-Love-Is-A-Micro-Moment-Of-True/PKVWLSXKUZ3Q.

Frost, Bryan-Paul, and Paul Hollander. "Extravagant Expectations: New Ways to Find Romantic Love in America." *Society* 49 (2012): 302–304.

Fuchs, Susanne, and Tamara Rathcke. *Laugh Is in the Air? Physiological Analysis of Laughter as a Correlate of Attraction During Speed Dating.* Laughter Workshop Conference,

Bibliography

Paris, August 2018. https://www.researchgate.net/publication/3271 77342.

Ghaziani, Amin. "Post-Gay Collective Identity Construction." *Social Problems* 58, no. 1 (2011): 99–125.

Giddens, Anthony. *The Transformation of Intimacy: Sexuality, Love & Eroticism in Modern Societies.* Palo Alto: Stanford University Press, 1992.

Gillett, Rosalie. "Intimate Intrusions Online: Studying the Normalization of Abuse in Dating Apps." *Women's Studies International Forum* 69 (2018): 212–219.

Gleason, Marci E. J. "Relationship Formation on the Internet: What's the Big Attraction?" *Journal of Social Issues* 58, no. 1 (2002): 9–31.

Gonzalez, Marti Hope, and Sarah A. Meyers. "Your Mother Would Like Me: Self-Presentation in the Personal Ads of Heterosexual and Homosexual Men and Women." *Personality and Social Psychology Bulletin* 19, no. 2 (1993): 131–142.

Good, Erich. "Gender and Courtship Entitlement: Responses to Personal Ads." *Sex Roles* 34, no. 3–4 (1996): 141–169.

Hall, Kira. "Lip Service on the Fantasy Lines." In Kira Hall and Mary Bucholtz, eds., *Gender Articulated: Language and the Socially Constructed Self* (pp. 188–216). New York: Routledge, 1995.

Hall, Stuart, and Paul Du Gay. *Questions of Cultural Identity.* Thousand Oaks: Sage, 1996.

Hardin, Russell. "Distrust: Manifestations and Management." In *Distrust,* edited by Russell Hardin (pp. 3–33). New York: Russell Sage Foundation, 2004.

Harrison, Albert A., and Laila Saeed. "Let's Make a Deal: An Analysis of Revelations and Stipulations in Lonely Hearts Advertisements." *Journal of Personality and Social Psychology* 35 (1977): 257–264.

Hill Collins, Patricia. *Black Feminist Thought: Knowledge, Consciousness, and the Politics of Empowerment.* New York: Routledge, 2000.

Hirschman, Elizabeth C. "People as Products: Analysis of a Complex Marketing Exchange." *Journal of Marketing* 51 (1987): 98–108.

Hobbs, Mitchell, Stephen Owen, and Livia Gerber. "Liquid Love? Dating Apps, Sex Relationships, and the Digital Transformation of Intimacy." *Journal of Sociology* 53, no. 2 (2017): 271–284.

Hollander, Matthew M., and Jason Turowetz. "'So, Why Did You Decide to Do This?' Soliciting and Formulating Motives for Speed Dating." *Discourse and Sociology* 24, no. 6 (2013): 701–724.

Hollander, Paul. *Extravagant Expectations: New Ways to Find Romantic Love in America.* Chicago: Ivan R. Dee, 2011.

Houser, Mairan, Sean M. Horan, and Lisa A. Furler. "Dating in the Fast Lane: How Communication Predicts Speed-Dating Success." *Journal of Social and Personal Relationships* 25, no. 5 (2008): 749–768.

Houser, Mairan, Sean M. Horan, and Lisa A. Furler. "Predicting Relational Outcomes: An Investigation of Thin Slice Judgments in Speed Dating." *Human Communication* 10, no. 2 (2007): 69–81.

Jagger, Elizabeth. "Is Thirty the New Sixty? Dating, Age and Gender in a Postmodern, Consumer Society." *Sociology* 39 no. 1 (2005): 89–106.

Jagger, Elizabeth. "Marketing the Self, Buying Another: Dating in a Post Modern, Consumer Society." *Sociology* 34, no. 4 (1998): 759–814.

Jarrett, Christian. "Why Meeting Another's Gaze Is So Powerful." *BBC News,* January 8, 2019. http://www.bbc.com/future/article20190108-why-meeting-another's-gaze-is-so-powerful.

Jauk, Emanuel, Aljoscha C. Neubauer, Thomas Mairunteregger, Stephanie Pemp, Katherina P. Sieber, and John F. Rauthmann. "How Alluring Are Dark Personalities? The Dark Triad and Attractiveness in Speed Dating." *European Journal of Personality,* 30 (2016): 125–138.

Kass, Leon, R. "The End of Courtship." *The Public Interest* 126 (1997): 39–49.

193

Bibliography

Kimmel, Michael. "Hooking Up: Sex in Guyland." In *Guyland: The Perilous World Where Boys Become Men* (pp. 190–216). New York: Harper, 2009.

Kirca, Nurcan, and Turkan Pasinlioglu. "The Effect of Yoga on Stress Level in Infertile Women." *Perspectives of Psychiatric Care* 55, no. 2 (2019): 319–327.

Klinenberg, Erick. *Going Solo: The Extraordinary Rise and Surprising Appeal of Living Alone.* New York: Penguin, 2012.

Koestner, Richard, and Ladd Wheeler. "Self-Presentation in Personal Advertisements: The Influence of Implicit Notions of Attraction and Role Expectations." *Journal of Social and Personal Relationships* 5, no. 2 (1988): 149–160.

Konrath, Sara. "What the Pandemic Has Done for Dating." *The Atlantic*, December 31, 2020. https://www.theatlantic.com/ideas/archive/2020/12/-what-pandemic-has-done-dating/617502/.

Korobov, Neil. "Mate-Preference Talk in Speed-Dating Conversations." *Research on Language and Social Interaction* 44, no. 2 (2011): 186–209.

Kumar, Saravana, Kate Beaton, and Tricia Hughes. "The Effectiveness of Massage Therapy for the Treatment of Nonspecific Low Back Pain: A Systematic Review of Systematic Reviews." *International Journal of General Medicine* 6 (2013): 733–741.

Ladd, Everett C. "The Data Just Don't Show Erosion of America's Social Capital." *The Public Perspective*, June/July 1996: 1–22.

Laner, Mary Riege, and G.W. Levi Kamel. "Media Mating I: Newspaper 'Personals' Ads of Homosexual Men." *Journal of Homosexuality* 3 no. 2 (1977): 149–162.

Larson, Jeff A., and William Tsitsos. "Speed Dating and the Presentation of Self: A Teaching Exercise in Impression Management and Formation." *Teaching Sociology* 41, no. 3 (2013): 307–313.

Lee, Catherine. *Prostitutes and Picture Brides: Chinese and Japanese Immigration, Settlement, and American Nation-Building, 1870–1920.* Faculty Working Paper 70, University of California at San Diego: The Center for Comparative Immigration Studies, 2003.

Lester, Neal A., and Maureen Daly Goggin. *Racialized Politics of Desire in Personal Ads.* Lanham, MD: Lexington Books, 2007.

Lin, Ken-Hou, Celeste Curington, and Jennifer H. Lundquist. "Dating Partners Don't Always Prefer 'Their Own Kind': Some Multiracial Daters Get Bonus Points in the Dating Game." *Council of Contemporary Families*, 2015. http://contemporaryfamilies.org/multi-racial-dating-brief-report.

Lopez-Gil, Teresa, Cuihua Shen, Grace A. Benefield, and Nichaolas A. Palomares. "One Size Fits All: Context Collapse, Self-Presentation Strategies and Language Styles on Facebook." *Journal of Computer-Mediated Communication* 23 (2018): 127–145.

Luchetti, Cathy. *"I Do!": Courtship, Love and Marriage on the American Frontier: A Glimpse at America's Romantic Past Through Photographs, Diaries, and Journals, 1715–1915.* New York: Crown Trade Paperbacks, 1996.

Lynn, Michael, and Barbara A. Shurgot. "Responses to Lonely Hearts Advertisements: Effects of Reported Physical Attractiveness, Physique, and Coloration." *Personality and Social Psychology Bulletin* 10, no. 3 (1984): 349–357.

Madden, Mary, and Amanda Lenhart. "Online Dating." Washington, D.C.: Pew Research Center, 2006. https://www.pewresearch.org/internet/2006/03/05/online-dating/.

Martinez, Jesus A. Ramirez. "Swiping Your Life Away Failing to Find Love Through the Dating Apps." Master's Theses, California State University, 2018. https://digitalcommons.csumb.edu/caps_thes_all/427.

Marwick, Alice E., and Danah Boyd. "I Tweet Honestly, I Tweet Passionately: Twitter Users, Context Collapse and the Imagined Audience." *New Media & Society* 13, no. 1 (2011): 114–133.

McCarthy, Ellen. "Marriage-Minded Do Better Online Than at Bars, Survey Claims." *The Washington Post*, Sunday, April 25, 2010.

Bibliography

McClure, M. Joy, and John E. Lydon. "Anxiety Doesn't Become You: How Attachment Anxiety Compromises Relational Opportunities." *Journal of Personality and Social Psychology* 106, no. 1 (2014): 89–111.

McFarland, Daniel, Dan Jurafsky, and Craig Rawlings. "Making the Connections: Social Bonding in Courtship Situations." *American Journal of Sociology* 115, no. 6 (2013): 1596–1649.

McKenna, Katelyn Y.A., Amie S. Green, and Marci E.J. Gleason. "Relationship Formation on the Internet: What's the Big Attraction?" *Journal of Social Issues* 58, no. 1 (2002): 9–31.

McRobbie, Angela. "Post Feminism and Popular Culture." *Feminist Media Studies* 4, no. 3 (2004): 255–264.

Mendelsohn, Gerald A., Lindsay Shaw Taylor, Andrew T. Fiore, and Coye Cheshire. "Black/White Dating Online: Interracial Courtship in the 21st Century." *Psychology of Popular Media Culture* 3, no. 1 (2014): 2–18.

Merskin, Debra L., and Mara Huberlie. "Companionship in the Classifieds: The Adoption of Personal Advertisments by Daily Newspapers." *Journalism and Mass Communication Quarterly* 73, no. 1 (1996): 219–229.

Murphy, Alyssa. "Dating Dangerously: Risks Lurking Within Mobile Dating Apps." *Catholic University Journal of Law and Technology* 26, no. 1 (2018): 100–126.

Muurlink, Olay, and Cristina Poyatos Matas. "From Romance to Rocket Science: Speed Dating in Higher Education." *Higher Education Research & Development* 30, no. 6 (2011): 751–764.

Naruse, Sayuri. M., and Mark Moss. "Effects of Couples Positive Massage Programme on Wellbeing, Perceived Stress and Coping, and Relation Satisfaction." *Health Psychology and Behavioral Medicine* 7, no. 1 (2019): 328–347.

Naruse, Sayuri M., Piers L. Cornelissen, and Mark Moss. "'To Give Is Better Than to Receive?' Couples Massage Significantly Benefits Both Partners Wellbeing." *Journal of Health Psychology* 25, no. 10–11 (2020): 1576–1586.

Ng, Kenneth C. W., and Marc Cohen. *The Effectiveness of Massage Therapy: A Summary of Evidence-Based Research.* Global Wellness Summit, Australia, 2011. https://www.globalwellnesssummit.com/wp-content/uploads/Industry-Research/Australia/2011-AAMT-Research-Report.pdf.

Ortutay, Barbara. "U.S. House Subcommittee Investigates Sex Offenders Use of Dating Apps." *Associated Press,* 2020. U.S. House subcommittee investigates sex offenders' use of dating apps | PBS NewsHour.

Parigi, Paolo, and Karen Cook. "Trust and Relationships in the Sharing Economy." *Contexts* 14, no. 1 (2015): 18–19.

Parigi, Paolo, and Rachel Gong. "From Grassroots to Digital Ties: A Case Study of a Political Consumerism Movement." *Journal of Consumer Culture* 14, no. 2 (2014): 236–253.

Parigi, Paolo, and Warner Henson II. "Social Isolation in America." *Annual Review of Sociology* 40 (2014): 153–171.

Parker, Clifton B. "Interpersonal Trust Erodes Over Time in the Online World, Experts Say." https://phys.org/news/-2015-03-interpersonal-erodes-online-world-experts.html, March 19, 2015.

Pasley, Jeffrey L. "Politics, Citizenship, and Collective Action in Nineteenth-Century America: A Response to Stuart Blumin and Michael Schudson." *Communication Review* 4 (2000): 39–54.

Paxton, Pamela. "Is Social Capital Declining in the United States?" *American Journal of Sociology* 105, no. 1 (1999): 88–127.

Paxton, Pamela. "Trust in Decline?" *Contexts* 4, no. 1 (2005): 40–46.

Phua, Voon Chin. "Sex and Sexuality in Men's Personal Advertisements." *Men and Masculinities* 5 (2002): 178–191.

Phua, Voon Chin, and Allison Caras. "Personal Brand in Online Advertisements: Comparing White and Brazilian Male Sex Workers." *Sociological Focus* 41, no. 3 (2008): 238–255.

Phua, Voon Chin, and Gayle Kaufman. "The Crossroads of Race and Sexuality: Date Selection Among Men in Internet

Personals Ads." *Journal of Family Issues* 24, no. 8 (2003): 981–994.

Pin, Emile J., and Jamie Turndorf. "Staging One's Ideal Self." In *Life as Theater: A Dramaturgical Sourcebook* (pp. 163–182). New Brunswick: Aldine Transaction, 2009.

Platt, Gerald M., and Michael Fraser. "Race and Gender Discourse Strategies: Creating Solidarity and Framing the Civil Rights Movement." *Social Problems* 45, no. 2 (1998): 160–179.

Poling-Kempes, Lesley. *The Harvey Girls: Women Who Opened the West.* New York: Marlowe, 1994.

Pooley, Kamarah, and Hayley Boxall. "Mobile Dating Applications and Sexual and Violent Offending." *Trends and Issues in Crime and Criminal Justice* 612 (2020): 1–16.

Poulin, Colleen, and Virgina Rutter. "How Color Blind is Love? Interracial Dating: Facts and Puzzles." *Council of Contemporary Families,* 2011. www.contemporaryfamilies.org/marriage-partnership-divorce/how-color-blind-is-love.

Prince, Gail. *CoffeeMating: Connecting Through Circulating and Percolating.* www.datingtomating.com.

Putnam, Robert, D. *Bowling Alone: The Collapse and Revival of American Community.* New York: Simon & Schuster, 2000.

Quiroz, Pamela A. "From Mail Order and Picture Brides, Lonely Hearts and Social Clubs, to eHarmony, 'Just Lunch,' Speed Dating, and Coffee Mating: The Evolution of Personal Advertising." In *Dynamics and Interconnections in Popular Culture,* edited by Ray B. Brown and Ben Urish (pp. 114–129). Newcastle Upon Tyne: Cambridge Scholars, 2013.

Räisänen, Jaana, Arto Ojala, and Tero Tapio Tuovinen, "Building Trust in the Sharing Economy: Current Approaches and Future Considerations." *Journal of Cleaner Production,* 279 (2021): 1–30. https://doi.org/10.1016/j.jclepro.2020.123724.

Rajecki, D.W., Sharon B. Bledsoe, and Jeffrey Lee Rasmussen. "Successful Personal Ads: Gender Differences and Similarities in Offers, Stipulations, and Outcomes." *Basic and Applied Social Psychology* 12, no. 4 (1991): 457–469.

Ramon, Mora Ripoll, and Isabel Quintana Casado. "Laughter and Positive Therapies: Modern Approach and Practical Use in Medicine." *Revista de Psiquiatria y Salud Mental* 3, no. 1 (2010): 27–34.

Ranganath, Rajesh, Dan Jurafsky, and Daniel A. McFarland. "Detecting Friendly, Flirtatious, Awkward, and Assertive Speech in Speed-Dates." *Computer Speech and Language* 27, no. 1 (2013): 89–115.

Recker, Nancy. "Laughter Is Really Good Medicine." Ohio State University, Family and Consumer Sciences, 2007. https://www.dartmouth.edu/eap/library/Laughter_Good_Medicine.pdf.

Rifkin, Jeremy. *The Age of Access: The New Culture of Hypercapitalism, Where All of Life Is a Paid-for Experience.* New York: J.P. Tarcher/Putnam, 2001.

Robnett, Belinda, and Cynthia Feliciano. "Patterns of Racial-Ethnic Exclusion by Internet Daters." *Social Forces* 89, no. 3 (2011): 807–828.

Rosenfeld, M.J., and R.J. Thomas. "Searching For a Mate: The Rise of the Internet as a Social Intermediary." *American Sociological Review* 74, no. 4 (2012): 523–547.

Rothman, Ellen K. *Hands and Hearts: A History of Courtship in America.* New York: Basic Books, 1984.

Ruffin, Paula Thomas. "A History of Massage in Nurse Training School Curricula (1860–1945)." *Journal of Holistic Nursing* 29, no. 1 (2011): 61–67.

Rutledge, Thomas. "How Meditation Improves Emotional and Physical Health." *Psychology Today,* August 4, 2019. https://www.psychologytoday.com/us/blog/the-healthy-journey/201908/how-meditation-improves-emotional-and-physical-health.

Samuelson, Robert J. "'Bowling Alone' is Bunk," *The Washington Post,* April 10, 1996, 1–22.

Santana, Jessica, and Paolo Parigi. "Risk

Bibliography

Aversion and Engagement in the Sharing Economy." *Games* 6, no. 4 (2015): 560–573.

Shapiro, Susan. *Wayward Capitalists: Targets of the Securities and Exchange Commission.* New Haven: Yale University Press, 1984.

Small, Meredith F. *What's Love Got to Do With It? The Evolution of Human Mating.* New York: Anchor Books, 1995.

Smith, Aaron, and Maeve Duggan. *Online Dating & Relationships.* Washington, D.C.: Pew Research Center, 2013 (accessed November 2, 2020), https://www.pewresearch.org/internet/2013/10/21/online-dating-relationships/.

Smith, Jane E., V. Ann Waldorf, and David L. Trembath. "Single White Male Looking for Thin, Very Attractive..." *Sex Roles* 23 (1990): 675–685.

Steinfirst, Susan, and Barbara B. Moran. "The New Mating Game: Matchmaking Via the Personal Columns in the 1980s." *Journal of Popular Culture* 22, no. 4 (1989): 129–139.

Stokoe, Elizabeth. "'Have You Been Married, or...?': Eliciting and Accounting for Relationship Histories in Speed-Dating Interaction." *Research on Language and Social Interaction* 43, no. 3 (2010): 260–282.

Stryker, Sheldon. "Identity Salience and Role Performance: The Relevance of Symbolic Interaction Theory for Family Research." In *Social Psychology and the Self-Concept,* edited by Morris Rosenberg and Howard B. Kaplan (pp. 200–208). Arlington Heights, IL: Harlan Davidson, 1982.

Sumter, Sindy R., Laura Vandenbosch, and Loes Ligtenberg. "Love Me Tinder: Untangling Emerging Adults' Motivation for Using the Dating Application Tinder." *Telematics and Informatics* 34, no. 1 (2017): 67–78.

Swidler, Ann. "Culture in Action: Symbols and Strategies." *American Sociological Review* 51, no. 2 (1986): 273–286.

SWNS. "Distanced Dating: Sixty Percent of Americans Say the Coronavirus Pandemic Changed the Dating Game for Good." *The U.S. Sun,* November 11, 2020. https://www.the-sun.com/news/1785487/-sixty-percent-americans-coronavirus-pandemic-changed-dating/.

Thornton, Arland, and Linda Young-DeMarco. "Four Decades of Trends in Attitudes Toward Family Issues in the United States: The 1960s Through the 1990s." *Journal of Marriage and Family* 63 (2001): 1009–1037.

Tierney, John. "Romantic Revulsion in the New Century: Flaw-o-matic 2.0." *The New York Times,* April 10, 2007.

Timmermans, Elisabeth, and Cédric Courtois. "From Swiping to Casual Sex and/or Committed Relationships: Exploring the Experiences of Tinder Users." *The Information Society* 34, no. 2 (2018): 59–70.

"Tinder vs. Bumble...Which Is Better for You?" Virtual Dating Assistants, 2016. https://www.virtualdatingassistants.com/tinder-vs-bumble.

Tolentino, Roland. "Bodies, Letters, Catalogs: Filipinas in Transnational Space." *Social Text* 48, no. 3 (1996): 49–76.

Turowitz, Jason, and Matthew M. Hollander. "Assessing the Experience of Speed Dating." *Discourse Studies* 14, no. 5 (2012): 635–658.

Useem, Bert. "Solidarity Model, Breakdown Model, and the Boston Antibusing Movement." *American Sociological Review* 45 (1980): 357–369.

Ward, Janelle. "Swiping, Matching, Chatting: Self-Presentation and Self-Disclosure on Mobile Dating Apps." *Human IT* 13, no. 2 (2016): 81–95.

Warner, Leah R. "A Best Practices Guide to Intersectional Approaches in Psychological Research." *Sex Roles* 59 (2008): 454–463.

Werber, Cassie. "Nobody Knows How Dangerous Online Dating Really Is—And Dating Sites Won't Talk About It." *Quartz,* March 31, 2017. https://qz.com/890320/nodobdy-knows-how-dangerous-online-dating-really-is-and-dating-sites-wont-talk-about-it/.

West, Candace, and D.H. Zimmerman. "Doing Gender." *Gender & Society* 1 (1987): 125–151.

Bibliography

Westman, Kathryn F., and Cathy Blaisdell. "Many Benefits, Little Risk: The Use of Massage in Nursing Practice." *American Journal of Nursing* 116, no. 1 (2016): 34–39.

Whitty, Monica, and Adrian Carr. *Cyberspace Romance: The Psychology of Online Relationships*. New York: Palgrave Macmillan, 2006.

Wilkins, Julia, and Amy Janel Eisenbraun. "Humor Theories and the Physiological Benefits of Laughter." *Advances in Mind-Body Medicine* 24, no. 2 (2009): 8–12.

Willis, Frank N., and Roger A. Carlson. "Singles Ads: Gender, Social Class, and Time." *Sex Roles* 29 (1993): 387–404.

Wilson, John. "Dr. Putnam's Social Lubricant." *Contemporary Sociology* 30, no. 3 (2001): 225–227.

Wilson, Shauna B., William D. McIntosh, and Salvatore P. Insana II. "Dating Across Race: An Examination of African American Internet Personal Advertisements." *Journal of Black Studies* 37, no. 6 (2007): 964–982.

Wolfe, Rachel. "Online Dating in the Coronavirus Era: How to Get with the Game." *The Wall Street Journal*, June 9, 2020. https://www.wsj.com/articles/-online-dating-in-the-coronavirus-era-how-to-get-with-the-game/.

Yancey, George, and Sherelyn Yancey. "Interracial Dating: Evidence from Personal Advertisements." *Journal of Family Issues* 19, no. 3 (1998): 334–348.

Yin, Robert K. *Case Study Research: Design and Methods*, fourth edition. Los Angeles: Sage, 2009.

Zelizer, Vivian. *The Purchase of Intimacy*. Princeton: Princeton University Press, 2005.

Zug, Marcia A. *Buying a Bride: An Engaging History of Mail-Order Matches*. New York: New York University Press, 2016.

Index

Index

interracial dating 75–76, 78–85
intersectionality framework 76
intersectioning identities 74–76
Irish immigrants 26
"It's Just Lunch" 28

Jagger, Elizabeth 33
Japanese arranged marriages 15
Just Eye Contact 29, 103–105

Kataria, Madan 121
Kegel devices 32
Klinenberg, Eric: *Going Solo: The Extraordinary Rise and Surprising Appeal of Living Alone* 2
KY Intense 32

Ladd, Everett 88
Laughter Yoga for couples 120–121
Lavalife 41
learning to trust strangers 92–94
Lester, Neal 78
location-based dating 29, 48, 135–138
lonely hearts 30
"long-term relationships" 19
Luchetti, Cathy 15

mail-order brides 13; "Casket girls" 17; "King's daughters 17
Manchester Weekly Journal 13
marital immigration 16, 26
Maryland Gazette 15
Match.com 41
Matrimonial News 12, 20–24
Meet and Greet 109–111
Meet Moi 49
Mercer maids 15–16
Methods 10
Mirror 34–40
mobile dating apps 50
mobile hookups 30
Morrison, Helen 13
Must Love Dogs 52–54, 62

new forms of trust relations 91
New York Daily Mirror 12, 15
New York Times 12

online and offline impression management 112–113
online dating sites 28
Operation Match 113–114

"paradox of choice" 158
partners chair massage 124
PerfectMatch.com 41
performing identity 2

personal advertising: defined 2, 27; and deviant behavior 17–18
PEW Internet & American Life Project 2, 152–155
picture brides 14
post-pandemic dating 158–159
proxy marriages 15
Putnam, Robert: *Bowling Alone: The Collapse and Revival of American Community* 88

Quota Act of 1921 27

race-mixing 13
racial dividends in personal advertising 75
relationship tourism 33
The Right Stuff 44
romance novels and mail-order brides 13
romantic tourism 4, 71

Safari Flirting 29, 47, 129
Samuelson, Robert 89
Sarah, Plain and Tall 13
Schwartz, Pepper 42, 66
self as organized structure 55
serendipity in personal advertising (defined) 116
"shape shifter" 63
sharing economy 92
significance of the telephone in American courtship 134–135
Skout 48
social clubs 15
Social Connections 21–24
"social types" 19
sources of trust-building 131–133
speed dating 28, 46; boot camp 103, 105–106; characteristics 100; scholarly appeal 102
speed relating 47
speed tennis 47, 108–109
spicy personals 20
strategic identity performance 52
Stryker, Sheldon 55, 63

technology and romance 142
testosterone boosters 32
thick trust 89
"thin slicing" 113
thin trust 89, 96
Tinder 48
"transitory moments" 27, 29
Tribune 34–40
True.com 41
trust: building 95; and dating apps

200

Index

142–145; defined 90; and social isolation 94; and strangers 130
Turkle, Sheryl: *Alone Together* 148

virtual context of personal advertising
41
virtual relationships 148
vocal pornography 134

Washington Post 12
Wedding Bell 12
Winks 48
WooPlus 159

Zandy's Bride 13
Zug, Marcia: *Buying a Bride: An Engaging History of Mail Order Matches* 14,
17, 26